The Massachusetts Miracle

High Technology and Economic Revitalization

edited by David Lampe

The MIT Press
Cambridge, Massachusetts
London, England

This book was set in Bembo by Achorn Graphic Services and printed and bound by Halliday Lithograph in the United States of America.

Library of Congress Cataloging-in-Publication Data

The Massachusetts miracle.

  Bibliography: p.
  Includes index.
  1. High technology industries—Massachusetts.
2. Massachusetts—Economic policy. 3. Massachusetts—
Economic conditions. I. Lampe, David.
HC107.M43H536   1988   338.4′762′0009744   87-35291
ISBN 0-262-12134-4

To S. R. R.

Contents

Foreword

Lester C. Thurow

Economic miracles like instant stardom don't really occur. Good actors or actresses may suddenly become famous, but they almost always have become good actors or actresses over a long period of time with a lot of hard work on the fundamentals. So too with an economic miracle. Economic success may suddenly become visible, but such miracles are almost always produced by solid fundamentals and these solid fundamentals always have a long history.

The Massachusetts high tech miracle actually began almost thirty years ago, but it has only been noticed in the past ten years. The reasons are simple. For the first part of that period of time old industries (shoes, textiles) were dying as fast or faster than the new industries were being born. By the mid-1970s, however, the last of the shoe factories and textile mills had essentially died, and declining employment in these industries no longer offset employment gains in the new, growing, high tech industries.

Why did today's high tech industries start growing in Massachusetts? There are essentially two answers. First, these high tech industries did not need a lot of energy or raw materials, and the transportation charges necessary to deliver their products to their customers were small relative to the costs of what was being sold. The traditional economic handicaps of New England (high energy costs, high raw material costs, high transportation charges) were not handicaps for these industries.

Second, Massachusetts has always been a high cost place to buy low skill labor but a low cost place to buy high skilled labor. High skill people were not cheap, but they were to be had at lower wages than elsewhere in the country. Industries that needed a lot of low skill labor could always find much cheaper places to locate—that is why shoes and textiles left the region. But the new high technology industries used very little low skill labor and a lot of high skill labor. What they needed—low cost, high skill labor—Massachusetts and New England had in an abundance because of good education and skill-training systems. The net result was a set of industries whose needs fit the traditional comparative advantages of New England.

This is not to say that the boom has not been helped by the great research institutions of New England, such as MIT, or by good government policies and labor management cooperation. They have all played a role. All too often in history a region has had a real comparative advantage in some type of production and found ways to throw that comparative advantage away. Massachusetts did not do so, and that is to the credit of the citizens who lived there and to the leaders, public and private, who lead them.

The Massachusetts Miracle

Introduction:
The Making of a Miracle

In the early 1970s it looked as though the economy of the Commonwealth of Massachusetts was on its last legs. The unemployment rate
had soared to more than 11 percent, one of the highest in the nation.
The region's aging industrial base was losing jobs to other regions
and nations. And taxes were among the nation's highest.

But by the mid-1980s Massachusetts was healthier than it had
been in decades. Unemployment dipped below 3 percent, the lowest
of any other industrialized state in the nation. Hundreds of successful
new high technology firms dotted the landscape, applying expertise
in such diverse fields as computers, software, artificial intelligence,
biotechnology, novel materials, electronics, and medical equipment.
And taxes had plunged below the national average. Massachusetts
had become a "model" for others to follow.

Mesmerized by this stunning turnaround, other states and nations flocked to the area to discover the secret to its success. Could
other regions engineer a similar boom? What type of leadership
guided the state from the edge of despair to prosperity? Were specific
governmental policies responsible for such a dramatic revival?

Some began to call it the "Massachusetts Miracle." But the real
story of Massachusetts' economic recovery is not quite so mysteri-
ous. Although specific executive and legislative actions, as well as
events from beyond its borders, no doubt played a part in the turnaround, Massachusetts' ultimate success owes more to the state's "natural" strengths and advantages than to any public policy decisions.

But these natural advantages—which include its Yankee entrepreneurial tradition and its extraordinary concentration of universities and research labs, as well as its community of venture capitalists and aggressive commercial banks—do not tell the whole story. All of these elements had been on the scene for decades without causing any miracles.

What triggered the change? First, there was a dramatic shift in the technology in the 1970s as many high technology businesses began to tap a wide array of profitable commercial applications for their products and services. In the computer industry, for example, advances in engineering design that began in the 1960s and continued into the 1970s drastically reduced the size and cost of computers while simultaneously expanding their capabilities. These advances opened up vast new markets for computers and computer-related products and services—markets that Massachusetts was poised to exploit.

Second, and at the same time, there was a basic shift in the relationship between business and state government. The desperate state of the Massachusetts economy in the early 1970s goaded the historically aloof business and banking community into taking a series of actions that have led to greater involvement and more clearly defined roles for both the state and the business community in shaping the state's economic development.

These two broad and fundamental developments together lie at the heart of the state's success. While the exploding high technology markets set the boom in motion and gave it momentum, the changing attitudes of leaders in business and government allowed the state to take advantage of the boom, laying the groundwork for sustaining a robust business environment in the Commonwealth.

The collection of papers in this book shows how a number of forces, few of them explicitly planned, came together to produce the booming economy and low unemployment of Massachusetts in the 1980s. Arranged roughly chronologically, they document the evolving understanding of the region's problems and of the recovery itself, which, in truth, caught many by surprise. Because these papers were written as the story unfolded, some of them repeat the same thoughts, while others contradict each other, but each one contributes key insights into the process by which the region's economy revived. By weaving these threads together, we get an intriguing picture of how the "miracle" happened.

The Seeds of a Turnaround

If high technology has played such an important role in the revitalization of Massachusetts, how did the state become a mecca of high technology business in the first place? Although many have traced its origins to the post-World War II era, Massachusetts has in fact been a center of industrial and technological innovation for much longer.

With its ready supplies of water power, its location on important trade routes, its sophisticated financial community and its inherent disadvantages in agriculture, New England became the first industrialized region in the United States. By the early nineteenth century New England—particularly eastern Massachusetts—was the capital of American industry, using the latest techniques and equipment to produce leather goods, textiles, and machine tools.

This concentration of industry in the Commonwealth was one of the factors that led to the founding of the Massachusetts Institute of Technology in Boston in 1861. The establishment of MIT merged the area's industrial tradition with a firmly seated academic tradition begun by the founding of Harvard University over two centuries earlier. With its uniquely practical focus, MIT developed a singularly strong orientation toward the needs and interests of the industrial community.

MIT spin-off companies began to appear before the turn of the century, as individuals saw opportunities to take their ideas and expertise to the marketplace. Companies such as Arthur D. Little, Inc., Raytheon Co., and EG&G, Inc. were among the firms spun off in the period prior to World War II. A number of other successful technology-oriented companies were also founded in the area during this era, including such giants as the Bell Telephone Co. (now AT&T Co.) in 1877 and Polaroid Corp. in 1937.

Another innovation emerged in Massachusetts that reinforced this trend: the venture capital firm. In 1946 several members of the academic and business community—including representatives of Harvard, MIT, and the Federal Reserve Bank of Boston—met to discuss ways of boosting the supply of capital available to entrepreneurs seeking to start new companies based on the ideas and expertise emerging from area institutions. Backed by capital primarily drawn from the traditionally conservative insurance industry, they founded

American Research and Development under the leadership of General Georges Doriot. This pioneering company set the pattern for the venture capital firms that proliferated in New England and other areas in later decades.

World War II brought millions of federal research dollars to area universities to support the military effort—$117 million to MIT alone. The successes brought about by this spending, which included the perfection of radar and the development of self-aiming antiaircraft weapons, inspired the military to continue the funding of basic research on a large scale after the war. Since universities refused to conduct classified research on campus because it would interfere with the academic community's policy of sharing ideas freely, new companies and organizations sprang up to handle these jobs.

The result was the development of a defense oriented research complex with strong ties to the academic community. In the 1950s MIT started up Lincoln Laboratory, an off-campus facility that conducts research primarily for the Air Force. Other key research firms are Draper Laboratories and MITRE Corp., both MIT spin-offs. Well-established defense contractors such as Raytheon benefited from this trend as well. The launching of Sputnik in the late 1950s led to another major influx of money into the region, this time from NASA.

A host of small firms with high tech expertise began to appear in the 1950s and 1960s, often to conduct research and development for the federal government. Many of them were MIT spin-offs. Studies by MIT professor Edward B. Roberts in the 1960s identified over one hundred companies started since 1950 by people who had worked in just four of MIT's laboratories or departments. Others have spun off from spin-offs. Lincoln Labs alone has spawned thirty-nine new companies since its founding, for example. And former employees of firms such as Data General Corp., Raytheon Co., and Digital Equipment Corp. have started up a host of others.

Boston's financial community took the financing requirements of these new high tech companies in stride, adapting their practices to accommodate the special needs of the emerging firms at the appropriate stages of development. In the late 1950s, for example, the Bank of Boston (then The First National Bank of Boston) became the first bank in the nation to establish a policy of accepting federal research contracts as collateral for loans to high tech entrepreneurs. In addition to providing credit to meet immediate needs, such loans also helped entrepreneurs' efforts to obtain additional support from venture capital firms.

One of the great legacies of this period was the minicomputer. In the late 1920s researchers at MIT had began studying and developing the basic concepts of automatic computing. During World War II MIT researcher Jay Forrester embarked on a federally funded project which resulted in the design and construction of Whirlwind, the world's first reliable real time electronic digital computer in 1953. Efforts to refine the concept for military application went to Lincoln Laboratory in the early 1950s. There Kenneth Olson, formerly one of Forrester's assistants, worked on ways to make computers smaller and more versatile.

Olson eventually left the laboratory to apply his expertise to the design of computers for a broader clientele. In 1957 he founded Digital Equipment Corp. just outside of Boston in an abandoned textile mill. The company not only became one of the world's largest computer manufacturers, but it laid the groundwork for an entirely new industry in Massachusetts that was to play a major role in the state's economic recovery in the 1970s.

Significantly, the Department of Defense was not the only federal agency interested in basic research. In the decades following World War II, others jumped on the bandwagon, including the Department of Energy, the National Institutes of Health, the National Aeronautics and Space Administration, the Department of Transportation, and the National Science Foundation. Thus the federal government assumed a new role as the principal source of funding for basic academic research in the United States.

Advances in academe have continued to provide ideas for new products, improved processes, and entirely new industries. Biotechnology, for example, which has potential for application in a broad spectrum of industries, evolved from basic research in the life sciences. And the diversity of companies that started up in the area to make electronic devices, sophisticated medical equipment, advanced computers, and software attest to the importance of the academic backdrop. The sixty-five colleges and universities in the greater Boston area have also provided a critical source of professional labor, including physicians, managers, and lawyers as well as engineers and scientists.

By the late 1960s high technology had taken firm root in Massachusetts, accounting for nearly 10 percent of total employment. An array of new technology-based firms lined Route 128, a highway that swings a wide arc around Boston; the area's universities were cranking out the ideas and people needed to keep the trend going; government funds were pouring into the area's defense and research establishment; and the financial community had acquired a taste for funding new technology ventures.

Even though technology-related businesses were doing well, they had grown too dependent on defense- and space-related work, and the traditional manufacturing sector of the economy was deeply troubled. The high tech sector was not to really come into its own and emerge as a major force in the Massachusetts economy until well into the turbulent decade of the 1970s.

The Downward Spiral

In 1970 the nation experienced a recession that merely slowed down the pace of growth in most states. But it set the Massachusetts economy reeling. When the national unemployment rate peaked at just over 6 percent in early 1971, unemployment in Massachusetts continued to climb, reaching as high as 8 percent in early 1972.

The 1970 recession abruptly worsened a long slide that had begun as far back as the mid-1920s, when the Commonwealth's bread-and-butter manufacturing industries—namely textiles, apparel, and leather—had reached maturity. For almost half a century these industries had been losing ground to their competitors in other regions of the United States and overseas as the general wage level rose in New England, driving production costs up along with it. As competition stiffened, these Yankee businesses grew more and more reluctant to invest in updating their aging capital base of machines and buildings in New England as they saw an increasing return on their investments in such rapidly growing areas as the South.

From 1967 to 1972 the state lost more than 112,000 manufacturing jobs as the region's industrial base—textiles, apparel, and leather goods—slowly crumbled in the face of mounting competition from the southern states and foreign nations. Even the new high technology companies, which had seen something of a boom in the 1960s, were laying off scientists and engineers at a record rate. In 1971 alone, more than 50 manufacturing plants closed.

As bad as things looked, the future looked worse. The state's budget deficit rocketed into the hundreds of millions of dollars. News reports showed both blue- and white-collar families fleeing chilly northern states for the warm promise of America's Sunbelt—states such as California, Texas, Arizona, and North Carolina—where the weather was more hospitable, and rapid development promised a bounty of job opportunities. Both new and established businesses, according to these accounts, were rushing off to other regions, lured by cheaper labor, lower taxes, and a pro-business environment.

Even the promising high tech sector was posting disappointing results. The federal government's shifting priorities in the late 1960s and early 1970s showed how weak the underpinnings of the fledgling industrial sector were. From 1967 to 1971, defense contracts awarded in New England nose-dived about 40 percent in real terms as the Vietnam War wound down. And waning interest in the space program caused funds from NASA to drop off sharply. Nearly 15 percent of the manufacturing jobs Massachusetts lost from 1967 to 1971 were in the high technology industries. Scientists and engineers were also joining the ranks of the unemployed at an unprecedented rate, and many left the region for opportunities elsewhere.

Unfortunately, the state government was in no condition to channel resources into programs for economic revitalization. Indeed, rising unemployment had added to the Commonwealth's considerable fiscal woes. The state budget presented for 1971 totaled more than $2.5 billion, and 22.5 percent of it—$576 million—was for welfare. Between 1965 and 1971 payments to aid families with dependent children skyrocketed from $54.2 million to $252.9 million. Overall, the ranks of the state's welfare recipients mushroomed from just 170,000 in 1960 to a staggering 750,000 in 1972.

Total per capita expenditures by state and local government in Massachusetts had nearly doubled to more than $750 from 1965 to 1971. In fact, these expenditures ranked just behind those of New York and California, two states with economic bases better able to support the cost. The number of bureaucrats at the state and local levels shot up by 33,000 to more than 268,000 in the period from 1968 to 1971.

Although many of the programs and services paid for by these outlays were no doubt politically necessary, they cut deeply into the state's ability to devote resources to shore up its sagging economy. Soaring spending rates drove up the state deficit into the hundreds of millions of dollars. These deficits in turn forced the government to keep taxes high in order to make ends meet.

The result was a downward spiral. Disgruntled taxpayers joined with the business community in branding the state "Taxachusetts," and the Commonwealth acquired a growing reputation for being hostile to the business community. Publicity accorded companies expanding outside the state, coupled with rumors of firms leaving the state in search of a more favorable business climate, soured the image further. The state's chances of attracting and retaining existing industry—and thus jobs and a strong tax base—were dwindling fast.

As the decade progressed, other concerns robbed the region of what little luster it had left. Energy costs in New England were higher than in other developing regions, not only because it is colder but, far more important, because nearly 80 percent of its energy came from costly oil, a problem exacerbated by the 1973 oil embargo. In addition pollution control became a hot issue, and many firms complained that the web of environmental regulations and restrictions in the Commonwealth were unreasonably expensive and time-consuming. A staunchly liberal Democratic state politically, Massachusetts' concerns over such issues as environment and social welfare contributed to the alienation between the state government and the business community.

Attempts to overcome this raft of problems were frustrated by the absence of any real economic planning in the state. Indeed, economic development had historically not even been regarded as a central concern of state government. Thus any efforts that existed for monitoring economic trends and coming up with plans for economic development were scattered among such agencies as the Departments of Commerce, Manpower, and Community Affairs, as well as a virtually powerless Board of Economic Advisors.

Late in 1972 a pamphlet appeared that brought the state's economic crisis into dramatic focus. Produced by the normally conservative Bank of Boston at the inspiration of chief economist James Howell, *Look Out, Massachusetts!!!* presented a blunt and forceful analysis of the causes and cures of the state's deepening economic crisis. Although it undeniably reflected the concerns of the business community, it did not dwell on the demands of any particular industry group. Its primary message—to bring state spending under control and to develop incentives to stimulate business investment in much-needed plant and equipment—was aimed at the underlying needs of the entire Massachusetts economy.

Over 75,000 copies of *Look Out, Massachusetts!!!* circulated throughout the state, alerting both the government and the business community to the severity of the economic crisis. More important, the pamphlet set the scene for getting the business community involved in shaping state economic policy. It also helped push the state into action.

Meanwhile, by the beginning of 1972, the need for economic revitalization had already emerged as a major political issue. In a speech delivered in March of that year, Republican governor Francis Sargent acknowledged that rising unemployment and the mounting cost of doing business in the Commonwealth were causing economic stagnation and cutting into the tax revenues needed to provide basic services.

Sargent promised no miracles, but he presented two specific ideas aimed at giving the sagging economy a shot in the arm. First, he proposed to triple the investment credit to 3 percent for a period of a little over a year, allowing firms to deduct $3 from their corporate excise taxes for every $100 of investment in the state. The reasoning was that lost revenues (estimated at about $12 million) would be more than made up in the expanded tax base from new jobs coupled with shrinking welfare rolls. In addition he proposed to gradually eliminate the tax on inventories and machinery. For those small companies with high inventory-to-sales ratios, this tax could amount to as much as half of their total state tax bills.

Both of these ideas were incorporated in a broader package of incentives passed into law by the legislature in 1973. Some of the measures were a direct result of the growing efforts of business leaders to exert their influence on public policy. Collectively called "Mass Incentives," these initiatives were designed to create new jobs both by luring out-of-state manufacturing and R&D firms to Massachusetts and by encouraging existing companies to expand. Other key features included a $500 tax credit allowance for each person hired from public assistance rolls, provided that a company's payrolls grew by at least 3 percent over the previous year. A loss carry-forward incentive provided that losses incurred in other taxable years could be applied to the current year income for a period of up to five years.

Although these moves were lauded at the time, it is difficult to determine the effectiveness of such incentives. In retrospect, there is little evidence that these incentives were responsible for any of the new jobs that eventually were created in the state, or for any of the relocations into the state. Perhaps the greatest impact they had was to signal Massachusetts' determination to take some concrete action against the economic crisis.

But still harder times lay ahead. In 1973 the nation headed into the deepest recession since the Great Depression. Unemployment in the state was high and on the rise. Federal contracts had continued to decline, putting pressure on many of the region's high tech businesses. By the end of 1974 oil prices shot up by 150 percent, driving up the cost of living.

When Michael Dukakis was elected to his first term as governor of Massachusetts in 1974, the state had slipped deeper into fiscal turmoil. State spending was out of control, and the deficit had run up to more than $350 million. Unemployment had topped 9 percent, and it was still on the rise. It eventually peaked at 11.2 percent in 1975, far above the 8.5 percent national average.

The magnitude of the deficit, which eventually mounted to $500 million, so alarmed the financial markets that no one would buy the state's short- or long-term notes, effectively plunging the Commonwealth into bankruptcy. But working with the Boston financial community, the Dukakis administration put together a long-term strategy in which local institutions backed an issue of $500 million in long-term bonds at 9 percent. Dukakis imposed a 7.5 percent surcharge on state income taxes to cover the cost of servicing the $500 million debt.

Under pressure from the often conflicting demands of consumer and environmental interests, on one hand, and the growing clamor of business interests, on the other, Dukakis had some tough choices to make. To help ease the state's deficit, for example, he cut back on welfare programs. But on the whole, he remained faithful throughout his term to his liberal Democratic ideals, earning the enmity of the high technology community, which insisted he was not doing enough to support business in the state.

In August 1976 Dukakis released a seventy-page document entitled "An Economic Development Plan for Massachusetts," detailing a sweeping array of nearly one hundred proposals for controlling state spending and cutting the costs of doing business in Massachusetts. The loosely defined "plan" drew on the resources of a wide variety of state agencies to focus in particular on controlling energy costs, making capital available at affordable rates, improving in-state transportation, encouraging growth in industries with high potential, and managing state spending.

As with the incentives package passed in 1973, however, it is not clear what impact any of these initiatives had on stimulating the state's economy. Its greatest significance was that it made economic planning and development a clear responsibility of state government for the first time.

The Road to Recovery

But by 1976 a number of other forces—mostly beyond the control of state policy—were coming together to turn the economy around. The recession, for example, had finally begun to ease in 1975. Shifting concerns in Washington, D.C., also began to bring billions of dollars of defense work back into New England, giving the high tech industries a much-needed boost. The real value of contracts awarded to plants in the region rose by 42 percent from 1976 to 1979.

In 1980 firms in Massachusetts—a state with just 2.5 percent of the nation's population—won 5.6 percent of prime federal defense contracts. More recently, the region's research establishments have garnered a significant share of funds for the development of the technologies behind the Strategic Defense Initiative. In 1985 defense production added up to $12 billion or 8.3 percent of state net product, one of the highest percentages in the nation.

But perhaps more significant for the long-term health of many high tech businesses was their determination to escape their dependence on inherently narrowly focused or unpredictable markets, such as the federal government. Instead, they began to diversify into commercial markets. Minicomputer makers, for example, one of the largest segments of the high tech sector, had been working to break out of purely scientific and technical markets, and were experiencing an explosion of growth in a diverse number of business and industrial applications.

In the late 1970s and into the 1980s minicomputers and powerful microcomputers, often linked together with sophisticated network technology, began to find countless applications in virtually every business, from banking and retail stores to manufacturing. Spurred by the availability of cheaper and more versatile computer hardware, firms developing the software to tailor these machines to a vast variety of specific tasks also saw spectacular growth.

Similarly, broad interest in and applications for biotechnology products, robotics, materials, artificial intelligence, and countless other leading-edge developments drove the creation of hundreds of new companies in Massachusetts. By the end of the 1970s few of the remaining successful high tech businesses focused solely on government research and development. In the period from 1965 to 1980 the share of high tech business conducted for the federal government fell from 60 to 25 percent in Massachusetts.

Foreign markets proved to be receptive to this emerging commercial focus as well. From 1972 to 1976 shipments overseas from New England rose from 5.2 to 9.2 percent of total sales.

Fueled by the expanding markets for their products, the high technology sector was playing a leading role in the economic revitalization by providing much-needed new jobs. By 1978 unemployment rates in Massachusetts were finally approaching national averages. In 1979 total high technology employment reached nearly 200,000.

Spin-offs from the Commonwealth's research and educational institutions were a key element in the economic boom. By 1986, for example, MIT alone had spun off at least 400 companies in the state, most of them since 1950. According to one MIT study, these firms represented sales in excess of $29 billion, and in-state employment of more than 175,000.

Nearly three-fourths of all new high tech manufacturing jobs in the state were roughly evenly divided between two areas: office machinery (such as computers) and electronic components. Fortunately for the stability of these industries, markets for both of these types of products are extraordinarily diverse.

As high technology manufacturing jobs increased by 47.4 percent from 1975 to 1983, non-high tech durable manufacturing slipped downward by 5.1 percent and non-high tech nondurable manufacturing fell off 6.7 percent. Total manufacturing employment climbed by nearly 4 percent during this period.

With the total number of manufacturing jobs in Massachusetts nearly stable, the prime contributor to the growth in jobs was the thriving service sector, led by business services. Between 1975 and 1983 the service sector grew at a rate of 46 percent, three times faster than all other sectors combined. By 1983, 664,230 people were employed in services, more than in any other job category. Business services such as computer services, data processing services, management consulting, advertising and public relations, and software grew at the fastest rate—95 percent—accounting for more than 30 percent of all new service jobs.

Other services also did well. During the same eight-year period, health services contributed 26.8 percent of all new service jobs, social services ranked third at 13 percent, and education accounted for 10.8 percent.

Many of these service businesses have proved capable of strengthening the region's economic base by drawing income into the area. The Boston area's sixty-five colleges and universities, for example, draw nearly a quarter of a million students to the city each year, many from out of state and overseas. These students pay rent, buy food and clothing, and patronize a wide range of the area's businesses.

Significantly, small businesses played the largest role in providing new jobs. Indeed, the smaller businesses were the critical source of job growth in New England, as they were in the rest of the United States. Although they have a far greater failure rate than larger firms, their birth and expansion rates are also great. In landmark studies of the dynamics of small business, MIT economist David Birch found that for the period from 1969 to 1976, firms with twenty or fewer employees created almost 92 percent of net new jobs. And in 1983 about 88 percent of all business establishments had fewer than twenty employees.

Demographic trends were also working in the state's favor. During the 1970s and early 1980s the number of jobs actually grew at the same rate in the Commonwealth as it did, on average, in the rest of the nation. But the population of Massachusetts remained almost stable from 1970 to 1984 while the overall U.S. population rose by more than 16 percent. Not only did New England have a lower birthrate than much of the nation, but many people had decided to leave the area, limiting the growth of the labor force and holding down unemployment.

Shaping the Business Environment

But despite significant economic progress, many business leaders were still irate about the high cost of doing business in Massachusetts. They argued that the steadily rising tax burden in the state—particularly for individuals—was seriously hindering their ability to keep or attract people with the critical management and engineering skills they needed for growth. In fact, Massachusetts' tax burden was 11 percent higher than the national average in 1979. Other regions, they insisted—including Texas, Arizona, and North Carolina—offered a comparable quality of life at a lower cost. As key professionals left, they took with them the potential for employing dozens of others in manufacturing and services.

This state of affairs finally jarred the emerging high tech sector into flexing its political muscle. In October 1977 a group of the region's high tech companies had banded together to form a political lobbying organization called the Massachusetts High Technology Council. The guiding force behind the Council was Ray Stata, president of Analog Devices, Inc., an electronics company he had founded in 1965. By 1979 their ranks had swelled to eighty-nine firms, which together employed about 140,000, mostly in Massachusetts. In a much-publicized move the MHTC drew up a nonbinding "social contract" in which they promised to provide 60,000 new high technology jobs, and an additional 90,000 jobs in manufacturing and support services, if the state would take "substantive" steps to cut taxes and establish a "healthy" business climate. The new jobs, they maintained, would lead to a $300 million annual growth in state and local tax revenues.

Democratic Governor Edward King, who had taken over from Dukakis in 1978 by narrowly defeating him in the primary, had publicly promised to work with the business community to lower taxes and create jobs. He signed the agreement on February 8, 1979.

As it turned out, the agreement was largely symbolic. Members of the Council knew that they could provide the jobs no matter what the state did. Not only were they flush with the success of growing markets for their products and services, but wage rates in Massachusetts had become competitive with those in other regions. Over the preceding decades, wage rates and manufacturing costs in such growing areas as the South had climbed steadily while the economic stagnation in Massachusetts had held down increases. Moreover labor costs were inherently lower in the nonunionized high tech sector.

But by signing the agreement, King made a direct gesture of friendship to the business community and took a big step toward erasing the negative image the state government had endured in the eyes of business leaders for years. It set a precedent of cooperation that prevailed into the ensuing administrations of Michael Dukakis as well.

The agreement also helped a grass roots tax revolt gain momentum. On November 4, 1980, voters passed a referendum popularly known as Proposition 2½. The measure had been originated by an organization called Citizens for Limited Taxation headed by tenacious lobbyist Barbara Anderson. The group's goal was to ease the growing burden of high property tax on the elderly and other economically disadvantaged groups. In an unusual alliance, the affluent MHTC joined CLT in backing Proposition 2½ and devoted considerable resources to the task. The MHTC felt that a lower tax burden would help the region attract and hold the professionals high tech firms needed for growth. The measure, which had been put on the ballot by a petition signed by more than 60,000 voters and which was supported by Governor King, slashed the individual property tax burden by limiting annual aggregate state and local property taxes to 2½ percent of "full and fair cash valuation."

Proposition 2½'s opponents—which included former Governor Dukakis—had maintained that the law would cripple central municipal services and the local governments' ability to pay for them. Although no such disasters occurred, it did indeed cause some belt tightening. It also forced the traditionally independent-minded local communities to rely more on state funds, and thus to have a greater vested interest in the state's overall plans. Most important, it demonstrated the strength of an emerging conservative sentiment in the state that was more receptive to the needs of business.

Much had changed since the days of *Look Out, Massachusetts!!!*

when Dukakis was again elected governor in 1982—this time with a more cautious and accommodating approach to the business community. Political leaders throughout the state acknowledged the expanded role of state government in promoting and maintaining a healthy state economy. Employment in state and local government, which had peaked at 372,000 in 1978, had been steadily declining as a result of efforts to streamline government operations. With an extra push from Proposition 2½, government employment fell to 319,000 in 1981. And with business booming and unemployment plummeting, not only were tax revenues rising but welfare rolls were shrinking as well. In almost every year since 1975, the state had enjoyed budget surpluses.

In 1985 the surplus hit $457 million. In addition the 7.5 percent income tax surcharge was dropped—despite the Governor's opposition—following voter approval of a ballot initiative to remove it. The cost of debt service had fallen when the $500 million loan had been refunded at a lower interest rate earlier, but the state had kept the surcharge as an extra source of revenue. By 1987 Massachusetts' tax burden had fallen to 10 percent below the national average. The "Taxachusetts" label finally disappeared.

The Massachusetts Miracle

Compared to the influence of changes in the market, state government's role in the Massachusetts economic revival has been minor. But it has not been unimportant. It is true that a host of tax incentives, training programs, and other innovative ideas were implemented at the urging of the business community to promote business growth in the state, but whether any of them achieved their specific goals is open for debate. More than anything, they represented an attitudinal shift toward accommodating the concerns of the business community. By thus shedding its "anti-business" image, the state was able to foster a supportive atmosphere of stability and cooperation that has helped to silence its critics.

This change in attitude and the resulting improved business environment can have important consequences in the longer term for the Massachusetts economy. Both existing firms from out of state and maturing home-grown companies value a stable and supportive environment when making decisions to expand or relocate. Thus the state has an advantage in its efforts not only to hold onto jobs from expansions of in-state firms but also to entice companies from other regions to set up operations to tap into the Commonwealth's unique high technology infrastructure.

The state's transformation has not been without its darker side. While the area extending from Boston north to the New Hampshire border saw a cumulative employment growth of 8.5 percent from 1979 to 1983, employment in the southern and western areas—where nearly 44 percent of the population lives—grew at only 0.7 percent. In addition the cost of living in Massachusetts is one of the highest in the nation. The cost of single-family homes in the Boston area, for example, shot up by 70 percent from 1984 to 1985 alone, far outpacing average family income growth and cutting many families out of the market. Some critics have also noted that with the proportion of manufacturing and blue-collar jobs shrinking, the income gap between the higher and lower ends of the range is widening. Although unemployment is remarkably low, many of the available positions are low-wage and low-skill jobs with little potential for growth and advancement.

But these concerns do little to tarnish the image of Massachusetts. Whatever its problems, it remains the envy of many ailing industrialized states as well as mature and developing regions of the world, which are now seeking to invoke the magic of high technology to cure their economic woes.

Yet the lesson of the Massachusetts experience is that these firms developed here not by design but because an elaborate complex of institutions and traditions gave them a reason to grow. Knowledge has become Massachusetts' most prized resource. In addition to providing local entrepreneurs with ideas to take to the marketplace, the expertise represented by the area's academic institutions and its high tech infrastructure has become a key attraction for research and development operations of companies based elsewhere, particularly from Japan and Europe.

Massachusetts benefited particularly because one of the technologies developed in the region—the computer—unexpectedly proved to have enormous international market potential. Not only did this create a wealth of new manufacturing jobs in the region, it also spawned a host of related high-growth businesses, ranging from software to data processing. Having a major branch of a new industry come to life in Massachusetts proved to be an incredible windfall for the state. Even the people who designed the machines had no idea of the impact they would have.

However, partly because of the success of computers, society is much more attuned to the potential of emerging technologies today than just a couple of decades ago. It may be possible for astute regional governments to attract or nurture the development of specific high growth, job-producing technology-oriented companies in other areas.

Certainly some of the conditions present in the Commonwealth are likely to be important to the encouragement of high technology business elsewhere. Strong research institutions, an entrepreneurial spirit, and an aggressive financial community are just some of the key ingredients to the state's success. A better understanding of these influences and how they interact is essential to the task of transplanting a success story from one region to another.

Massachusetts too must seek to understand the specific dynamics of what happened in order to extend and sustain the "miracle" within its own borders. Furthermore, as markets change, industries mature, and new technologies emerge, the state must be prepared to meet the continuing challenges of keeping the economy vital.

In its current position of strength Massachusetts is set to actively take advantage of its traditions of entrepreneurialism and academic excellence. It was these traditions—with the right market conditions and the nurturing business environment that evolved in the 1970s—that were able to produce a new broad-based and vital industrial sector, sparking an economic revival just as the state's mature industries were no longer able to carry the burden.

Looking back over the period of 1971 to 1987, there can be no question that Massachusetts experienced an extraordinary turnaround and that the high technology sector played a central role in revitalizing the region. It is also clear, however, that no individual or organization from business, academe, or government can claim credit for consciously engineering this development. It happened by itself, fostered by a remarkable combination of favorable conditions that emerged from the particular culture of the region and by chance.

That is the real miracle of Massachusetts.

The Dilemma of a Mature Economy and Excessive Government Spending

Economics Department
The First National Bank of Boston
December 1971

In 1971 Massachusetts' economy was seriously ailing. But while government representatives, business leaders, the press, and the general public complained about many of the symptoms—including rising unemployment, poor business conditions, and skyrocketing welfare costs—no one had diagnosed the disease. The following piece for the first time brought together the growing concerns expressed by diverse groups throughout the state, and sounded an alarm that awoke Massachusetts to the severity of its ailment.

The alarm was all the more startling because it came from The First National Bank of Boston, a Brahmin bank founded in the eighteenth century which, like many other banks, had historically avoided making waves in the business community. The piece, inspired by the bank's chief economist, James Howell, appeared in The New England Letter, *a small newsletter put together by the bank's economics staff. This publication was circulated to about 35,000 business executives, government officials, academics, and members of the press throughout the region and around the world.*

It was soon clear that the article had struck a nerve. More than fifty newspapers in New England reported on the essay, and many of them wrote editorials supporting its message. In addition to describing the dangers inherent in Massachusetts' maturing economy, the piece suggested the formation of a partnership among the business, government, and academic communities to study ways to produce jobs and restore economic growth. This was a radical proposition in a state where no individual or organization had direct responsibility for economic development.

Bank's Year-Long Study Charts Path to Restore Growth, Profits, and Jobs to All in Bay State

Massachusetts has just about run out of wealth-creating energy, and its economic engine needs an overhaul.

Signs of trouble have been with us for more than two decades, and some observers say that the Commonwealth has had a disproportionate amount of bad luck. Whether it is bad luck or a lack of essential economic maintenance really doesn't matter: Massachusetts has a real problem with a catastrophic potential. This problem must be corrected now.

It started with the decline of textile, apparel, and leather industries. These losses cut into the state's income payments and raised unemployment. More recently, winding down the Vietnam War caused cutbacks in defense contracts, and changing socioeconomic priorities reduced space expenditures. Again, Massachusetts has been dealt a severe blow leaving a deep imprint of personal economic hardship. Taken together, these forces have spawned a wide range of views concerning the interrelationships between economic growth and economic hardship.

For more than a year now, The First National Bank of Boston has been engaged in an analysis of socioeconomic problems in Massachusetts and New England. We have assessed the changes, identified forty-one key growth industries, and spotlighted vital areas for improvement in the socioeconomic environment.

At the core of the immediate problem is discovery of a way to trigger sound economic growth while at the same time reducing the difficulties of retraining workers in declining industries for jobs in growth industries.

In a young, growing economy, reconciling these two objectives is relatively easy. When you have growth, new jobs in new industries are readily available to reassimilate the worker in occupational transition. In other words, those who become unemployed due to the decline of one industry are soon offered jobs in an expanding industry.

But in a mature economy such as exists in Massachusetts, growth is not self-generating. We have no inherent or latent growth momentum. All new job opportunities must be consciously and deliberately created and nourished by helping existing firms get into activities with growth potential and by attracting industries from other regions into Massachusetts and New England.

New job opportunities here, therefore, are not easily discernible, nor are they readily available in a mature economy at a rate consistent with labor demands and labor growth rates. Too many times in this situation the only place for a displaced worker is on welfare.

When such a condition is created, negative momentum is started which steadily drags the state or region down to a slower economic pace or pushes the area into economic retrenchment. It is this sequence of events that cuts the heart out of new economic growth.

Mushrooming welfare costs are subtracted from local productive resources which create the real wealth necessary for jobs and financing local and state government services. The vicious chain reaction then forces governments to tax business and citizens at ever-higher rates, and a new ball and chain is attached to the economy.

Destructive Process Sets In

In time this chain of events creates a less attractive business environment because more and more industries begin to move from the state or become reluctant to expand their operations within the state. Many firms openly seek a more friendly economic environment in other parts of the nation. At this stage, the state loses more tax revenue and must hike the taxes of those that remain, while the welfare rolls grow.

To close the revenue gap all sorts of new taxes and tax schemes are proposed such as a lottery or general sales tax.

Soon this destructive process becomes self-sustaining and a strong anti-business environment emerges. In such an environment, the worker losing his job in a dying industry has little alternative today but to go on welfare.

To a large extent this unhappy pattern of events has been occurring in Massachusetts during the past several years. In 1968 the unemployment rate was about 4 percent, roughly in line with the United States average. But today it is much higher than the national rate.

The record of the six years between 1965 and 1971 traces the true nature of economic hardship here. In 1965, payments to aid families with dependent children amounted to $54.2 million; in 1968, this amount climbed to $91.6 million; last year it soared to $252.9 million.

At the same time, general welfare payments rose by more than $47 million to $56.7 million. This year, the drain has been compounded as more than fifty manufacturing plants have closed, representing the loss of more than 7,000 prime jobs in the Commonwealth.

Everyone Loses a Little

A tragic picture emerges from these unhappy economic events. The standard of living in Massachusetts has been reduced:

• For the businesses and their employees who remain in the state, taxes are being increased to support the unemployed on welfare.

• For those out of work and unable to find jobs, the lack of growth and deteriorating business environment condemn them to a life of bare survival.

In these two factors we find a fundamental truth: the redistribution of income to reduce the pain of unemployment in a mature economy has the effect of stopping economic growth or further eroding the business base. We are forced to rob ourselves of our own economic future.

Although these facts are alarming, our studies do not indicate that we must sink into an Appalachian-type poverty environment here. The current dilemma between economic growth and welfare can be reconciled by an all-out effort through a partnership of business and government to redirect the economy into growth channels and to improve the business environment.

What is required is a new program capable of reversing the current trend of little or no real growth in Massachusetts. The logical way out is rapid industrial expansion. But the key question is: What industries should be expanded?

The First's studies concentrate on three key tasks:

• Identification of growth industries and development of a growth program through accelerated capital investment.

• Job retraining to ensure a supply of trained labor able to work in the growth industries.

• Major actions by the Commonwealth's government to foster a rational business environment which will attract new enterprises into the state and nourish expansion of those already here.

The solutions to the first two problems are at hand as a result of more than one year's intensive and extensive research by bank officers and economists. We have pinpointed the forty-one key growth industries which should be expanded. Nearly all of them are represented to some extent in Massachusetts.

They are in six broad industry groupings—processed food, converted paper products, book publishing, communications equipment, electronic components, and ophthalmic goods. All seem to hold unusual promise for new jobs in the Commonwealth.

A Strategy for Growth

But translating this economic research into practical business activity requires leadership. The immediate challenge, of course, is to develop a practical strategy to accelerate industrial expansion in these key industries.

We plan to initiate a series of discussions with the key executive officers of the state's growth industries. The purpose of these meetings will be simply to explore ways to produce new jobs.

Several business leaders have indicated acceptance of this approach as direct means to job creation. And, undoubtedly, these meetings will significantly improve our understanding of the complex industrial interfaces in Massachusetts, but they will be of little value unless we can get the Commonwealth going again on the road to productivity and economic expansion.

Seeking a Partnership

A sober view of the current situation tells us that our efforts will certainly fail unless a business environment that encourages industrial expansion and new capital spending can be created. We are currently researching this problem and seeking answers from a wide variety of sources. One source of financial salvation would be complete Federal takeover of the Commonwealth's welfare burden.

The creation of a favorable environment for business, new business development, and generation of job opportunities are part of the government's role; but the situation requires concerted effort. At the moment, we can only say that business seeks a partnership with government and the academic community to produce jobs and to reconcile the current dilemma between economic growth and welfare cost expansion. It is our hope that the Commonwealth government will agree with our appraisal of the problems and join with business in a partnership for progress and opportunity through productivity and jobs.

A contest for political "one-upsmanship" between the executive and legislative branches in Massachusetts can be particularly troublesome at a time when industrial recovery is so urgent. It is our hope that both branches will moderate their enthusiasm for putting the Commonwealth well ahead of all other states in matters of spending for social benefits and for anti-pollution measures which deceive the public by producing barely measurable improvements at great economic cost.

Surely the governor and the legislative leaders must some day come to the understanding that Massachusetts cannot stay out of line with other states in the cost of doing business without destroying the base that is the sole support of our economic well-being.

The Economic Development of Massachusetts

Francis W. Sargent
Governor of Massachusetts
March 1972

On March 13, 1972, Governor Francis Sargent appeared before the Boston Citizens Seminar in the city's historic Faneuil Hall to deliver what was billed as an important economic policy statement. Although economic development had been officially declared a state priority as far back as 1959, Massachusetts' relative prosperity through the 1960s had kept economic planning issues on the back burner. Although many of the old mill towns had continued to decline, the area around Boston in particular had been doing well, largely due to the emergence of new high technology-based businesses.

Now the importance of these issues could be ignored no longer. Unemployment and high taxes in particular had become pressing concerns throughout the state. In his first major speech since delivering the State of the State Address earlier that year, Sargent sought to answer some of the criticisms then being raised about the state's economy by emphasizing the Commonwealth's strengths and by proposing some specific incentives to spur business expansion and new jobs in the state.

Sargent, a progressive Republican, ardent environmentalist, and member of a prominent Massachusetts family, had become in 1970 the first governor to be elected to a four-year, rather than a two-year, term as part of an effort to strengthen the executive branch of state government. Among his primary goals as governor were to revitalize and reform the state's moribund network of social service agencies, which dealt with everything from education and prison reform to welfare.

Sargent approaches the issues of economic development within this context, emphasizing the importance of a vigorous economy in providing the tax base to support effective social services programs. This address was a tentative first step toward getting the state more actively involved in shaping the business environment.

These efforts were to continue into early 1973 when Guy Rosmarin, Sargent's director of federal-state relations, and James Howell convened a meeting of Massachusetts' business leaders and the Governor's senior policy aides. As a result of that meeting, Sargent directed Lieutenant Governor Donald Dwight to coordinate formally the state's economic development activities, serve as liaison to the business community, and to assist Sargent in developing new economic initiatives. The ultimate outcome was the passage by the legislature, in 1973, of a package of initiatives called "Mass Incentives" designed to stimulate the state's economy.

It is easy to preach gloom about the Massachusetts economy.

The cost of doing business mounts while employment opportunities plummet.

One hundred and ninety-five thousand Massachusetts citizens are out of work. For the unemployed, who cannot find new jobs, the economy is indeed in crisis. Hard-earned savings don't last long when coupled with today's high prices.

For state government a stagnant economy also means austerity, without sufficient tax revenues, the state cannot provide the educational, environmental, and social programs which our citizens expect, and which they have a right to expect.

So a vigorous economy is vital to us all.

It is not just the giant corporation of the wealthy businessman who cashed in on a booming economy. It is each and every citizen in this state who needs a flourishing economy—those on welfare, and the working man; big business, and small business; management, and the labor forces.

All of us depend on a healthy economy. We are endowed with features which can spark economic vitality. Features few other states enjoy.

Massachusetts is a good place in which to work. We possess already a labor force skilled in the latest techniques.

Our sophisticated technology places us above our peers in the development of new products.

And Massachusetts is a very good place in which to live. Our social investments, our educational resources, and our recreational resources give us a quality of life that attracts the best in brainpower, and keeps it here—as long as we have jobs to offer.

So we must build upon our strengths. We must exploit our own advantages in order to get things moving again. But let us not pretend that we can stage miracles. There are indeed limits to what a governor can do.

In recent years, changing priorities have had a severe impact on the economy of this state. Cutbacks in space and defense department spending have left many Massachusetts residents jobless.

At the same time foreign competition has sliced deeply into our domestic shoe industry and textile operations. And the high cost of fuel adds an extra burden to doing business in this region.

There are conditions over which a governor has little or no control. By one stroke of his pen, the president of the United States can radically improve an economic situation.

I do not have that kind of power. I cannot act unilaterally, in an instant, and revolutionize the Massachusetts economy.

But I can call on you, and together we can undertake specific actions to make Massachusetts more competitive with other industrial states.

Today I want to outline a plan by which we can begin to turn this state's economy around, to move us from stagnation to a vibrant and sustained period of economic activity.

If Massachusetts has great strengths to build on, we must admit that we also have weaknesses.

What we can do is to counteract those weak points with specific programs. To a lot of people, this state is "Taxachusetts." Businesses, we are told, are reluctant to locate here. We are reputed to have exorbitant tax rates.

But let us take a look at the facts. Our total tax burden is nearly identical to the national average. Nationwide, the average paid in state and local taxes is 11.2 percent of personal income. We have a rate of 11.8 percent, only fractions higher.

If taxes are not much higher here—then why are there so many complaints. Perhaps some people fear that this state is unconcerned with the burden imposed on business by state taxes. Perhaps they feel we disregard costs to business when we plan state programs.

But, they are wrong. And I intend to demonstrate our concern. I will take specific steps to regain the confidence of industry . . . the type of confidence that will encourage expansion and the creation of more jobs. In that way we will all share in the benefits of a dynamic economy.

I am directing the Secretary of Communities and Development to draw up an economic impact policy review. This policy commits state agencies to a rigorous and systematic review of the economic consequences of their decision.

Where proposed programs might damage the economy, we will be able to consider possible adjustments or alternatives.

That process will parallel the legislation I have already filed for an environmental review of policy decisions. When we have experience with the procedures, we will formalize them in specific legislation. In this way, we will have achieved a balance between environmental and economic considerations in determining state policy.

But let one thing be clear. This administration is committed to cleaning up the environment. There can be and will be no let up in our fight against pollution. We will make every effort to assist business in compliance with environmental regulations . . . , but we will not relax standards of permit violations. There is simply too much at stake.

A healthy environment can be our most precious asset . . . we must not surrender the future for the convenience of today. Under the policies I have outlined we will have an overview of the economic and environmental impact of our future decisions. This will go a long way toward helping us make balanced and rational judgments.

I would venture to predict that this kind of balanced review policy will trigger a trend across the nation. We have successfully experimented in other areas in the past, when most states have feared to try. Here especially, we cannot be afraid to be first.

High taxes and lack of concern are not the only myths which sap confidence in our state's economy. Our programs of unemployment compensation costs are borne exclusively by Massachusetts employers.

Unemployment compensation has mushroomed into one of the major costs of doing business in this state.

That burden must be eased.

We have already restricted the use of unemployment compensation to supplement retirement income. But more must be done. I have directed my new commissioner of the Division of Employment Security to make this matter his first priority. Confidence in the economy can only be restored if citizens can rely on their state government. But we cannot expect that confidence if we do not employ first-rate people in state service.

Our present state-hiring procedures often deny us the most qualified personnel. In Massachusetts civil service job applicants wait an average of one year to receive notification of employment.

It is one year from the time they take the exams until their names are sent to the agencies which might hire them. Other states complete this process in less than two weeks. Frequently, the best people leave to take jobs in private industry. If government is to contribute to an economic upswing, or any other kind of improvement, then state government must make itself competitive with private industry.

Streamlining the administration of our civil service system is a major priority of our development program.

But the state needs to do more than put a new face on government to spur on economic growth. It needs to enact specific measures to encourage expansion of existing firms. And it might recruit new industries to bolster its job market.

Therefore, I am proposing concrete new tools to augment economic growth potential.

I will file legislation to institute state guarantees for mortgages. Firms unable to obtain commercial credit to build new plants will be able to rely on state government to guarantee their mortgages.

Other New England states offer mortgage assistance. This financial incentive can spell the difference between holding and attracting industry or watching it go elsewhere.

I have requested funds for highway construction projects. Portions of those monies already allocated will be used to assist industry. I have instructed my secretary of transportation to use portions of those funds for the construction of highway access roads, so frequently needed for new plants.

Massachusetts has always been able to lure businesses to its shores with a plentiful supply of trained workers. But in a period of stagnation, government must exert control over what kind of skilled labor we offer. Workers trained for jobs that don't exist go away frustrated—and go on welfare. Industries with jobs that can't find suitable workers move away.

Therefore, I am proposing that a portion of federal manpower funds coming into Massachusetts be reserved for training men to match specific jobs. We will tailor our programs to fit the exact requirements of new facilities.

I will ask the legislature to appropriate additional training funds. These state funds will free us of the delays and restrictions so often accompanying federal grants.

Such flexibility gives Massachusetts an edge over sister states in the competition for new industry. Now when a firm is ready to open a new plant, its labor force will be ready. And when a worker concludes his training, he will be confident that a job is waiting for him.

State government also has an obligation to advise troubled industries. The State Department of Commerce should act as a primary resource for business.

To augment its expertise, I am directing the department to hire technical and management specialists in the major industries in our state. We will then be in a position to assist struggling companies. As an example, our specialist in the manufacture of computer hardware could provide the quick and accurate economic data to a computer firm that will convince it to locate a branch in our state. Struggling firms would then be able to turn to the proper expert within state government for guidance.

But we cannot ignore the small entrepreneur while we support the giant corporations. Small businesses are as vital to a healthy economy as large ones. They are simply not as well equipped to obtain expert advice and financial assistance. For this reason I am establishing a Bureau of Small Business Assistance, within the Department of Commerce and Development. This agency will be able to provide small businesses with technical aid, marketing information, and financial advice. In addition the Bureau will assist small business in their dealings with the federal government.

However, the level of technical assistance the state can offer businesses could be vastly increased through a partnership of industry and government.

Through a personnel loan arrangement the expertise of the private sector could broaden and deepen the state's ability to cope with the profound economic problems which confront it.

In the coming months I will work to interest business in loaning some of their key people to give government more flexibility and greater breadth in the aid it can offer struggling businesses.

Direct assistance to business to protect and expand the job market will begin to create a better economic climate. But I believe that concrete financial incentives will also tempt new industry to locate within our borders. In addition, we must use tax incentives to encourage existing business to expand, thereby creating new employment opportunities.

Specifically, I will recommend to the legislature that we triple the present Massachusetts investment credit. I will ask them to make this increase effective from today until July 1, 1974. We must encourage firms to expand now—to create more jobs today.

The investment credit allows a firm to deduct $3 from its corporate excise tax for every $100 of investment in the Commonwealth. This really means Massachusetts is investing some $12 million per year. But this revenue loss will be doubly compensated. The expansion of industry leads to increased future tax revenues. And a growing, healthy economy guarantees a job for every individual.

Investment credits do not, however, completely neutralize heavy taxes. The Massachusetts tax, most bitterly resented, is the property measure of the corporate excise tax. I believe this to be an unfair tax. It nullifies our strongest efforts to attract new businesses. And by invoking a financial penalty against a firm for all of its inventory and machinery, this tax discourages investment.

I will file legislation to phase out the property measures of the excise tax on manufacturers. This tax on inventories would be reduced by 1 percent per year. In eight years there will be no tax. Further, I will recommend that we completely exempt, from the tax, all machinery purchased after today.

In addition, I will establish a tax review panel. It will be chaired by the lieutenant governor. This panel will assess the total economic impact of any new tax proposal . . . and where necessary, recommend alternative programs. But economic growth will not result from tax incentives alone.

We will need experimentation.

I promised in my annual message to review my proposal for a state development corporation. This year's legislation emphasizes the economic development potential of this promising vehicle.

Such a corporation would be empowered to assemble sites for private projects. It can construct buildings which might be sold or leased to new firms. Its flexibility makes it an ideal tool for stimulating economic development at local and state levels.

With these proposals we can refurbish our image in the business community. We can attract new firms. These new industries will tend to locate in the urban centers of our state, where they find the highly skilled workers.

But what of those parts of our state where unemployment levels are dangerously high? We cannot gloss over those regions of chronic unemployment—they will not go away if we ignore their claims.

We must persuade industry to move into areas of high unemployment. Into areas where the traditional industries have fared poorly. And where workers have had no opportunity to acquire sophisticated skills.

This Commonwealth has already passed the Urban Job Incentive Act. I plan to implement that legislation. We will provide tax rebates to firms which located in low-income areas.

The state will return a portion of the property taxes and wages paid by businesses locating in low-income areas. Taxes are often higher in depressed communities. Retraining workers, to assure them permanent employment, costs business more money. This program will compensate the socially concerned businessmen . . . to provide sound incentives for investments and job development in poorer communities.

With these proposals, we can strengthen the economy of the state, as a whole.

Economic pressure from foreign competition is responsible for much of our state's unemployment. Ten years ago, the federal government passed the Trade Adjustment Act to help workers and firms affected by imports. They can receive extra unemployment compensation and training money for workers. They are eligible for grants and low-interest loans to develop new products or new production techniques.

Unfortunately, the application process is complicated. Few Massachusetts people have managed to benefit from the law.

We will correct this situation. The U.S. tariff commission will lend us a tariff expert. He will train our staff at the Department of Commerce and Development in the procedures which will bring federal help to Massachusetts. We will hire a grant expert. He will direct us to the fullest use of grants and low-interest loans available from the Federal Economic Development Administration.

Minority businessmen in our state still face special obstacles in the struggle for economic survival. So we must give them systematic assistance if they are going to flourish.

I will establish an Office of Minority Business Enterprise with available federal funds. The office will promote public and private contracts to stimulate these emerging businesses.

Technological progress has weighed heavily on our natural resources industries. Some of the most depressed areas in the state lie along our seacoast.

So I am reactivating the Commission on Ocean Management. I am ordering it to prepare a comprehensive program for shoreline development. The Commission will focus primarily on commercial fishing, as well as port and recreational development.

Today state government is not the prime mover in the field of economic development. Local communities now possess their own development agencies. Strong local efforts constitute an important part of the development mechanism.

I am filing legislation to give local agencies the power and flexibility to determine their own projects. Under this legislation local agencies can assemble sites and construct buildings for new firms.

In addition, this legislation allows local development agencies to float low interest, tax-free bonds. The proceeds will finance pollution abatement equipment for local industries . . . , thus, allowing industry to meet the new pollution regulations at reasonable cost.

The measures I have outlined today should infuse new life into our present economy.

But what of tomorrow? Will today's high growth industries continue to rise? Will the stimulants we apply today work equally well tomorrow?

I believe we must prepare now for future growth. I will file legislation to acquire $100,000 in economic research funds. The immense technological resources of the state can be enlisted to pioneer new product development. And to explore avenues of sustained growth potential in the years to come.

Successful prototypes will convince the rest of the nation to buy new products. A small investment of state funds today could mushroom into new jobs for Massachusetts residents a few years from now.

The steps that I have outlined today are but a beginning. I do not expect that they alone will resolve all of the problems of a sluggish economy.

Many of the obstacles to a full economic recovery are beyond our control.

We cannot expect to build a strong vibrant economy in Massachusetts while the rest of the nation agonizes through an economic slump.

We can, however, set the stage for a complete recovery . . . and that we shall do.

A healthy economy is in the best interest of everyone . . . citizen and taxpayer, labor and management, business and government.

Working together we can achieve a sound balanced economy. An economy which will support our cherished life-style, respect our natural environment, and provide for effective human development.

I ask you to join me in this effort.

The Governor's Message on the Economy of Massachusetts

Economics Department
The First National Bank of Boston
April 1972

Buoyed by the enthusiastic reaction to the December 1971 issue of The New England Letter, *The First National Bank of Boston chose the same forum in April of the following year to respond to Governor Sargent's March address. While it welcomed the Governor's proposal to implement tax incentives for Massachusetts firms, the article also questioned whether this move alone would be enough to stimulate new business capital spending and, in turn, employment growth.*

In addition to Sargent's proposed measures, this article advanced several additional ideas for aiding an economic turnaround. To boost in-state investment, for example, it suggested specific tax credits for "value added" in manufacturing. And it endorsed a proposal by Tom Sampson from the Boston office of the Chicago-based accounting firm of Arthur Andersen & Co. that would give each company that added more than ten full-time jobs to its payroll an annual credit of $500 per job. Furthermore it challenged the state's stringent pollution control laws, claiming that the business community found them restrictive to growth.

Like the previous piece, this article gave voice to many of the concerns of the business community as a whole. In the process it challenged some of the basic tenets of the existing state government, including its reluctance to make commitments to the business community along with its strong endorsement of environmental protection. The Andersen proposal—along with some other business-backed proposals—were incorporated in the "Mass Incentives" package passed by the legislature in 1973.

The most pressing need that faces the Massachusetts government is reversal of the effects of economic stagnation:

• Reduction in unemployment
• Revival of industrial activity
• Removal of social hardships

The governor's economic message, delivered on March 13, 1972, recognizes the urgency of this tripartite need. Indeed, the message may mark a turning point in the state's fortunes if the economy of Massachusetts can command the concern of the legislature as well as the governor.

This *Report* recommends a series of specific steps, in the spirit of the governor's message, that will lead to the immediate creation of new jobs and to the resumption of sustained economic growth in the Commonwealth.

The First National Bank of Boston has been emphasizing for some time the dangers that lie ahead if new measures are not taken to stimulate the economy of the state. In our December *Letter,* for example, we outlined the findings of a year-long study undertaken by the Bank to identify obstacles which prevent restoration of growth, profits, and jobs in the Commonwealth of Massachusetts.

Since then, in presentations before the state's government, labor leaders, and businessmen, we have described the dismal economic situation that would prevail by 1975 if a "do-nothing" policy were adopted. We have consistently emphasized the need to create jobs and to secure full employment in the state's economy. Time and again we have warned of the consequences of inaction.

The Governor's Economic Message

From this perspective, the governor's recent economic message is welcome as a clear recognition of the state's highest priority problem: the stagnation of Massachusetts' economy resulting from its economic maturity. Further, the message is evidence of a resolve by the state government to do something decisive. At the core of the message is the proposal to reduce the tax on inventories and machinery and to triple the investment tax credit from one to three percent for manufacturing firms. Both of these proposals indicate that the governor is committed to reducing unemployment by increasing investment incentives for firms residing in Massachusetts. But as welcome as these tax measures are, there is a question if they are sufficient by themselves.

The primary objective of reducing unemployment can be accomplished in the short run by the Andersen proposal. We endorse it as a direct and immediate way of creating jobs.

The Proposal by Arthur Andersen & Co.

In a recent meeting with state officials, a tax proposal was put forward by Arthur Andersen & Co. for providing an immediate employment opportunity incentive to manufacturing firms located in the Commonwealth. According to the proposal "each employer who adds jobs to his payroll, starting with a minimum of ten jobs, shall receive an annual credit of $500 per full-time job added. The credit will continue as long as the job is continued, but for no less than five years in total."

One of the advantages of such an employment incentive is that it will cost the state nothing in terms of lost tax revenue. In fact, revenues will actually increase as a result of these tax credits. A new job for Massachusetts means a new worker earning a new wage to be taxed by the personal income tax, and the firm with expanded employment will also pay more taxes to the state. These new revenues alone would offset the $500 cost to the state; but if the new worker was formerly on the welfare or unemployment rolls in Massachusetts, the state would enjoy a substantial expenditure reduction in addition to the increased revenues.

This tax credit proposal is sound only as an initial step to stimulate employment in the immediate future. If such an incentive were to remain in force for long, it could cause inefficient distortions of the production process. Firms artificially encouraged by tax exemptions to hire more labor will naturally tend to use more labor in relation to capital equipment than economic efficiency requires. This excessive use of labor could lead, in turn, to a reduction in the productivity of workers.

Despite its adverse impact on efficiency in the long run, the Andersen proposal has great merit as an emergency short-run measure for increasing employment in Massachusetts. Eventually the state must adopt a tax program that would deal with the long-run causes of unemployment as well as the symptoms.

We propose a tax credit program based on value added in manufacturing. Our proposal follows logically from the Andersen plan because it is designed to encourage efficiency in the utilization of labor and capital.

Tax Credits for Value Added in Manufacture

As we have stated on numerous occasions, the immediate policy objective in Massachusetts is to stimulate employment. But the long-run goal of the state's economic policy must be to sustain vigor in an efficient manufacturing sector. Investment which brings current technology to our industries must be encouraged, because modern methods will open rapidly expanding markets to these industries, which will then generate sustained employment and render our labor force highly productive and highly paid.

We believe that this objective can be achieved by introduction of a system of credits against state taxes based upon the value added in manufacturing. By "value added" we mean the sales revenue of each firm less the value of all its purchases from other firms. The system we propose will reward firms by offering them tax exemptions in direct proportion to the value of output which they generate through the activity of the workers, capital equipment, and technical expertise used in their production processes.

Existing firms will be encouraged by a tax credit to expand their output and create jobs. For these firms, the tax credit should be calculated on the basis of the percentage increase in their value added from the preceding year.

New firms—less than five years in Massachusetts—will be granted a tax credit based upon the actual level of their value added in production.

There are three direct benefits of this program; these are:

• The program will stimulate employment and investment
• The tax exemption contains built-in safeguards
• The program will increase total tax revenue

Employment Stimulation

The proposed program of tax credits will stimulate higher utilization of the state's existing capital equipment, thereby adding new jobs. It will also encourage new capital spending by the state's manufacturing firms, and this new capital spending will further stimulate employment. Finally, by inducing firms to remain technologically up-to-date, the program will ensure a productive labor force.

Safeguards

The program provides safeguards against intentional adjustments in value added for the purpose of maximizing tax credits. During a year in which value added by a firm declines, the firm would not qualify for the tax credit and would, therefore, be taxed at a higher rate. During a recession, the loss of the tax credit could be an undue burden for many firms. Under these circumstances, the credit may be maintained.

Tax Revenue

The overall effect of this program on the state budget will be extremely favorable. As output and employment are expanded, total tax revenue from businesses and their employees will grow and increase the tax base.

The concept of stimulating efficient growth in Massachusetts through the use of tax credits is a sound one. Some may be critical of this tax proposal on the grounds that it will accentuate the squeeze on business profits during a recession, and thus introduce unnecessary instability into our state economy. We accept this criticism but believe that it misses a fundamental point.

Without a doubt, the Massachusetts economy is now locked in the trap of economic stagnation as a consequence of maturity. Our outmoded capital stock and loss of comparative advantage in large parts of manufacturing are clear characteristics of this trap. This means that we have reached the point where new growth in manufacturing will not be encouraged by traditional economic policies. Rather, an economic strategy is needed to provide the incentive to get the economic base of Massachusetts out of this maturity trap.

The value-added credit is aimed specifically at this need by encouraging existing firms to become more efficient by balancing their investment in new plant and equipment. Thus, to dismiss the value-added credit as being unstable is to overlook the fact that it is only through careful unbalancing that new capital spending and new employment will take place. This is the most direct path to a growing economy and full employment.

A more detailed description of the value-added credit will be published shortly in the Bank's monograph series.

Need for Control of Government Spending

Whenever plans are made to implement new taxes and increase revenues, it seems reasonable to look also into the uses of these revenues. The government of Massachusetts has experienced a 250 percent increase in spending during the past five years: so it is now imperative to review these spending increases and to bring under control some programs in which spending is too high for the sluggish economy to support. For example, expenditures by the Department of Public Welfare had risen 1,200 percent by 1971 from their 1966 level. Clearly, increased employment and more rapid economic growth in Massachusetts is needed to stem this fantastic rate of increase in welfare spending.

Taxes which add downward pressure to an already lagging economy cannot be tolerated. Thus, control of spending is critical in the next few years while programs are instituted to revitalize the economy.

Tax Reform

Various plans have been suggested that deal with revising the Massachusetts income tax. Indeed, a number of people wish to see the Commonwealth adopt a graduated income tax system at this time.

But redistributing the tax burden and raising more tax revenue from the existing group of taxpayers should not be the primary objective of tax policy at this time. Instead, Massachusetts needs a tax program that increases the tax base by creating more job opportunities at higher wage levels. The ultimate goal of the value-added tax reform proposed in this *Report* is to create better employment prospects for everyone, to bring about an increase in the productivity of labor which will lead to higher wage rates, and to broaden the tax base.

The urgency of the contemporary economic situation requires that the issue of graduation in our tax structure be set aside momentarily—until the acute unemployment situation in Massachusetts is ameliorated, and government spending is under better control. Otherwise, in the midst of current debate, we may lose sight of the overriding issue in our state—job creation.

Cleaning Up and Protecting the Environment

In his economic message, the governor stressed the necessity of a clean environment; in his own words:

But let one thing be clear. This administration is committed to cleaning up the environment. There can be and will be no let up in our fight against pollution. We will make every effort to assist business in compliance with environmental regulations . . . but we will not relax standards of permit violations. There is simply too much at stake.

A healthy environment can be our most precious asset . . . we must not surrender the future for the convenience of today. Under the policies I have outlined we will have an overview of the economic and environmental impact of our future decisions. This will go a long way toward helping us make balanced and rational judgments.

I would venture to predict that this kind of balanced review policy will trigger a trend across the nation. We have successfully experimented in other areas in the past, when most states have feared to try. Here especially, we cannot be afraid to be first.

We fully support the governor in his search for an economically rational method to improve our physical environment. In our eagerness to halt pollution, we must not debilitate our economic system.

In dealing with the environment problem, the governor must not lose sight of the fact that the imposition of pollution control requirements on firms—however desirable such controls might be—increases the costs of doing business in Massachusetts. Clearly, firms must not be given a free license to pollute our environment at will, but neither should they be forced to adopt control programs which will raise costs of production disproportionately to pollution-control costs in other states.

Proposal to Hire Technical and Management Specialists

The proposal by the governor to hire technical and management specialists "to assist struggling companies" is aimed at a serious problem; however, we don't believe that state-employed consultants can solve it.

There are persuasive reasons which argue against having the state hire technical and management specialists. First, the federal government—specifically the Small Business Administration—has consultants available at no cost to troubled companies. Private groups also exist to provide free technical and management advice to minority enterprises; so the state's entry into this field seems superfluous. Second, competent private consultants should be worth their fees and more to companies that use them well. A specialist's diagnosis of a firm's problems should lead to enough improvement in that firm's profit position to pay the consulting fee. If such improvement does not occur, the consultant was either poorly utilized or not competent. Free state aid would probably lead to excessive and inefficient use of technical and management consultants.

Thus, we believe that a firm must be allowed to hire, on its own, the technical and management consulting specialists that it needs. Even to a "struggling company" advice may only be worth what it costs.

The Goal . . . Efficient Growth in Manufacturing

In conclusion, we admire the theme of the governor's economic message but find some of his specific proposals lacking. The governor's recognition of Massachusetts' acute economic problem—unemployment—paves the way for an immediate tax credit for job creation as proposed by Arthur Andersen & Co. The longer-run goal of sustained economic growth can be better met with our proposed tax credit for efficient growth in manufacturing. We believe that spending by the state government must be more carefully controlled. We oppose imposition of any new taxes in the currently stagnant economic environment. Improvement of the physical environment is, as the governor mentioned, a high priority goal that must be approached in an economically rational way. Finally, we agree with the governor that struggling companies need skilled consulting help, but the consultants should belong to private firms and be chosen by the struggling companies.

The State's Fiscal Crisis

Francis W. Sargent
Governor of Massachusetts
April 1972

The problems of the state's economy were inextricably intertwined with the state's fiscal management problems. Rising inflation and an eroding tax base were cutting into state revenues. And with the money to pay for the Commonwealth's extensive social service programs drying up, the state budget was plunging into the red, just at a time when the sagging economy created a greater need for many of these services.

Governor Sargent addressed this crisis on April 8, 1972, in a speech to the Massachusetts Taxpayers Foundation. In this address he lamented the bind he found himself in: a rising demand for services, on one hand, and increasingly strident calls for budgetary control, on the other.

While promising to tighten the state's budget, and to "gamble" on tax incentives to stimulate the economy, Sargent also proposed "substantive" tax reform, including a reevaluation of the state's "oppressive" property tax, which had long served as the principal source of income for cities and towns. Sargent also proposed a graduated state income tax similar to the federal system, a concept which had long been vigorously opposed by both individual taxpayers and the business community.

It will come as no surprise to anyone in this room when I tell you that the state of Massachusetts is in the grip of a severe financial crisis.

What is not so well known perhaps is that this unhealthy fiscal condition is shared not only by nearly every state in the nation . . . but also by the federal government.

For the past few years we have heard much about the desperate financial plight of state and local governments . . . but most people assumed that federal resources were boundless.

Recently, however, it has begun to appear that even the federal reservoir has a bottom . . . and that bottom is quickly being reached.

Citizens and taxpayers groups, like your own, have been asking how did this happen? How did governments run out of money . . . and why have they not then cut back on spending?

These are certainly valid questions . . . , but they do not lend themselves to easy answers.

This afternoon I would like to take a look at some of the factors which have contributed to our present unhealthy financial condition in the Commonwealth.

It is the primary function of government to provide its citizens with services which they cannot otherwise obtain.

In recent years a better-educated and widely informed public has begun to demand more from its government. Increased social awareness has prompted government to enact badly needed, but costly, social programs. High unemployment coupled with crippling inflation have placed unprecedented strains on government . . . , while sharply curtailing government tax resources.

The result is an increase in demand for services at the same time that the tax base is shrinking. It consequently becomes more difficult each year to balance the state's budget.

There is of course a growing concern over how the state spends the money it raises. Yet misconceptions and a good deal of misinformation on this issue abound.

Let's look at the facts.

In fiscal 1973, Massachusetts will spend 22.5 percent of its income for welfare. This is the biggest single area of state expense and probably the most unpopular.

Yet the caricature of the welfare mother with seven illegitimate children riding the gravy train to riches at the expense of the working man has distorted the reality of the welfare program.

Welfare in Massachusetts is far broader than rebellious taxpayers suspect. It includes aid to the elderly, aid to the disabled, children services and food programs, as well as the AFDC program.

It is popular to exaggerate the cost of abuse and fraud in welfare. But such theories cannot be supported by facts.

Survey after survey has determined that abuse in welfare is minimal. That in fact the vast majority of recipients are honest victims of their surroundings.

The second largest portion of the state's budget goes to education. After that, aid to cities and towns consumes over 13 percent of tax revenues.

Most of the state's spending is already essential. We cannot let people starve. Nor can we default on our obligations to local communities.

It is easy for concerned citizens to demand budget cuts and call for reductions in spending . . . , but Massachusetts *must* continue to meet its obligations in a responsible manner. That makes budget cutting nearly impossible.

Individuals and groups like your own have suggested paring the budget to the bone.

I have done just that; the problem is this. I receive letters from individuals complaining about extravagant governmental spending and outrageously high taxes . . . , then two weeks later I get a letter from the very same person berating me for cutting the budget request of the University of Massachusetts . . . or some other, equally worthy, institution. . . .

One of the problems with budgets is that you can't have it both ways. You can't cut expenditures and still maintain programs.

Almost daily we are attacked in the newspapers for pruning one program or another. Yet in the same paper you find articles criticizing the administration for spending too much or raising taxes. But you simply cannot have your cake and eat it too.

We have taken steps to control the seemingly runaway cost of government.

We have begun a reorganization of state bureaucracy. This administration is committed to making order out of what was a chaotic situation in Massachusetts.

Already reorganization holds out great promise. Through a better coordination of departments and agencies, we will be able to reduce the costly and needless duplication of services, and we will be able to make government more acceptable.

In addition we have selected priorities with economy in mind. For example, the community-based concepts, which we are applying in the areas of adult and juvenile corrections and in mental health, are not only sound from a rehabilitative standpoint, they also invite hope for much greater economies in government. We will no longer be forced to pay for costly institutions long after they have lost their justification.

We have also begun a real austerity program in the executive branch. I have issued a directive which states that no vacant position in state service will be filled . . . unless a legitimate urgency can be documented. Moreover I have called a halt to all temporary employment in state government.

These are actions which will save the taxpayers' money.

But more will have to be done.

Last month I outlined a series of proposals to stimulate the economy of the state and create more jobs.

At the time I pointed out there is only so much a governor can do. With a stroke of his pen, the president can turn the economy of a state around. But a governor's power to affect the economy is limited to providing tax incentives to encourage business expansion.

Thus we did what we could.

We took a gamble that the tax incentives we hold out will be translated into substantial economic expansion and many new jobs.

This will help our sagging economy. It will check our soaring unemployment rate. But it will be some time before we can expect to reap substantial rewards. In the meantime we must act immediately to hold the line on spending.

Tomorrow I shall return the state employees' pay raise to the legislature. I am requesting that their cost of living adjustment become effective only on January first, 1973.

I take no pleasure in this action.

Most state employees are hardworking people who are often underpaid. And like the rest of us, they need more money, now, to meet soaring prices.

But the plain fact is that we cannot afford to pay an across the board increase at this time. We simply do not have the money. Approval of the pay raise, retroactive to January first of this year . . . would seriously jeopardize the state's financial solvency.

As much as I would like to sign this measure, I simply can not.

In the next few weeks we in government are going to have to make some tough decisions. The legislature is currently reviewing the budget.

If they add one dime to that budget, Massachusetts will find itself faced with a tax program this year.

This is not a threat, it is the truth of the matter. The simple, depressing truth.

But we must also look beyond the next few weeks. To meet future fiscal needs, dramatic reform of the state's tax structure is essential.

Talk of budget cutting may be enticing, but it is not realistic. The indications are that in the foreseeable future demands on state government will not lessen. Rather they will continue to multiply. So we must come to grips with that reality.

I have fought for a national takeover of welfare. I believe that the responsibility for an equitable program properly belongs to the federal government. I believe that in the not too distant future we will get a national welfare program and states will be relieved of a crushing burden they can no longer meet. But that will not solve all our problems.

Courts in several states have already ruled that the property tax is an unfair means of financing education. Without a doubt, the states will eventually have to absorb the bulk of education costs.

There is also the hope that Congress will soon enact a revenue-sharing proposal to funnel cash to hard-pressed states as well as cities and towns.

But in the final analysis, the financial crisis which threatens the well-being of Massachusetts citizens will be resolved right here by those of us in state government.

It is our first responsibility to submit tight and efficient budgets. But we must also move aggressively to initiate substantive tax reform.

The property tax in Massachusetts has climbed to the point where it is absolutely oppressive.

It hits hardest those who are least able to pay. It is an archaic tax form which was never intended to provide the bulk of revenue for our cities and towns. And the basic inequity of the tax is often magnified by abuses in its application.

The property tax has become the flash point of the taxpayers' rebellion. It is in urgent need of drastic reform, and that reform must come soon.

But we can overhaul our existing tax structure just so much. And in the long run a lottery or steep taxes on "forbidden" luxuries like cigarettes and liquor cannot really do the whole job.

We must begin to look at other alternatives. Even at those which may not seem so appealing at first glance.

I am well aware that many members of the Taxpayers Foundation shudder at the thought of a graduated state income tax.

But it is a levy that has worked well on the federal level. And it is considered by many to be the fairest and most effective tax form available.

We may have reached the point where we will have to review the value of a graduated tax, not because we want to but because feasible alternatives are running out.

The next few weeks and months will demand some hard decisions from those of us in government.

To make these decisions properly, we will need the help and advice of all our concerned citizens and groups.

The Taxpayers Foundation has offered its assistance in helping to trim the budget. I have gratefully accepted that generous offer. Let it be clear: this administration is ready and willing to work with the Taxpayers Foundation, the legislature, or any other groups who have constructive suggestions to offer.

The state's fiscal situation is indeed critical. Resolution of our problems will only come if we can work together to create an efficient government that is responsive to the needs of all its people.

The Impending Fiscal Crisis

Economics Department
The First National Bank of Boston
August 1972

The Bank of Boston's outspoken criticism of state policy continued with the August edition of The New England Letter, *which responded to Sargent's April 8 speech. Stating flatly that control of state spending is an essential ingredient of economic revitalization, the article blamed Massachusetts' excessive spending for the high cost of doing business in the Commonwealth.*

To solve Massachusetts' problems, the piece argued, Sargent's administration should concentrate on keeping taxes and other costs of doing business in the state under control. This would encourage the business community to expand in the state, creating more jobs and a larger tax base. The increased revenues from the expanded tax base could then fund the state's programs for social services.

To bring some immediate relief, the article suggested boosting the state sales tax. Simultaneously, it maintained, the state should take concrete steps to better plan and manage its $2 billion budget as part of an overall effort to bring its taxes in line with those of other states.

Once again, The New England Letter *allowed the business community to air some of its specific complaints about the relatively high cost of doing business in Massachusetts. To many businesses, one of the most irksome costs was the unemployment compensation tax, which was funded entirely by business. It was this cost more than any other, some claimed, that was driving firms to relocate in the South and other regions where unemployment compensation taxes were significantly lower. As unemployment rose in the state, so did the tax, putting even greater pressure on companies that stayed behind.*

- The Massachusetts *state government is confronted with a fiscal crisis*—government spending outrunning revenues.
- This fiscal crisis is the direct *result* of the *state's economic stagnation*. Massachusetts industry suffers from a substantial competitive cost disadvantage relative to other states.
- As the Bay State *experiences economic difficulty, welfare rolls grow.* Indeed, the number of welfare recipients has risen to 519,000, up 349,000 from 1960.
- A strong and growing state economy can come only after the *competitive position of the state's industry* in the national and international marketplace has been restored.

Our Massachusetts state government is confronted with a fiscal crisis—government spending outrunning revenues available under the current revenue structure. For fiscal year ending June 30, 1973, last minute spending cuts of about $70 million had to be made in an attempt to bring the state budget in balance. The Massachusetts Tax-payers Foundation estimates that the revenue shortfall may be as much as $300 million by 1974. Why is the state government in this bind? And how may the crisis be averted?

We believe that the deteriorating fiscal situation here in Massachusetts—which has been aggravated by the fiscal imprudence of the state government—is a direct result of the economy's stagnation. Any long-run solution to the fiscal problem must involve revitalization of the state's economy and reassessment of the priorities and goals of state government. Any stopgap solution must not delay achievement of these goals.

The Economy's Stagnation

Since 1967, 95,000 jobs have been lost in the Commonwealth's manufacturing sector. The growing part of our economy—durable goods production and services—is not creating jobs at a rate fast enough to absorb new workers and to offset job losses in the declining industries—especially the textile and leather industries. In fact, total private employment in Massachusetts has remained virtually unchanged during the past five years, while the number of workers without jobs has increased by nearly 100,000.

As we warned in the Bank's December *New England Letter,* "Massachusetts has just about run out of wealth-creating energy, and its economic engine needs an overhaul." This overhaul must trigger sound economic growth and smooth the social and economic adjustments for workers employed in our declining industries. Concerted action on the part of government, business, and labor is needed to restore growth momentum in Massachusetts.

State Government Spending

While the private economy has been troubled, state government spending has mushroomed. In the fiscal 1973 budget for the Commonwealth, spending is two and one half times as large as it was in 1967. State government expenditures have increased more than four times as fast as gross state product during the past five years, as is shown graphically in the chart below.

Both the executive and legislative branches of the state government have demonstrated considerable enthusiasm for putting the Commonwealth ahead of other states by setting high standards for antipollution measures and social benefits. They may have improved our ecology and social welfare, but the improvements are barely perceptible. But they have succeeded in raising the cost of doing business in Massachusetts. They have neglected to give adequate attention to protecting our tax base with the result that the funds are not—and will not—be available to sustain essential governmental programs.

Relative Cost of Doing Business

Massachusetts suffers from a substantial competitive disadvantage relative to other states. For example, local property taxes in Massachusetts are the second highest in the nation, power costs are 8 percent above the national average, and unemployment compensation tax rates are 41 percent above the national average. The table that follows contains actual cost figures for a company that does business in both Massachusetts and Texas.

In each instance, the Massachusetts costs are substantially higher. The company pays a total of $969,000 more for these four items in

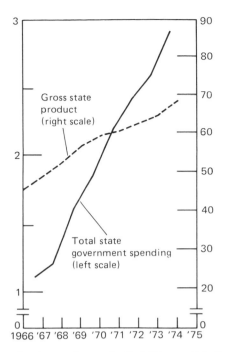

The destructive cycle (in billions of dollars)

	Massachusetts	Texas	Difference (as % of Massachusetts costs)
Power	$ 456,000	$252,000	45%
Unemployment compensation	401,000	44,000	89
Workman's compensation	299,000	177,000	41
State taxes	382,000	96,000	75
	$1,538,000	$569,000	63%

Massachusetts than in Texas. Comparison of real estate taxes would, in most instances, considerably worsen the Massachusetts cost picture. They have not been included because the real estate tax burden would vary considerably depending upon the particular communities selected. Massachusetts cannot stay this far out of line with other states in the cost of doing business without destroying the base that is the sole support of our economic well-being.

The Destructive Cycle

This is the destructive cycle: our economy weakens as state government spending grows out of control. As the state takes over an ever-larger portion, the private sector is crushed under the burden of supporting extensive government activities. Then some businesses move to more favorable economic climates in other states, and the support burden on remaining business is further increased. One statistic summarizes the situation: state tax payments per person employed in the private sector of the Massachusetts economy have nearly doubled since 1967. Clearly, the brakes must be applied to the juggernaut of state spending while the spending machinery and appetites for new programs are reexamined.

Control of State Spending

Control of state spending is an essential ingredient of any plan of economic development. It is the only way costs here can be kept in line with those in other states. It is the foundation for keeping our tax system competitive.

The need for improved management of all state government activities is most obvious in the welfare programs. The state is confronted with near financial disaster due to a breakdown in welfare services. The Federal Department of Health, Education, and Welfare has teamed with the state Public Welfare Department to modernize the department.

State budgeting, like welfare administration, has long been a seriously neglected area. Improvements in the budget process have not kept pace with the tremendous growth of state government. The need for the recent across-the-board budgetary cuts is glaring testimony to this fact.

What is needed is realization that state government—with close to 70,000 employees and a budget exceeding $2 billion—is the largest single enterprise in New England. Then it will be recognized that budgetary reform is imperative! Zero-base budgeting—a system in which each spending program must justify itself each year—should be instituted. Under the zero-base system, older programs that have been virtually unquestioned because of stable spending patterns would be scrutinized in light of each year's constraints and priorities. Also program planning should be more closely linked to the budgeting process, with annual spending and appropriations considered as part of a long-term program of objectives and requisite spending.

This rationalization of the budgeting process would allow the state legislature to see more clearly the costs and benefits of various spending programs. Priorities could be more easily ordered. Within the state government bureaucracy, savings could result from better administration and control. It is our recommendation that budget reform be vigorously pursued forthwith.

But these reforms, even if assiduously pursued, will not solve our immediate problem. More tax revenue is needed in the short run to meet the impending budget deficit.

The Sales Tax—The Short-Run Solution to Our Fiscal Crisis

As a result of fiscal imprudence in the past, the state government now needs additional revenue to supplement careful spending cuts in realigning receipts and expenditures. A comparative study of state income taxes shows that Massachusetts relies far more heavily on the personal income tax than do most states. Indeed, 42 percent of Massachusetts' tax revenues are derived from the income tax, versus a 20 percent average for all states. Clearly, the income tax cannot be raised further, even in response to the fiscal crisis. An increased sales tax is the most logical source of major new revenue. In Massachusetts, we rely on the general sales tax for only 12 percent of our state tax revenues; but nationwide, the tax provides more than 40 percent of the state tax-take.

To put this disparity in more personal terms, the average resident of Massachusetts pays about one-fourth as much in sales taxes as his counterpart in the rest of the nation. For example, a family of four with an $11,000–$12,000 income pays about $37 a year in Massachusetts sales tax. In the other forty-five states that have a sales tax, this family would pay an average of $151 a year. Clearly, there is room to raise the sales tax in Massachusetts without significant harm to our competitive position relative to other states.

The Advisory Commission on Intergovernmental Relations

commissioned a nationwide survey on the public's fiscal preferences, and the results showed that the sales tax is the most popular tax. Almost one-half of the respondents said that if a state government must raise substantial new revenue, then the sales tax is the best vehicle. Only one-quarter of the respondents to the nationwide survey favored an increased state income tax. Opinion research polls show that taxpayers in Massachusetts have an even stronger preference for the sales tax relative to the income tax as a source of additional state revenue.

Revitalization of Massachusetts' Stagnant Economy—
The Long-Run Solution to Our Fiscal Crisis

Emergency spending cuts and a higher sales tax can be merely stopgap measures. But these measures will grant us valuable time to improve the economic climate of our state and to effect reforms in the government's management and spending policies. Policymakers must use this reprieve to formulate a cohesive strategy to revitalize the state economy. Government, business, and labor leaders must unite in their efforts to attract new industry to Massachusetts and to encourage existing industries to expand.

Restoration of our competitive position in the national and international marketplace can only result from stabilizing the cost of doing business in the Commonwealth. A richer, more vital economy will create more jobs and generate more resources for the state to pay the cost of combating social ills.

Unbalanced Growth in Manufacturing—
The Consequences

Our current economic problem arises largely from loss of jobs in the manufacturing sector. Job creation among nonmanufacturing industries continues to be quite strong.

In a recently completed, more detailed study of the manufacturing base of our economy, we analyzed the forces that create jobs and, therefore, studied the interaction of changes in employment and changes in output during a period (1963–1967) in which the state economy followed the national economy to full employment. During the expansion, Massachusetts' growth industries undertook substantial new capital spending on plant and equipment, even at a more rapid rate than in the same industries nationally. This, combined with the continued intensive use of labor in declining industries, built in an unemployment vulnerability during periods of slack national demand and left our employment base especially sensitive to the slackening of demand in the 1969–1970 recession. Hence, our current unemployment problem.

The basis for these generalizations rests on analysis of production functions for twenty-eight traditional and expanding industries.

Among the state's fourteen traditional industries, we found:

• Five Massachusetts traditional industries experienced both output and labor declines despite the overall expansion in the national economy. Nationally, there was no case where both output and labor declined simultaneously in these industries.

• Five Massachusetts traditional industries increased output mainly through a greater relative expansion of capital and less in expanding employment. In the same five industries in the nation, the increase in output was accompanied mainly through an increase in job creation.

• Four traditional industries expanded output and increased the share of labor both in Massachusetts and the nation. But even here the relative rate of job creation in these industries in Massachusetts was considerably slower than in the nation.

Among the state's fourteen expanding durable goods producing industries, we found:

• Six industries in both Massachusetts and the United States simultaneously increased output and employment. Four of these increased the share of labor relative to the United States while expanding output. But the use of capital was expanded at a much sharper rate in Massachusetts in the remaining two.

• Eight industries were rapidly expanding output locally and nationally. However, Massachusetts substituted capital for labor in these industries and actually decreased the absolute amount of labor used.

Interpretation of these relationships is valuable in assessing the near-term outlook for the Massachusetts economy. Many of the state's durable goods producing industries that are currently expanding output, in response to a booming national economy, are likely to do so with a greater relative reliance on capital that still is in excess of the national average. On the other hand, the state's traditional industries which are labor intensive continue to reduce employment. The consequence of these forces is the tendency for the unemployment rate to stay well above the nation as a whole. In other words, the current growth in aggregate demand may be adequate to push the national economy into the zone of full employment, but it will probably be inadequate to restore full employment in the Commonwealth.

Look Out, Massachusetts!!!

Economics Department
The First National Bank of Boston
November 1972

When the December 1971 issue of The New England Letter *roused such widespread praise for is message on the dangers facing the state, it also captured the imagination of the bank's own executive vice-president, Ephron Catlin. Fired up by the implications of the state's economic deterioration, Catlin asked the economics department to prepare a series of charts outlining the problem in detail, and then presented the story in a series of private meetings with business leaders, bankers, community leaders, and legislators to solicit ideas on what could be done. Encouraged by these meetings, he got the idea to assemble the material, along with some simple words of explanation, into a pamphlet for wider dissemination.*

Prepared by bank economists Howell and Mary Ellen Byrn, the twenty-eight-page booklet was distributed in November 1972 to a broad audience throughout the state, including all chief executive officers and key elected officials. The cover showed the outline of Massachusetts slipping beneath the waves, with just the northeast corner of the state and the tip of Cape Cod still visible above the waterline. Demand was so great that eventually 75,000 copies were produced in five printings. A number of newspapers reprinted some of the charts, especially those showing the growth of welfare expenditures in the state.

Whereas the 1971 article had merely tested the waters, Look Out, Massachusetts!!! *plunged the business community into the political arena. It also brought economic development to the forefront of public concern, eventually helping to make it the primary issue debated by candidates in the 1974 gubernatorial election.*

The Problem: In recent years it has become painfully clear that the Massachusetts economy has gotten out of line with the rest of the nation. Since 1967, more than 100,000 jobs have been lost in the Commonwealth's manufacturing sector. The overall impact on the state's general economic health of this severe shrinkage in manufacturing jobs has been great.

The unemployment rate has jumped from around 4 percent to the 7.5-8.0 percent zone — that's more than 225,000 breadwinners who are currently unemployed. Fewer jobs mean an eroding tax base and, hence, a significant falloff in tax receipts.

Simultaneously, the ranks of welfare recipients have swelled by 200,000. And, by mid-1972, the total number of persons on one form of welfare or another has risen to the staggering total of more than 750,000.

The purpose of this booklet is to pinpoint the causes of our current economic difficulty and to recommend solutions to restore our economic vitality.

. . . The Massachusetts unemployment situation is out of line with the nation.

For over a decade, the unemployment rate in the Commonwealth of Massachusetts moved very close to the rate for the nation as a whole. But in recent years local business activity has been unable to increase employment and output to get our economy going again; consequently, the state's unemployment rate has jumped upward to an unacceptable level.

The fundamental cause that is holding down our current business expansion, and increasing unemployment, is simply this:

The cost of doing business has gotten out of line with other competitive states. Current estimates clearly show that rapidly escalating business costs are pricing many Massachusetts-produced goods out of the marketplace. Private studies by Honeywell and Acushnet show that Massachusetts costs are as much as 200 to 400 percent higher than costs elsewhere.

The state government has been unable to develop a sensible economic blueprint for our recovery. Rather than constructively building for our common economic future, many politicians have consistently maintained that our current economic problems should be placed at the doorstep of the federal government in Washington.

The Solution:

The ultimate solution of the current problems of our state rests on two factors: (1) fiscal responsibility and (2) a strong state economy.

As we must do in our personal affairs and as business must meet accepted and prudent financial and accounting practices, as taxpayers **we must demand greater fiscal responsibility** in state government. The Commonwealth is spending two and one half times as much as it was in 1967, and revenue shortfalls have become commonplace because our state's economy is no longer strong and growing.

Both the executive and legislative branches of the state government must moderate their enthusiasm for placing the Commonwealth ahead of all other states in matters of spending for social benefits and for ill-advised environmental measures that produce barely measurable benefits at great cost.

The first step must be **a two-year ceiling on all state spending.** Expenditure increases in any area must be met with reductions of expenditures for the outmoded programs that no longer serve their original purpose and other economies.

This ceiling on all state spending will provide valuable time **to improve the economic climate of the state.** Policy makers should use this time to formulate a bold new economic strategy to revitalize the state and to accelerate job creation in key growth industries. Restoration of our competitive position in the national and international marketplace can result only from stabilizing the cost of doing business in the Commonwealth. And, in turn, a richer, healthier state economy can generate resources to use in combating social and environmental ills.

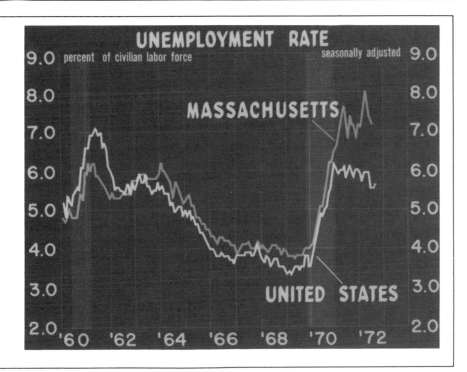

. . . In the face of a deteriorating economy, the state continues to spend precious tax receipts on programs of questionable economic value, while state and local government employment has increased by 42,000 in the past four years.

In terms of state spending for social programs, Massachusetts is considered to be the most liberal state in the nation. This chart shows state and local expenditures per capita for Massachusetts and seven other representative states. Note that the per capita expenditures in Massachusetts are only slightly behind New York and California — two states whose economic bases can better support higher spending rates.

. . . Total spending per capita in Massachusetts, Connecticut, and Illinois is roughly the same, but one dollar in five in Massachusetts goes for welfare, approximately twice the spending rate in Connecticut and Illinois.

Shown in this chart are per capita expenditures for welfare. Note the explosive increase in welfare spending per capita in Massachusetts over the past several years. The recent buildup in the state's welfare staggers one's imagination. In 1960 there were 170,000 recipients; by mid-1972 this number has swelled to more than 750,000. These spending demands for welfare leave only small amounts for education and critical economic and business programs.

Our views about this explosive increase are straightforward: the solution to our welfare crisis can only be solved through better control and management, not through a reduction in the level of payments to recipients.

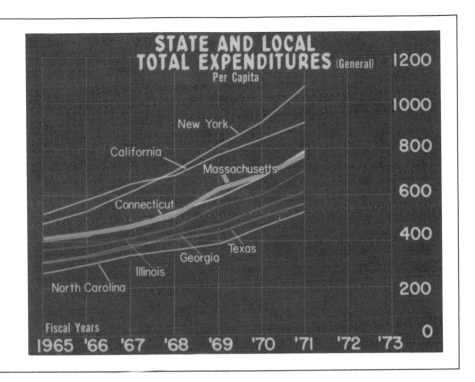

STATE AND LOCAL
TOTAL EXPENDITURES (General)
Per Capita

New York
California
Massachusetts
Connecticut
Texas
Georgia
Illinois
North Carolina

Fiscal Years
1965 '66 '67 '68 '69 '70 '71 '72 '73

1200
1000
800
600
400
200
0

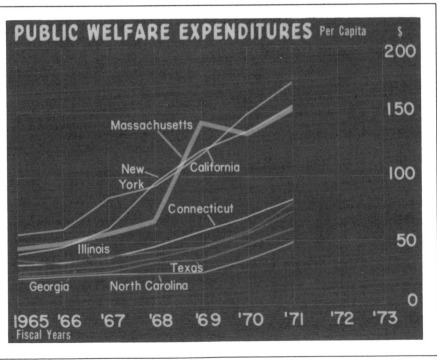

PUBLIC WELFARE EXPENDITURES Per Capita $

Massachusetts
New York
California
Connecticut
Illinois
Texas
Georgia
North Carolina

1965 '66 '67 '68 '69 '70 '71 '72 '73
Fiscal Years

200
150
100
50
0

. . . Massachusetts has lost control of spending on the MEDICAID program.

Shown in this chart are the results of a private study conducted for the United States Department of Health, Education, and Welfare in Washington, D.C. These figures show that the Massachusetts Department of Welfare has completely lost control of spending of the state's MEDICAID program. Cost per recipient for a physician's services in the Commonwealth is currently running three times greater than in New York, while the cost per recipient for pharmaceutical services is more than five times the New York rate.

The average costs for the nation as a whole are $55.00 per recipient for physician's services and $45.00 per recipient for pharmaceutical services, only about one third the Massachusetts rate.

. . . Taken together, the consequences of uncontrolled state spending and a weak economy mean that workers in private businesses must carry more and more publicly-supported individuals.

This chart vividly shows the consequences of excessive spending on social programs while ignoring the increasing weakness in our private economy. In 1960 there were four workers in the private economy for every person either employed or supported by the state. By 1971 this ratio had halved to 1.9 private workers to 1 person either employed or supported by the state.

Those persons either employed or supported by the state include: (1) state and local government employees, (2) those supported by unemployment compensation, and (3) those supported by welfare in one form or another.

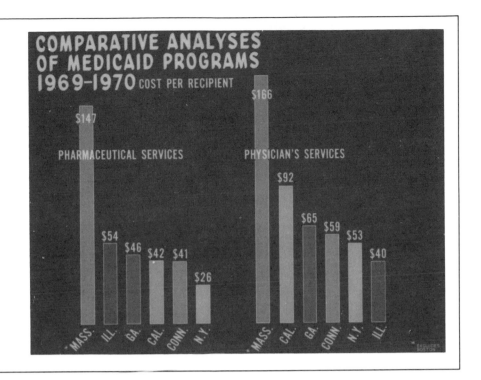

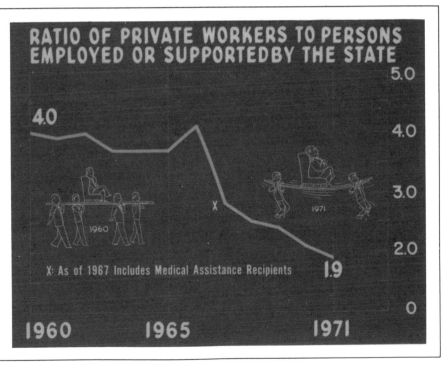

. . . Total private employment has remained constant at slightly less than two million, while manufacturing employment has declined by 95,000 in the past four years alone. Simultaneously, those employed by or supported by the state have increased to more than 1,000,000 today, or roughly one person in five.

Shown in this chart are the underlying trends that explain the sharp decline in the private-public sector ratio in the preceding chart. The fact that may be seen so clearly in this chart is the near economic stagnation of the private economy in the Commonwealth. Yet in the face of this stagnation, the total number of persons either employed or supported by the state continues to rise at a disturbing rate. If this trend continues, businesses in the existing economic base of Massachusetts may soon be unable to function competitively as a result of the excessive tax pressure to finance state spending programs.

. . . The effects of spending so much on welfare in the Commonwealth mean that less is available to be spent on stimulating economic development.

Shown in this chart are the spending priorities for the eight states. For instance, in Massachusetts nearly 20 percent of total state and local spending is for public welfare, the highest among the eight states. Note also that Massachusetts spends more for fire protection than the other seven states. And because we spend so much on welfare, there is less to be spent on stimulating local economic development. Note the small amounts that Massachusetts spends in key areas such as highways and education.

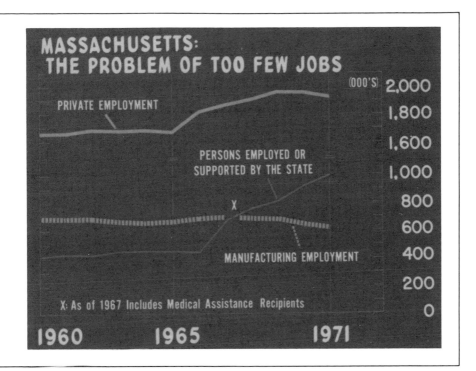

MASSACHUSETTS:
THE PROBLEM OF TOO FEW JOBS

PRIVATE EMPLOYMENT

PERSONS EMPLOYED OR SUPPORTED BY THE STATE

X

MANUFACTURING EMPLOYMENT

(000'S) 2,000 / 1,800 / 1,600 / 1,000 / 800 / 600 / 400 / 200 / 0

X: As of 1967 Includes Medical Assistance Recipients

1960   1965   1971

STATE AND LOCAL SPENDING IN PERCENT

Education	Pub. Wel.	Highway	Health & Hosp.	Other
0 20 40	0 10 20	0 10 20	0 10 20	0 10 20
N.C.	Mass.	Tex.	Ga.	Cal.
Tex.	Cal.	N.C.	N.Y.	N.Y.
Ill.	N.Y.	Conn.	Mass.	Mass.
Ga.	Ga.	Ga.	N.C.	Conn.
Conn.	Conn.	Ill.	Tex.	Ga.
Cal.	Ill.	Mass.	Ill.	Ill.
N.Y.	Tex.	Cal.	Cal.	N.C.
Mass.	N.C.	N.Y.	Conn.	Tex.

Int. Gen. Debt	Police	Sewer & San.	Fire	Parks
0 10 20	0 10 20	0 10 20	0 10 20	0 10 20
Conn.	N.Y.	Conn.	Mass.	Ill.
N.Y.	Ill.	Ill.	Conn.	Cal.
Tex.	Cal.	N.Y.	N.Y.	N.Y.
Mass.	Conn.	N.C.	Cal.	Conn.
Ga.	Mass.	Tex.	Ill.	Tex.
Ill.	Tex.	Mass.	Tex.	Mass.
Cal.	N.C.	Ga.	N.C.	N.C.
N.C.	Ga.	Cal.	Ga.	Ga.

. . . Relative to other competing states and the average for the nation, the Massachusetts taxpayer has consistently paid a larger part of his income for taxes.

Shown in this chart are the amounts of state and local taxes paid per $1,000 of personal income in the eight states. For instance, in 1971 the average taxpayer in Massachusetts paid $127 per $1,000 of income earned, compared with averages of $119 for the nation and $116 for the seven competing states. The underlying cause of the significantly higher taxes in Massachusetts is clear: excessively liberal social programs and inadequate management and insufficient spending controls in state and local government.

. . . Per capita taxes in the Commonwealth have been consistently higher than in states with which we compete.

The relative tax burden on the individual among the various states directly affects the cost of doing business in the state. Shown in this chart are total state and local taxes per capita. Note the steady acceleration in state taxes in Massachusetts that has significantly widened the tax differential between Massachusetts and Texas, Georgia, and North Carolina, states whose manufactured goods are in direct competition.

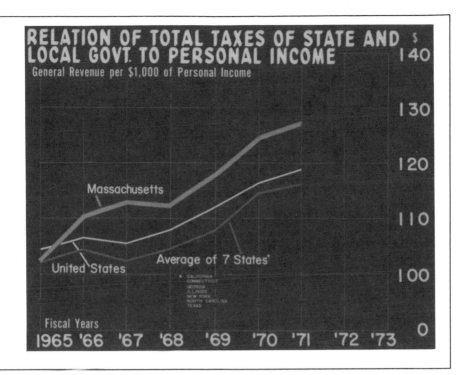

RELATION OF TOTAL TAXES OF STATE AND $
LOCAL GOVT. TO PERSONAL INCOME

General Revenue per $1,000 of Personal Income

Massachusetts

United States   Average of 7 States'

CALIFORNIA
CONNECTICUT
GEORGIA
ILLINOIS
NEW YORK
NORTH CAROLINA
TEXAS

Fiscal Years
1965 '66 '67 '68 '69 '70 '71 '72 '73

140
130
120
110
100
0

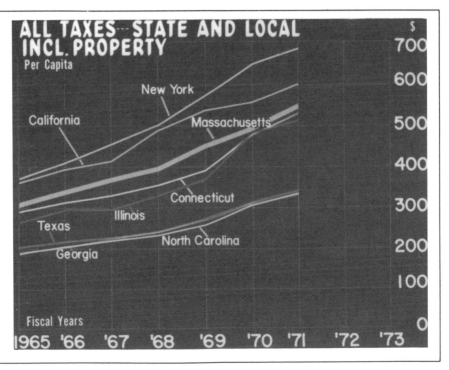

ALL TAXES--STATE AND LOCAL $
INCL. PROPERTY

Per Capita

New York

California   Massachusetts

Connecticut

Illinois

Texas

North Carolina

Georgia

Fiscal Years
1965 '66 '67 '68 '69 '70 '71 '72 '73

700
600
500
400
300
200
100
0

Look Out, Massachusetts!!!

. . . If current trends persist, the Property Tax in Massachusetts will be the highest in the nation.

The excessive pressure on the state government in Massachusetts to finance welfare has limited the amount of tax receipts available to be redistributed to local communities to finance education and other key town services, especially for education. Consequently, local cities and towns have had no alternative but to finance their needs through the only tax available to them — the property tax! The final resolution of the real estate tax crisis in Massachusetts depends on restraint in state and local spending, improved management and management controls in state and local government, revision of tax and cost allocation policies so as to lighten the excessive percentage burden which the property tax carries, and an improved system of distributing state tax receipts to the cities and towns.

The graduated income tax will not provide our towns and cities with property tax relief unless state and local spending is controlled. If Massachusetts copied New York state's graduated income tax — the highest of any major state — Massachusetts would raise no more money than from our current flat rate tax.

. . . Massachusetts has relied excessively on the real estate, personal income, and corporate income taxes to finance state programs. Sales taxes have played only a small part in producing greatly needed revenue.

Shown in this chart is the relative reliance on the four key sources of tax revenue in the eight states. Note that most states have relied principally on the combination of the real estate and sales taxes to finance expenditures, while New York and Massachusetts have relied on a combination of property and income taxes.

Only Massachusetts and New York have already turned to heavy personal income taxation. Studies have shown that high personal income taxation by states acts as a deterrent to local business expansion. Thus for competitive business reasons, we strongly believe that the income tax is not a realistic way of raising more income for the state. Increased use of the income tax could put Massachusetts at the very top in its reliance on the income tax as a source of revenue.

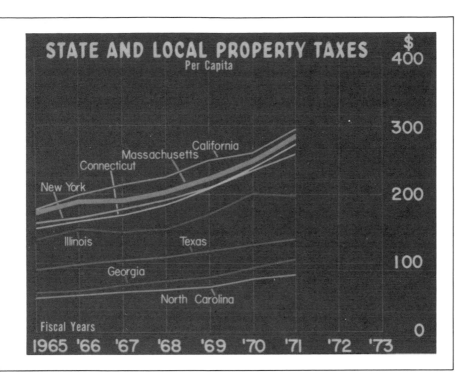

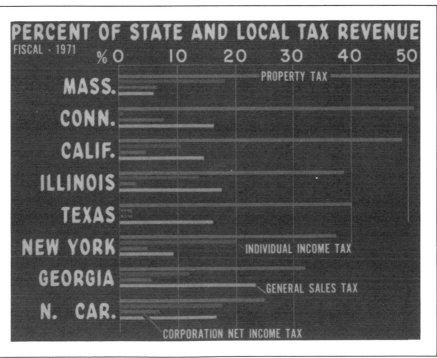

. . . The current Massachusetts flat rate income tax is progressive.

Shown in this chart is the calculated state income tax burden for six typical taxpayers in Massachusetts, New York, and a composite group of competing states.

The results of these calculations are indeed revealing to the current debate over the need for Massachusetts to abandon its current flat rate income tax for a graduated one.

A tax is considered to be progressive if higher income individuals pay a larger percentage of their total incomes than do lower income people. In actuality, the present Massachusetts income tax is progressive. Although many feel that equity would be better served by a more progressive tax — one with graduated rates — it does not appear that the current Massachusetts tax is grossly inequitable. Under 1971 income tax laws, a typical tax-payer in the $10,000 bracket paid a Massachusetts income tax of 3.5 percent of his income after federal taxes. In the $30,000 bracket the figure was 6.5 percent and rose to 8.5 percent for the $50,000 bracket. In fact, as the figures in the table below show, the flat rate in Massachusetts is a bit more progressive than is the graduated federal income tax.

	Percent of Total Income in Class	Percent of Population in Class	Percent of Federal Tax Paid by Class	Percent of Mass. Tax Paid by Class
under $5,000	11	23	6	3
$ 5,000 under $10,000	27	32	21	21
$10,000 under $15,000	28	28	25	27
$15,000 under $20,000	13	10	13	14
$20,000 and over	21	7	35	35

Source: Internal Revenue Service, *Statistics of Income*, 1969.

Postscript: The current debate over taxes and spending, on the one hand, and a strong, healthy economy, on the other, was stated very clearly in a recent column by the *Boston Globe*'s distinguished writer, David Wilson. Mr. Wilson wrote: ". . . the true choice is not between two sets of taxes but between taxes and no taxes, between the continued, unleashed expansion of the public sector and a cold-turkey fiscal crisis which would bring the state into harsh, even painful collision with economic realities." (The *Boston Globe,* September 23, 1972).

Author's Note:

Sources of state and local financial data in this booklet (with the exception of charts on pages 11 and 27) are *Governmental Finances* and *State Tax Collections*, published annually by the United States Department of Commerce.

Data source for the chart on page 11 is a recent survey by the United States Department of Health, Education, and Welfare.

Data source for the chart on page 27 is *State Tax Review*, Commerce Clearing House, Vol. 32, No. 51, 1971.

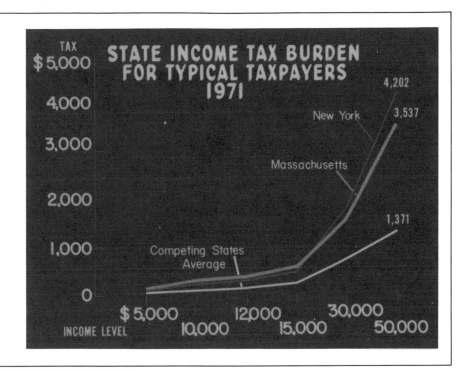

The Economic Development of Massachusetts

Bennett Harrison
Massachusetts Institute of Technology
November 1974

Look Out, Massachusetts!!! *stirred up considerable controversy not only over the severity of the Commonwealth's economic problems but also over how the state should handle them. Many members of the state legislature felt the need to respond to the issues raised, particularly as a reflection of their authority over the regulation of business. Some also felt that the business community was capturing the limelight at the expense of labor and seizing the traditional turf of the elected political leadership.*

Senator Alan McKinnon, a friend of labor and one of the most powerful members of the legislature as Co-Chairman of the Joint Commerce and Labor Committee of the Massachusetts Legislature, commissioned this study in January 1974. To lead the study, he chose Bennett Harrison, an economist and professor of Urban Studies and Planning at MIT with special expertise in labor economics and regional and urban development.

Between February and May, Harrison and his colleagues conducted more than fifty interviews with commerce and manpower agency personnel, business people, labor leaders, and community organizers. They gathered opinions on existing and proposed development legislation, goals for state economic development, appropriate policies for achieving the desired goals, and the reorganization of the state's commerce and manpower agencies.

The resulting report—which ran to almost 200 pages in its unedited form—was completed in November. Although Harrison's views were colored somewhat by his particular views on labor issues, he presented an intriguing picture of Massachusetts' economy from someone independent of the bias of both the state government and the business community. On one hand, Harrison challenged the business community's claims that the state had been anti-

business, that taxes were too high, and that all the costs of doing business were much higher than those of other states. And on the other hand, he faulted the state for its lack of any serious economic planning and claimed that the few programs that had been initiated to help the state economy had done more harm than good.

According to the business press and the more popular media, the economy of Massachusetts is in trouble. The three most frequently mentioned sources of difficulty for the state are the collapse in the demand for the products of the "defense" industry, the secular decline in employment in the mill-based industries, such as shoes and textiles, and the region's precarious location at the end of the national power and transportation systems.

Massachusetts ranked seventh in the country in "defense" contracts prior to 1969. Arthur D. Little, Inc. estimates that:

One out of every five people unemployed and seeking work in Massachusetts [in 1970] lost his job due to cutbacks in defense spending; the ratio [declined] to one in seven or eight individuals over the next two years. Over [the] period 1970–72, we estimate that 25,000 jobs [were] lost by civilian employees on military installations.[1]

The industries most affected have been electrical machinery, transportation equipment, ordnance, and nonelectrical machinery. The areas most seriously impacted were Boston, Lowell, the Lawrence–Haverhill region, and Pittsfield. Though most of the jobs lost were (as popularly thought) in the professional-technical category, probably one-fifth were in unskilled labor. Of course the multiplier effect of the reduced spending out of the reduced incomes of those laid off (or never hired because of the disappearance of the job) further depressed the economy, leading to still further layoffs in services, retail trade, and construction.

The secular deterioration in the mill-based and related labor-intensive industries' demand for labor is the second major structural problem in the state's economy. Until 1972, employment in the furniture industry had declined steadily each year since 1965; in 1972, it rose slightly (by 400 jobs). Work in the food industry has declined without letup since 1954. Until it gained 700 jobs in 1972, the textile industry underwent a steady reduction in employment since 1950. Apparel jobs have failed to grow every year since 1964. Rubber and plastics jobs increased by 400 in 1972; previously, they had been on the decline since 1966. Leather has not registered a single gain since 1955.[2]

In some cases, these declines in traditional mill employment are the result of increases in productivity through the introduction of new equipment and techniques; a separate and quite detailed study would be needed to verify this hypothesis. It is our best judgment that declining demand for the products themselves (or at least for those produced in New England relative to elsewhere) is a more important factor than increasing productivity.[3]

The problem has been exacerbated by a significant shift in the capital intensity of newer firms in the state. The First National Bank of Boston commissioned a statistical analysis of so-called "factor shares" in Massachusetts. The proportions of each dollar of output produced that end up as wages, salaries, and benefits to workers are given in table 1. It appears that Massachusetts' old industrial base was *more* labor intensive than the national average for the corresponding industries, whereas its newer, emerging base is much *less* labor intensive than the national average for the same industries. Perhaps the newer firms engage in capital-intensive research and development work in their Massachusetts plants, while reserving their production work for plants in other states (or other countries). In any case, a dollar of locally produced output produces fewer jobs in Massachusetts than it used to.

The third widely recognized problem with the Massachusetts economy is its location with respect to the sources of supply of energy, and the severely deteriorated state of its rail transport system. *These problems are interdependent.* For example, in 1968:

Table 1
Labor shares of state output in Massachusetts: 1963–1967

Type of industries	Labor share	
	United States	Massachusetts
Massachusetts' declining industries	35¢ per $1 of output	41¢
Massachusetts' growing industries	21¢	12¢

Source: James M. Howell, chief economist, The First National Bank of Boston.

The cost of industrial fuel, as measured at electric power generation plants, [was] higher in New England than in any other region of the country and at least 35% higher than in the country as a whole. The reason for this differential is again transportation costs resulting from having to import coal, gas and residual oil from outside the area as well as higher taxes. Electric power rates are also relatively high in New England (in large part due to fuel costs and taxes), exceeding the national average by at least 11% [in 1968] for comparable service.[4]

One large company with plants in several states has kindly provided us with comparative data on power costs in its different plants. In March 1974—with costs measured in dollars per thousand kilowatt hours of electric power, and an index number of 100 assigned to a North Carolina plant in this firm—comparative index costs in plants in New York, Maine, New Hampshire, and Massachusetts were 100.7, 176.3, 153.3, and 211.1, respectively (these figures are admittedly crude, as they do not take into account differences in plant capacity or efficiency in the five locations).

In July 1974, among the nation's 23 largest metro areas, only two (Buffalo and New York–northeastern New Jersey) faced higher fuel and utility prices than Boston.[5]

None of this should cause us to lose sight of the strengths of the Massachusetts economy. At least until recently, the Commonwealth had the ninth highest per capita income of all the states, and fewer poor people than all but three other states.[6] The core of our economic base is doing well: electrical and nonelectrical machinery (despite the military contract cutbacks), communications equipment, electronic components, most services (especially those associated with the operation of business offices), wholesale and retail trade, and government itself (employment in the public sector has grown since 1968 by 16 percent, to its present level of about 350,000 jobs). The new Hewlett-Packard plant in Andover is expected eventually to generate 5,000 direct jobs. During 1973, most of the industrial space vacated by R&D firms in the recession of the early 1970s, and as a result of cutbacks in defense and space programs, was reoccupied largely by diversified companies producing for civilian markets.[7] And we *do* have a highly skilled labor force. In 1970, the share of the labor force employed as laborers or household service ("domestic") workers was only 4.5 percent in Massachusetts, as against 7.2 percent in the United States as a whole. And the proportion of the adult population having completed high school was—even as far back as 1968—more than 6 percent greater in Massachusetts than in the United States as a whole.[8] The attractive and growth-stimulating impact of the Commonwealth's enormous education industry (with 125.1 thousand government and 84.3 thousand private paid employees in 1973[9]) is of course well-known.

One surprising strength grows out of the older decline itself. The abandonment of many of the old mills has created a lot of cheap space for a host of small Massachusetts businesses. Interviews with some of these companies revealed a real concern that urban renewal or other similar programs might mistakenly demolish these facilities, or make them less accessible.

An investment anticipations survey conducted in the fall of 1973 by the First National Bank of Boston revealed that "expenditures of $1.4 billion on new plants and equipment are planned by New England manufacturers in 1974, a 15 percent increase over the $1.2 billion spent last year."[10] The strongest sectors appeared to be primary and fabricated metals and electrical equipment. It could not be determined what share of these intended expenditures would be placed in Massachusetts. In a related analysis, the Secretary of Manpower Affairs has written:

Despite the attention which is given to the unemployment rate, we are encouraged by the economic performance of the Commonwealth during the past year. Non-agricultural employment increased by 56,000 jobs during 1973, with one-third of those jobs in the durable goods sector . . . This is particularly encouraging because employment growth in this sector generates large multiplier effects throughout the economy. These industries are (especially) dependent upon other industries for their input requirements and the incomes generated by their high wage payments are a significant stimulus to retail trade and service activity.[11]

High rates of job growth, *together with* high unemployment rates, are reconciled here in Massachusetts—as in the country as a whole—by the phenomenon of rapidly increasing labor force participation.[12]

It is also not entirely fair to compare Massachusetts' slow rate of economic growth in recent years with the booming South, as some writers have done.[13] As an older, mature industrial state with a full complement of infrastructure, industries, and services, we have a larger and deeper economic base upon which to grow; the larger the base employment, the harder it is to achieve large percentage gains in growth. In other words, we should not allow ourselves to be overwhelmed by pessimistic forecasts of slower overall economic growth for the state; the slowdown in our rate of growth is to a great extent a *normal function* of the age, size, and complexity of our economy. But this also means that Massachusetts' growth must be *qualitatively* different than the growth of younger regions.[14]

Thus, the economic picture seems to be a mixed one. Simplistic depictions of the state economy as undergoing catastrophic decline are clearly exaggerated—and based to a great extent on data which are admitted by all knowledgeable persons to be seriously defective.

Popular Explanations of the Declining Health of the Massachusetts Economy

Four explanations of the high unemployment and related problems of the Massachusetts economy seemed to appear again and again throughout the interviews that went into the development of this report. These explanations show up in media presentations. They are repeated so often on Beacon Hill that people have come to take them for granted. Sometimes they even become self-fulfilling prophecies. We could not avoid conducting an investigation of these beliefs, so prominent are they. As it turned out, it's a good thing we did investigate them, for they are at best only partially true and often proved to be substantially false. Continued uncritical acceptance of these "explanations" can only impede efforts to promote the economic development of the Commonwealth.

The four explanations are these: (1) "this is in every respect a high cost-of-doing-business state"; (2) "the state government is antibusiness"; (3) "economic development means *industrial* development" (and the corollary: "only blue-collar industrial jobs will meet the employment needs of our unskilled—especially black—workers"); and (4) "welfare and unemployment compensation are high and rising because so many Massachusetts workers don't want to work."

The extent of actual unemployment and the "high cost of doing business" indictment have both been exaggerated in Massachusetts.

In some ways, the costs of doing business *are* higher in Massachusetts than elsewhere. These are invariably the categories stressed by pessimists. But in many other ways, the costs of doing business here are *lower* (or at least no higher) than the corresponding national averages.

Massachusetts businesses (and consumers) do pay extraordinarily high prices for power and transportation. Unemployment insurance taxes on business are high—because unemployment is high and so many jobs pay very low wages—but most workers who leave their jobs in fact never draw either welfare or unemployment "comp." Other costs of business compare favorably with the other industrial states. In some cases—especially in terms of labor costs—Massachusetts is actually a *low-wage* state! State and local business taxes are not especially high, and in any case, the services they help to produce place the Commonwealth at the very top of most business executives' lists of desirable states in which to *live*.

There is no evidence that the present or past state administrations have been "antibusiness." And in any case, major industrial location decisions are seldom predicated on such insubstantial impressions. Certainly the state has done little to promote strong economic planning, but this is not something that the business community has actively sought anyway.

The transformation of the economic base from mill-oriented blue-collar manufacturing to service-oriented white-collar and blue-collar work *has* created serious problems. But they have been much misunderstood or misrepresented. The problem is *not* that services don't earn the Commonwealth export income—they do—or that unskilled workers laid off by the mill industries (or "new" black and other minority workers) cannot find suitable work in the new service sector because of a skill mismatch; services use as many or even more unskilled workers as do the manufacturers. The real problem caused by this structural shift is that many of the services tend to pay low wages.

Finally, welfare costs are *not* rising because people are unwilling to work. In fact, more people *want* to work than ever before—a fact that sharply contradicts the widespread belief on the part of many businessmen that the local population is "too lazy to work," or is "less interested in looking for a job." In fact, the rate of expansion of the Massachusetts labor force substantially exceeded the overall New England rate during the period 1970–73.

The Central Problems of the Massachusetts Economy

If these popular explanations of the ill-health of Massachusetts are in question, then what are the "real" problems?

Some costs of doing business (and of running a household!) are clearly high in Massachusetts, and growing. And there are clearly too many people out of work. These problems are shared in part by every other state; the entire country is, after all, undergoing a period of sustained "stagflation," suffering both inflation and unemployment simultaneously.

But even if the United States were experiencing the kind of modest price increases and very low (under 4 percent) unemployment enjoyed during the last years of the Johnson administration, Massachusetts would be experiencing serious economic problems, cutting to the most basic structure of the region within which we are located. These problems are *much* more fundamental than the "attitudes of the governor toward business," or the relative attractiveness of the state as a site for location by outside firms. High unemployment compensation and welfare costs are a *consequence* of these basic problems.

Apart from the general economic malaise in the country as a whole, the problems of Massachusetts are:

• High "subemployment"—too many low-wage, inherently unstable, "dead-end," or often seasonal jobs, which are inadequate to allow a worker to support his or her family. This is a major cause of our high welfare and unemployment insurance costs.

• High costs related to inadequate regional production of energy, transportation, and other infrastructure—key inputs into the production process.

• Institutional procedures that reduce the availability of private capital for sufficient economic development to fully employ the region's workers at nonpoverty wages.

• Virtually nonexistent economic planning in state government, to anticipate serious economic problems and to guide public and private investment into areas of the state and sectors of the economy which fall behind the rest.

Paradoxically, the things that the state *has* done in the name of economic development—job creation tax credits for private industry, public investment in the tourist industry, and the creation of public industrial development corporations or authorities backed mainly by revenue bonds—have made things *worse*.

The "$500 tax credits" for private sector "job creation" produce no new jobs, but they do cost the Commonwealth in foregone jobs and revenue—jobs and revenue that would have been generated had the taxes been collected and used for other purposes.

To stimulate the tourist industry (to the exclusion of paying attention to other sectors, such as metal-working and high tech) is to stimulate precisely the lowest-wage, least stable, most "dead-end" sector of the economy.

Since the various development corporations and authorities are backed by revenue bonds, they can't afford (or are afraid) to lend to (or invest in) risky ventures, for fear of endangering their privileged credit ratings. They therefore tend to subsidize firms or developers who could have as easily obtained their financing privately.

Thus, all three policies have been misdirected, and have not furthered the economic development of the Commonwealth. Tax subsidies to industry and revenue-bonded public development corporations constitute a redistribution of income from taxpayers to large corporations. Tourist industry subsidies reinforce and expand the size of the low-wage sector of the economy, putting even more pressure on workers to find additional sources of income (including welfare and unemployment compensation) with which to support their families.

A Program for Economic Development

Our analysis of the Massachusetts economy is by no means complete. Much more can and should be done to develop more precise descriptions of the structure of the economy, to test out the hypothesis of labor market duality, etc. The controversial conclusion that tax incentives do not significantly affect the production (and related hiring) decisions of private firms should be subjected to critical evaluation by other economists (and business persons), and the analysis extended explicitly to other components of the "Mass Incentives" package.

Still, we think that enough has been learned to permit at least the outlining of a comprehensive program of state economic development. It would be very difficult—and rather premature—to specify a detailed legislative package, with associated costs. Every element of this proposed agenda should be questioned (just as every *existing* policy of the state should be questioned).

With these qualifications, we propose that the legislature and the executive branch give careful consideration to a six-part economic development program consisting of:

1. The stimulation of the local sales of (and therefore the derived demand for labor by) Massachusetts producers in the primary labor market: existing private firms, new private or quasi-public enterprises, and state and local government agencies themselves. The main priority should be given to public investment in (and possibly ownership of) transportation, power, and other "infrastructure."

2. The stimulation of the *export* sales of (and therefore the derived demand for labor by) primary labor market producers of goods and services.

3. The upgrading and transformation of at least some low-wage secondary labor market jobs, to enable firms to pay higher wages and offer better working conditions.

4. More tightly planned, coordinated and *visible* manpower training and equal employment opportunity programs.

5. The maximum feasible substitution of locally produced for imported goods and services, and an increase in the share of capital investments of Massachusetts-based private capital institutions actually placed in Massachusetts.

6. The continued modest recruitment of national and foreign firms interested in building plants in Massachusetts, largely through personal contacts by state officials and through maintenance of a residential environment attractive to the families of company executives.

Implementing the Program

But how might these programs be implemented? What policy "instruments" are available to the state government to attain these objectives? How can they be financed? As before, the following suggestions are designed to arouse interest and debate, rather than to define a specific legislative program.

We propose for consideration, and "fleshing out," an eleven-point agenda:

1. Experimentation with both "indicative" and "target" economic planning. The former would have the state making forecasts of local activity, and impact analyses or projections for major public and private investments, *prior* to their realization. The latter would have the state's leadership regularly announce specific industry, occupation, and location targets on which both public and private investment should be focused, and which will receive priority in current state spending and technical assistance programs.

2. Upgrading selected secondary labor market jobs, through technical assistance to small- and medium-size firms willing to cooperate with the state's minimum wage and equal employment opportunity goals, and the removal of implicit subsidies (such as free access to manpower services) from at least some low-wage employers unable or unwilling to undergo upgrading. Technical assistance would be provided by pools of business consultants, through contracts with the state, with the costs being shared by the state and the client firms. There should be limits on the size of the firms eligible for technical assistance subsidies.

3. Expanded public service employment, targeted to workers dislocated by the other economic development policies of the state.

4. Manpower and vocational training, tied to job vacancies, emphasizing cooperative work-study programs, and subject to affirmative action goals.

5. Deliberate use of state public facilities location and procurement contracting to impact the target industries, occupations, and locations established by the economic planning office, and to ease the transition from a dual to a more integrated economy.

6. Export trade promotion, in the rest of New England, with Canada and the Maritime Provinces, and with the rest of the world. The state should help to organize associations of smaller businesses which might provide the scale sufficient to enable them to participate in international and interregional trade. Such assistance should be made conditional upon the participation of such businesses in the state's economic target and affirmative action programs, and would be subject to maximum size and minimum wage constraints.

7. Creation of a Massachusetts Land Bank, to rationalize the location and shape of new economic activity (especially within dense cities) and to provide a source of development capital through the appreciated value of those land holdings that are ultimately resold to the private sector over time.

8. Intrastate tax sharing à la a recent Chamber of Commerce proposal, as an interim mechanism for neutralizing the interjurisdictional competition for new plants, a competition that is only weakening the future tax bases of these jurisdictions. According to this plan, all the jurisdictions within a region would *share* the new taxes provided by any new economic activity developed in any one or more of the member jurisdictions.

9. Creation of a full-scale state Economic Development Bank, to finance both equity and low-interest debt for the expansion of the productive capacity of the Commonwealth's economy, especially through the creation or expansion of enterprises not normally having access to conventional capital markets. The bank would be financed by legislative grants, transfers from the appreciated assets of the Land Bank, a share (and perhaps a monopoly) of state treasury deposits, and only secondarily by revenue bonds.

10. Creation of a state Economic Development Corporation, to be the chief operating agency of the executive office ultimately designated as in charge of economic development policy. Initially, the existing Massachusetts Science and Technology Foundation would be subsumed into this agency, which would be organized on the model of the World Bank and the U.S. State Department, with different "desks" (area specialists) for different areas of the Commonwealth or the region.

11. Coordinated use of federal grants and shared revenue for state economic development, with particular attention to funds from the Departments of Labor, Commerce, Health, Education and Welfare, and (as in the case of Boston's Southwest Corridor Development Project) Transportation.

In sum, the Massachusetts economy faces some serious problems, and the solution to them is going to require a degree of deliberate, calculated state economic planning never before contemplated— let alone undertaken. The time to begin is now. If we wait for a new expansion of the national economy, or for large-scale revenue sharing, Massachusetts may be in too weak a position to benefit from these stimulants later on. Conversely, if we begin *now* to strengthen our economic base, we will be in a far better position later to take advantage of increased national and international ("export") demand for Massachusetts products and services, and new shared revenues or grants from Washington.

Postscript

In his now famous "job development" speech of June 26, 1974, at The First National Bank, Governor Sargent told his audience of businessmen, labor leaders, and representatives of the media:

Our problems do not originate within our borders. The energy crisis, base closings, cutbacks in housing funds, in defense, research and development all flow from national policies, national problems.

Would that it were so. Certainly, if these events hadn't occurred, if the Nixon administration had been more interested in domestic welfare and less interested in international grandstanding and internal subversion, the Commonwealth of Massachusetts (like the rest of the country) would be better off. At least measured *unemployment* would be lower.

But what about *subemployment*—and therefore welfare, unemployment compensation, the depreciation of worker skills, the dissolution of families? In 1968—under a Democratic president and with the substantial help of a wartime economic boom—the U.S. unemployment rate fell to 3.8 percent. Yet in that same year, according to one measure of subemployment, over a *tenth* of those Americans working, looking for work, or discouraged after a period of fruitless job search had no jobs at all, had given up looking, were involuntarily part-time employed, or were trapped in jobs paying poverty wages![15] In the Roxbury section of Boston, just two years earlier, almost 25 percent of the work force was subemployed.[16]

In the period 1966–68, there was no energy crisis, our military bases were flourishing with war orders, the Great Society's housing programs had a full head of steam, and R&D complexes (like those along Massachusetts' Route 128) were booming with contracts from the Pentagon and NASA. Apparently, we were all too mesmerized by our apparent good fortune to perceive that the structure of the economy—especially older economies like that of the Bay State—was undergoing a change: a change for the worse. Simply put, the Massachusetts economy split in two. The "glue" that had previously held it together—especially the older manufacturing industries requiring modest skills but paying relatively good wages—was drying up, and no one was prepared to make room in the emerging "glamour industries" for those displaced in the process, not to mention the unskilled newcomers to the state trying to find a place for themselves in the labor market. Instead, we proliferated low-wage, unstructured, "dead-end" service and manufacturing jobs. As this "secondary labor market" came to be the "world of work" for a growing number of our workers,[17] the social and private costs associated with keeping these workers alive have risen, to the point where *they* are now probably the most significant costs of doing business for most firms.

Unemployment is easy to see—and to blame on the actions of others. Underemployment is like the submerged seven-eighths of the proverbial iceberg: hard to see but massive in its ability to block further progress.

A distinguished MIT economist, Professor Charles Kindleberger, has said of the distinction between economic *growth* and economic *development*: "Economic growth means more output, but economic development implies both more output and change in the technical and institutional arrangements by which it is produced."[18] Massachusetts has exhausted the growth potential of its old economy. Old institutions and programs will no longer do. Social and economic change is needed. Economic development is needed.

Notes

1. Arthur D. Little, Inc., *Fostering Industrial Growth in Massachusetts*, Department of Commerce and Development, Commonwealth of Massachusetts, Vol. I, pp. 2–3. These are direct impacts only; the secondary effects on subcontractors and merchants were not estimated.

2. U.S. Department of Labor, Bureau of Labor Statistics, *Employment and Earnings in States and Areas: 1939–72*, Bulletin 1370-10, GPO, 1972, "Massachusetts" section.

3. One study did find that in Lowell at least, a *lower* proportion of the mill-based firms suffered declining employment from 1962 to 1972 than did other firms. Moreover, the proportion of very high employment growth for mill-based firms

exceeded the corresponding proportion for other firms in Lowell. See Lowell Center City Commission and Massachusetts Executive Office of Communities and Development, January–February 1973 survey of eleven firms in Lowell. "Mill-based" may, however, refer to small businesses that have moved into the abandoned mills to get cheap space, rather than to such traditional mill industries as furniture and textiles.

4. Arthur D. Little, Inc., *New England: An Economic Analysis,* New England Regional Commission, November 1968, p. 101.

5. U.S. Department of Labor, Bureau of Labor Statistics, "Retail Prices and Indexes of Fuels and Utilities," News Release, Washington, D.C., September 1974, table 3.

6. *Boston Globe,* March 19, 1973, p. 1.

7. Board of Economic Advisors, *Annual Report,* Commonwealth of Massachusetts, 1974, p. 17.

8. Department of Commerce and Development, *Massachusetts Fact Book,* no date, pp. 3–4.

9. Division of Employment Security, unpublished data, May 1974.

10. First National Bank of Boston, News Release, March 25, 1974.

11. Executive Office of Manpower Affairs, "Employment Trends 1970–1974," May 17, 1974.

12. The unemployment rate is defined as the ratio of the number of people looking for but unable to find work to the number working or looking for work. When new people enter (or re-enter) the labor force to look for work, but cannot find it, the ratio goes up.

13. See "New England: What Replaces the Old Industry?" *Business Week,* August 4, 1973, pp. 36–42.

14. In fact, after undergoing sustained economic growth for two decades at a pace exceeding the national (and *far* exceeding the New England) rate, the southern region has begun to experience a significant decline in its rate of growth. This has been described as "probably inevitable [since] the 'New South'. . . is becoming more and more like the rest of the country . . . We were behind everybody else. Now we're catching up." "South's Economy Lags After a Robust Decade," *New York Times,* Sunday, September 22, 1974, p. 1.

15. Sar Levitan and Robert Taggart, "Earnings and Employment Inadequacy," *Monthly Labor Review,* October 1973, table 4.

16. Harrison, *Education, Training, and the Urban Ghetto,* op. cit., p. 74.

17. Earlier, we showed that the share of average annual state employment in the most obvious secondary labor market-type industries has not declined much in a decade. Since turnover is much higher in the secondary than in the primary labor market, and since turnover has risen over time, it is a good bet that the total number of workers in secondary jobs has risen, too.

18. Charles P. Kindleberger, *Economic Development* (New York: McGraw-Hill, 1965, 2nd ed.), p. 3.

Alternatives for the Northeast: Choices and Costs

James M. Howell
The First National Bank of Boston
December 1975

In the mid-1970s Massachusetts was not the only state suffering from economic maturity. It appeared as though the economy of the entire Northeast was in trouble. In December 1975 Roger Thompson, secretary to New York state senate majority leader Warren Anderson, convened a three-day meeting in Albany, New York, of state legislative leaders from the northeastern states. The purpose was to discuss the common problems of the region and how to restore competitiveness with other regions. It was the first time such a joint meeting of state legislators had ever been called.

Among the meeting's presentations was the following paper by James Howell, which argued that the main objective of state and local economic development policy should be to revive the deteriorating industrial base by encouraging capital spending on new plants and equipment. Within this context Howell wrestled with a wide range of troubling concerns about the region's prospects.

For example, while crediting the emergence of high technology firms in the 1960s for substantially offsetting the loss of manufacturing jobs from traditional industries, he questioned whether the region can count on the high tech sector for economic health in the long term. These firms tended to be far less labor intensive than the declining industries, he cautioned. And although New England excelled at generating new high tech enterprises, its overall high tax structure was pushing the production jobs in these industries to the South and West.

Howell also raised the often-voiced doubts about whether the region's economy could depend on the growing service sector for replacement jobs. For the most part, he observed, the region's services—including health and social services—had tended not to be as "exportable" as manufacturing. Manufacturing also generally created a higher value per employee than services.

Furthermore Howell emphasized the critical role state government should play as a planner and coordinator of growth, balancing the needs of the expanding economy with the constraints of physical environment. This was a role that had been unnecessary in the past.

Defining Our Region's Common Problem: Economic Maturity

The current economic problems that beset the northeastern region of the United States date back a number of decades.[1] As the national economy grew rapidly in the early 1950s, the Northeast slipped into the rut of economic maturity as the area's historically vital industries migrated southward in search of cheap and unorganized labor. Difficult as these transitional years were, with chronically high unemployment and urban blight in the region's older cities and mill towns, the problems corrected themselves largely through unguided market forces that accompanied vigorous national growth and a substantial wave of replacement industry, especially among the high technology and research and development firms. By the early 1960s, the northeastern economy once again started to show favorable income and employment characteristics. Most contemporary observers believed that the worst was over and that the region's inherent growth momentum would be self-sustaining.

The impressive economic gains during the sixties should not be minimized, for they were indeed significant in job and income creation; but they also tended to gloss over a number of truly difficult problems. Each of these requires brief comment.

Replacement Industry

The problem of generating new manufacturing firms to replace those migrating southward is almost always overlooked. It should not be, because the swing to replacement manufacturing industry was most dramatic during the two decades ending in 1970. The relevant data are shown in table 1. That such a near job-for-job match-up took place during this period was vital to the maintenance of growth in income and jobs in the region. But today, it is important to look back

Table 1
Replacement industry in the northeastern economy, 1950–1970

Region	Change in manufacturing employment (in thousands)	
	Nondurable goods industries	Durable goods industries
New England	− 93.9	+ 81.0
Middle Atlantic (New York, New Jersey, Pennsylvania)	− 244.5	+ 230.6
Northeastern region totals	− 338.4	+ 311.6

on the fundamental preconditions that created this process; namely, there was a sharp rise in defense and NASA spending and the emergence of a unique regional comparative advantage in the nation's sophisticated service industries—educational, engineering, consulting, banking, and research and development institutions.

Looking forward today, there is a genuine need to question seriously whether this transformation will likely be duplicated in the next decade. As the region's manufacturing base continues to erode, there are a number of reasons that support the view that the region's future economic growth of replacement industry should not come solely from the services, but this is an economic policy issue that has yet to be adequately answered.

Labor Markets

As this process of industrial transition continues, labor markets function imperfectly, especially in terms of retraining the older production worker who has become unemployed because of the liquidation of a textile mill or a shoe factory for reemployment into expanding industries. Although the northeastern economy has been nearly studied to death, few if any analysts have really developed a clear understanding of how labor markets function in an economically mature region. Even today, there is virtually no meaningful long-run industrial and occupational forecasting, and what is done has a very limited impact on vocational-technical planning, worker counseling, and business planning. And it was only recently that one of the special market problems was identified—the significantly older work force of this region vis-à-vis the nation.

In a recently released special *New England Regional Commission Task Force Report to the New England Governors,* the unique characteristics of the older age composition of the New England labor force were analyzed. Proportionately, the region has more workers 55 years of age and over than the nation as a whole, and fewer young workers in many of the important industries to take their place. By the 1980s a significant labor market gap will develop as retirements take place. This unique regional problem has three pressing dimensions. First, some segments of the regional labor market will swing from their current situation of excess supply to excess demand. The increase in demand will produce selective tight labor markets in certain critical occupations. Assuming that there will be no dramatic inflow of labor from other regions, existing demographic patterns make this outlook inevitable. The result of tighter labor markets will, of course, be an upward wage pressure. Second, there will develop a large overhang of retired workers that must be supported by an economically mature industrial region with relatively few midcareer skilled workers. In the decades of the 1940s and 1950s substantial out-migration of young, new entrants into the labor force took place at an alarming pace. Today there is a noticeable midcareer shortage in most occupations. Third, tight labor markets and rising wages may induce greater pressures on existing businesses, especially manufacturing firms, to migrate to other regions where labor supply and demand balances are more satisfactory.

Tentative statistical analysis suggests that by the 1980s this exodus of the older worker from the labor force could become an important regional labor market problem. According to the 1970 U.S. Census of Population, 5.3 percent of New England's manufacturing labor force was 55 years of age or older, compared with 0.8 percent nationally. More detailed analysis allows for an estimation of the number of vacancies which need filling (based on existing employee positions in 1970) as a result of this exodus of older workers. Specifically, there are 76,000 job vacancies that will result from the greater number of older workers (relative to the national averages) who will exit from New England manufacturing during the current decade. Precise estimation of the labor shortfall because of out-migration of the new labor market entrants is much more difficult. Nonetheless, there is no doubt that the out-migration of the 1940s

Table 2

Percent of employment in industry, 55 years of age or older in 1970

Industry	New England	United States	New England age differential
Yarn, thread, and fabric mills	30.9%	18.4%	+67.9
Other textile mill products	27.3	16.8	+62.5
Machinery, except electrical	23.8	14.9	+59.7
Professional and photographic equipment and watches	19.3	12.8	+50.8
Primary nonferrous industries	24.1	16.0	+50.6
Paper and allied products	19.2	14.1	+36.2
Furniture and fixtures	23.0	17.1	+34.5
Apparel and other fabricated textiles	26.2	19.6	+33.7
Miscellaneous wood products	27.7	21.3	+30.0
Fabricated metal industries	20.9	16.1	+29.8
Primary iron and steel industries	22.6	18.0	+25.6

and 1950s will pose special labor market problems for some time to come.

A number of manufacturing industries are expected to be disproportionately impacted by these developments, especially given the older age composition of their employees. They are given in table 2. Most of these eleven industries are likely to continue operation in New England, but it is clear that they are going to face major labor turnover and shortages by the early 1980s. Additional study and evaluation must soon be initiated if this problem is to be adequately anticipated and appropriate policies developed. Unquestionably, this analysis understates the true magnitude of the problem because manufacturing employment accounts for only about 25 percent of the region's work force. When this special problem is considered from the vantage of our region's economic maturity, it becomes clear that policy steps must be taken to ensure orderly adjustment in meeting these labor market demands. Otherwise, the New England regional competitive position could become even more eroded. This situation demands better cooperation among business, organized labor, the vocational-technical schools and the state Divisions of Employment Security.

Capital Markets

A common assumption is that the various financial intermediaries are shortchanging their region's capital needs. Our challenge is to attempt to unravel the complexities of this often-stated generalization. To this end, it is valid to conclude that regional capital flows are significant and they are one of the critical determinants of regional growth disparities. More important, however, it may be concluded that in a market economy, capital should and will flow from the older, already industrialized areas to the faster-growing regions, and that great care should be taken before implementing policy tools that would interfere with this process.

The evolution of market forces has had its effect on the northeastern economy. As economic growth accelerated in the New South and the West, expanding markets have become more geographically dispersed. Newly constructed urban areas with numerous industrial expansion and construction incentives facilitated rapid growth, and capital has flowed to these growth areas. Meanwhile, the Northeast continues to struggle with the high-cost economic disadvantages. Since the turn of the century, capital export has become relatively commonplace. Simultaneously, the higher cost of doing business in the Northeast has produced a lower rate of investment in new plant and equipment vis-à-vis the younger, growing areas. The stock of plant and equipment in the Northeast has, therefore, not been renewed at a pace sufficient to maintain the region's growth rate at parity with the national average. Capital spending surveys indicate that the average age of plant and equipment in New England is eleven years compared with eight years in the entire United States. Thus, regional underinvestment has developed which has led, in turn, to obsolete and inefficient plant and equipment and lower productivity.

Another indication of the adverse impact of cost inequities on the region's economy is the declining New England share of total manufacturing investment in the nation. During the period 1958 through 1968, total New England manufacturing capital spending for new plant and equipment amounted to a relatively stable 4.3 percent of the nation's total capital spending. In the years following 1968, there has been a perceptible decline in this ratio, especially during the years 1973 and 1974. For the six-year period ending in 1974, the region's ratio amounted to 3.7 percent, or approximately 15 percent below the ratio that consistently prevailed in the 1950s and 1960s. According to both McGraw-Hill and The First National Bank of Boston estimates, 1975 could intensify this widening capital gap, for regional capital spending is expected to reach only 2.9 percent of total national spending. If this forecast becomes reality, the 1975 regional spending ratio would be about 30 percent below the norm of the preceding two decades. This trend is particularly alarming when judged against the fact that manufacturing activity is still relatively more important in the Northeast than in the country as a whole.

Another troublesome dimension is that new manufacturing capital spending is not creating many new jobs. To the casual observer, this is a surprising conclusion because new manufacturing start-ups and expansions of existing facilities are running substantially ahead of plant liquidations. A recent survey by The First National Bank of Boston showed that the dynamics of industrial change in New England are increasingly dominated by more sophisticated manufacturing processes as the region's more labor-intensive, low technology industries are phased out. Of the forty-five New England plant closings during the two-year period ending July 1974, twenty (or 44 percent) were in labor-intensive industries, and only eight (or 18 percent) were high technology firms, while 94 of 211 new plant openings (44 percent) were concentrated in high technology or high technology supporting industries. It is also noteworthy that 61 of 87 expansions of existing plants were also concentrated in these high technology and capital-intensive industries.

This progressive structural adjustment into high technology industries is not without problems affecting job creation. In support of this generalization, The First National Bank of Boston analyzed a number of production functions to determine labor's contribution to total output for declining and expanding manufacturing firms in Massachusetts and in the same industries nationally. The Massachusetts figures are considered representative of the region as a whole. The results of this analysis are shown in table 3. Interpretation of these data is easy: for every $1.00 increase in output in the declining industries in Massachusetts, labor contributed 41 cents, while in the same industries nationally, labor contributed 35 cents. Conversely, Massachusetts' expanding industries relied far less on labor (12 cents per $1.00) than their national counterparts (21 cents per $1.00). Hence, Massachusetts stands to lose more jobs, on the average, in the

Table 3
Labor shares of value added in selected Massachusetts industries, 1963–1967

Type of industry	Job content expressed as a percentage of output		National growth pattern of industry
	United States	Massachusetts	
Labor intensive	35%	41%	Declining
Capital intensive	21%	12%	Expanding

nationally declining labor-intensive industries than in the rest of the nation. Furthermore, this analysis relates to the economic situation during the preceding decade. Since that time the industrial situation in New England has worsened rather than improved.

This is an important conclusion that future regional policy initiatives should take into account, for these are the critical characteristics of industrial change in the Northeast. First, there is a cumulative widening in the capital spending lag in the Northeast vis-à-vis the nation, and, second, new capital spending in the region has consistently been capital-using and labor-saving. Again, it is important to remember that regional capital flows are drawn to those areas (the older, mature, and the young, growing alike) where attitudes toward business expansion, new investment, and profits are favorable. These attitudes are vitally important and their impact is significant, but they are complemented by institutional attitudes—especially among state and local governmental officials—toward new investment. Thus, state and regional policies to enable northeastern capital investment to catch up with the nation involve not only the design of regional capital investment incentive programs, including the possible creation of new capital market institutions, but also include major emphasis on qualitative improvement in regional attitudes toward business expansion, job creation, and new capital spending.

The Mill Towns
Scattered throughout the Northeast are the "mill towns." These towns are often known by other names, such as "economically depressed areas" and "stranded areas," but one of the main criteria for defining a mill town is substantial and persistent unemployment. Other criteria are the older age of the city, and the juxtaposition of a

decaying inner city and growing suburbs. Each of these requires additional comments.

The issue of higher-than-acceptable unemployment in these older urban areas may be analyzed from published data. For more than a decade, the performance of labor markets has been monitored through the U.S. Department of Labor's analysis of approximately 150 major employment centers according to the adequacy of their labor supply, many of which are easily defined as mill towns. The classifications are based on reports prepared by the state employment security agencies and a letter classification code is assigned to each major area;[2] the unemployment rate is a key factor in determining the area classification, but consideration is given to other factors, for instance, local employer estimates of manpower requirements and seasonal factors. Shown in table 4 are the relevant data for five selected dates.

A number of interesting conclusions may be derived from these data, but before discussing them, a brief comment is in order about the national economic conditions existing during the five data points. During four of the years—1958, 1960, 1970, and 1974—the national economy was in a recession. As for the final data point—1965—the economy was in the final phase of the unusually rapid growth period of the early to mid-1960s. To develop a better understanding about the magnitude of the unemployment situation, the national unemployment rates for these five data points are:

November 1958   6.2%
December 1960   6.6
December 1965   4.0
December 1970   6.0
January 1974   5.2

The persistent nature of the poor performance of the economically mature Northeastern economy and its impact on labor markets show through in the high ratios of major regional employment centers experiencing substantial unemployment. Note that though New England has persistently experienced high unemployment among its urban areas, the Mid-Atlantic has fared somewhat better. Finally, it is worth noting the consistently favorable economic performance of the East South Central, the West South Central, and the Mountain areas.

Table 4
Adequacy of labor supply in various major employment centers within the nine economic areas

Area	Percentage of employment centers with labor supply conditions classified in groups D through F, substantial unemployment				
	January 1974	December 1970	December 1965	December 1960	November 1958
New England	61.1% (18)	58.8% (17)	23.5% (17)	56.3% (16)	72.2% (17)
Middle Atlantic	20.0 (25)	32.0 (25)	16.0 (25)	48.0 (25)	91.3 (23)
East North Central	21.2 (33)	21.9 (32)	None (33)	39.4 (33)	65.6 (32)
West North Central	12.5 (08)	None (07)	12.5 (08)	12.5 (08)	37.5 (08)
South Atlantic	12.5 (24)	4.3 (23)	12.5 (24)	17.4 (23)	29.2 (24)
East South Central	None (08)	11.1 (09)	None (08)	25.0 (08)	75.0 (08)
West South Central	None (14)	14.3 (14)	None (14)	14.3 (14)	10.0 (10)
Mountain	None (04)	25.0 (04)	25.0 (04)	None (04)	None (04)
Pacific	84.6 (13)	85.7 (14)	28.5 (13)	23.1 (13)	38.5 (13)

Note: Figures in parentheses are the number of employment centers in the U.S. Labor Department survey.

This, of course, reflects the strong growth that these employment centers were undergoing during this period.

The pervasive nature of unemployment in these mill towns raises the serious question: "Why can't these towns devise programs to lift themselves up by their own bootstraps?" There are a number of reasons. First, there is the fact of local property taxes substantially out of line with the non-mill towns, making them less attractive to industry. Our tentative analysis in this area suggests that the property tax differential between the older urban areas and the younger suburbs may be as great as 20 to 25 percent. That's significant in terms of manufacturing costs. Furthermore, the fact that most, if not all, of these urban areas were fully developed before the turn of this century means that their underlying central city infrastructure is badly in need of repair—or outright replacement. This, in addition to being an inducement to manufacturers to locate elsewhere, is the cause of high property taxation to satisfy a rising demand for public services. In combination, these forces have worked in such a way to cause serious economic and financial erosion in these older urban areas. In recent years, these problems have worsened. The economic and financial deterioration of these older urban areas has not gone unnoticed and one excellent source that reflects the dynamics of these changes is the regularly reported municipal bond ratings.

Shown in table 5 are the Moody's and Standard and Poor's bond ratings for the central cities for the 150 labor markets discussed above. The data have been organized in such a way that the New England and Middle Atlantic urban areas are shown independently of those in the remainder of the country.

One specific conclusion that may be derived from the data is that for the Northeast region there is a substantially higher degree of downgraded bond ratings than for the remainder of the country as a whole. (When the data are broken down further, there is an even more profound instance of downgradings in the Middle Atlantic states than in either New England or the rest of the country. Although the reasons for this are not fully known, they may rest on the availability of more detailed and factual information on these cities.)

It is interesting to compare the changes in the labor market classifications (specifically the U.S. Department of Labor Supply Category Groups A through F) with the changes in the Moody's and the Standard and Poor's bond ratings for the labor market's central

Table 5

Municipal bond ratings for the center cities' 150 major labor market areas

	1970–1975 Moody's	June 1970–1975 S&P	1965–1970 Moody's	June 1965–1970 S&P
U.S. (excluding Northeast)				
Unchanged rating	61 (54%)	59 (86%)	76 (70%)	61 (82%)
Upgraded	44 (39)	4 (6)	26 (24)	7 (9)
Downgraded	8 (7)	6 (8)	7 (6)	7 (9)
U.S. (excluding New England)				
Unchanged rating	77 (55%)	66 (81%)	89 (66%)	74 (80%)
Upgraded	47 (34)	6 (7)	32 (24)	7 (7)
Downgraded	15 (11)	10 (12)	14 (10)	12 (13)
Northeast				
Unchanged rating	33 (69%)	12 (63%)	32 (68%)	19 (76%)
Upgraded	6 (12)	2 (11)	8 (17)	— (—)
Downgraded	9 (19)	5 (26)	7 (15)	6 (24)
New England				
Unchanged rating	17 (77%)	5 (83%)	19 (90%)	6 (86%)
Upgraded	3 (14)	— (—)	2 (10)	— (—)
Downgraded	2 (9)	1 (17)	— (—)	1 (14)
Middle Atlantic (New Jersey, New York, Pennsylvania)				
Unchanged rating	16 (62%)	7 (54%)	13 (50%)	13 (72%)
Upgraded	3 (11)	2 (15)	6 (23)	— (—)
Downgraded	7 (27)	4 (31)	7 (27)	5 (28)

city. The comparison shows that the vast majority of bond rating changes (both upward and downward) took place while labor market conditions were deteriorating. Our tabulation shows that of 50 cities whose bond ratings were upgraded by Moody's, there was a deterioration in the labor markets of 31. Obviously, more work needs to be done in this area, but it is interesting to note that our analysis suggests that changes in a community's bond rating may not fully reflect deteriorations in underlying labor market conditions. This is an important conclusion, for it is counterintuitive, but it may merely reflect the lag in adjusting bond ratings to changes in underlying economic conditions in the central cities.

Finally, there is the special northeastern situation that aggravates the unemployment in these older urban areas, and this is the strong presence and continuing arrival of European ethnic groups. The ethnicity of the Northeast has continued to attract immigrants despite a severe shrinking in job opportunities. In essence, Europeans have come into the region faster than we have been able to provide new job opportunities. This is the principal conclusion reached in a recent paper by Roger White of the University of Connecticut. He states that New England, with 5.8 percent of the nation's population, currently receives about 7.9 percent of the total immigrants to the United States. Furthermore, the region has continued to absorb a disproportionate share of immigrants even while sustaining a level of unemployment appreciably above the national average.

In his statistical analysis, White concludes that "immigrants have a strong and overriding preference for settling where their fellow countrymen have preceded them. Furthermore, this preference is expressed irrespective of, and perhaps in ignorance of, the relative economic conditions of the various regions of the country." By "relative economic conditions" he means relative wage and cost-of-living conditions. Shown in table 6 are White's immigration figures for the country as a whole, and for the nine census regions.

Table 6
Immigration as a percentage of total population of geographic regions, 1970

Geographic area		Percentage
United States		0.1847
New England		0.251
Maine	0.121	
New Hampshire	0.119	
Vermont	0.103	
Massachusetts	0.267	
Rhode Island	0.327	
Connecticut	0.289	
Mid-Atlantic		0.355
East North Central		0.112
West North Central		0.045
South Atlantic		0.096
East South Central		0.022
West South Central		0.109
Mountain		0.098
Pacific		0.336

Sources: U.S. Bureau of the Census, *Census of Population*, 1970, and U.S. Immigration and Naturalization Service, *Annual Report*, 1970.

Note especially the unusually high immigration ratios for the Middle Atlantic states and Rhode Island. Here again, the old mill towns seem to be particularly singled out, for the historical presence of ethnic groups attracts more Europeans to them. We may summarize at this point by saying that a confluence of economic and social conditions works to condemn these areas to an unhappy existence. Property tax differentials and greater ethnicity directly contribute to higher unemployment and greater incidence of poverty. The responsibility of regional economic policy is to take these special factors into consideration when developing new economic solutions.

Accepting the Implications of Economic Maturity

Our detailed economic and statistical analysis suggests that there will be three principal growth sectors in the Northeast during the balance of the 1970s and throughout most of the decade of the 1980s. These are:

- The high technology industries
- The sophisticated services
- State and local government

In the most general terms, all three of these broad industry groupings contain special growth promise as well as problems. Each requires special comment.

The economic significance of the high technology industries to our national economy was recently analyzed by John Flender and Richard Morse in a paper entitled *The Role of New Technical Enterprises in the United States Economy*. The principal thrust of their analysis was to analyze the job and sales creation potential of a number of different types of manufacturing companies. Their findings are summarized in table 7.

In commenting on these statistics, Flender and Morse write that "it is worth noting that during the five-year period (1969–74), the six mature companies with a combined sales of $36 billion in 1974 experienced a net gain of only 25,000 jobs, while the five young, high technology companies with a combined sales of only $857 million had a net increase in employment of almost 35,000 jobs. The five innovative companies with combined sales of $21 billion during the same period created 106,000.

Table 7

Type of manufacturing firm	Sales[a]	Employment[a]
Mature	11.4%	0.6%
Innovative	13.2	4.3
Young, high technology	42.5	40.7

a. Percentage changes are the average annual compounded growth rates. Mature and innovative firms cover the period 1945–74, whereas the young, high technology firms are for the period 1969–74. Data were collected from *Moody's Industrial Manual*.

In addition to this job creation dimension of the young, high technology firms, the Flender-Morse paper expressed great concern about fundamental changes in the late 1960s and early 1970s that have virtually eliminated the environment for the establishment of new high technology enterprises. As critical underlying causes they cite (1) the sharp cutbacks in government funding for research and development, (2) the deterioration of financial incentives to the enterprises, (3) the loss of the new issue equity market, thus severely reducing capital supply, and (4) the unfavorable impact of increased regulation. Unmistakably, all of these are pressing issues that cannot be pushed aside. Some will be largely self-correcting (for instance, the reemergence of the new issue market) when national growth and prosperity return. Others will not, but my point goes considerably beyond these issues. There is little doubt that the Flender-Morse paper clearly establishes the link between the young, high technology enterprise firm and substantial job creation. Prior to their analysis, I suspect that most of us would have staunchly maintained that the entrepreneurial capital input in these firms was the dominant characteristic. Not the other way around. As it turns out, this is a northeastern viewpoint, and it is consistent with the labor shares of value-added analysis in table 3. The point is simply that although the Northeast continues to enjoy a special comparative advantage in the creation and startup of high technology manufacturing, the production-line jobs resulting from the expansion are outside of the region. We are the father of these creations, but other regions are the benefactors of their payrolls. Thus, the policy option for the Northeast is clear: regional economic policy should create a business environment that will provide the incentive to keep more of these production-line jobs in the region.

The perfectly natural question that frequently arises in seminars such as this is: "Why can't a mature economy, like that of the northeastern region, thrive with an increasingly service-oriented economy? After all, a tax base derived from wages and profits in services is just as good as one derived from manufacturing." There are three reasons why we must make a conscious effort to maintain a vital core of high-value manufacturing. (What constitutes that minimum manufacturing core will, one supposes, forever be subject to debate.)

First, although a town may thrive on a total service-oriented economy, an entire region, and perhaps each of the states in our New England region, must have some local manufacturing base. The basic point is that most of our service activity is not "exportable" for more than a few miles. If we are going to import all our manufactured goods and food requirements from outside New England, we will not be able to earn in return enough from services (and investment income) to finance these imports. We may be able to sell our high-powered consulting services across the country and around the world, but the services of hospitals, child care, and printing, to name a few, can only be sold within a very local market. Second, it may be simply stated that manufacturing generates a much higher value created per employee than most services. Thus, efforts to develop manufacturing have a much higher payoff in terms of a growing tax base, thus avoiding the burden of higher tax rates on all sectors of society.

Third, although it is true that increases in exporting services (for instance in banking and in engineering services) do stimulate the region's internal growth, the smaller, secondary job effects make complete reliance on exporting services an unattractive route to regional growth. In one of our Bank's recent monographs, we attempted to isolate the export supporting job ratios for the New England economy. The relevant data are reproduced in table 8.

Several brief observations are in order. Note the limited number of job increases that occurred among the export service industries. Note also the growing imbalance between the exporting industry sector and this supporting sector. It is clear that this cannot continue for long without causing a potential structural imbalance in our regional economy. We may conclude this discussion at this point by saying that the regional economic policy should be the striking of a functional economic balance between the expansion of the region's

Table 8

Changes in employment in New England industries (in thousands)

	1950–55	1955–60	1960–65	1965–70
Total exporting sector	+ 19.6	− 15.3	+ 26.0	+ 3.6
Traditional exporting industries[a]	− 98.3	− 58.3	− 30.3	− 47.4
Other manufacturing exporting industries	+102.6	+ 22.1	+ 41.1	+ 24.8
Exporting services[b]	+ 15.3	+ 20.9	+ 15.2	+ 26.2
Total supporting sector	+184.0	+144.9	+303.4	+512.8

a. Traditional exporting industries consist of textile, apparel, and leather products industries.

b. Exporting services data are employment estimates for the region's key consulting firms, hospital and medical services, insurance, banking, and educational institutions.

high technology enterprises and sophisticated export services, on the one hand, and the region's employment and income needs, on the other. Achieving this trade-off within the context of promoting a full-employment regional economy where society's environmental objectives are met is the linchpin to policy. To many, these kinds of statements say little more than the oft-heard rhetoric that the future will be better than the past.

I believe that they say considerably more, that the next major period of economic transition will not be another wave of some unknown replacement industry but, rather, it will be largely based on additional growth among those industries already in our region's economic base. In my opinion, we should accept this as a fundamental working premise and develop regional economic policies to achieve this end. Of special importance are those steps to get regional capital and labor markets to work better.

Inasmuch as this was the objective of a recent special New England Regional Commission Task Force on Capital and Labor Markets, I shall not dwell on these policy issues. In their report the seventeen private sector Task Force members made twelve specific recommendations to the New England governors. In essence, these recommendations showed much in common. Most significant, the Task Force policy options to make capital and labor markets function more smoothly rest heavily upon minimizing existing frictions and obstacles that prevent their orderly interaction with the other sectors of the regional and national economies. In my opinion, this emphasis is important because it recognizes the imperative need to clear away first these structural impediments before any more sweeping policy options can be considered.

I submit that to achieve our long-sought-after goals of lower unemployment and a growing economy, there must be a fundamental restructuring of the role of state and local government in an economically mature region. The role of state and local government as an initiator, or coordinator, of a region's growth is generally overlooked. This is regrettable because historically these levels of government have contributed much to a region's growth patterns. First, state and local government spending for infrastructure has done much to determine the spatial distribution of the local economy's growth poles. Second, state and local government regulation and attitudes toward profits, business expansion, and growth have been important. As revenue sharing becomes more commonplace, the role of state and local government and its impact on regional economic activity will become even more important.

These are but broad generalizations. Clearly, much more work needs to be done in establishing the economic impact of state and local government on regional activity. Nonetheless, a part of our ongoing regional analysis suggests that the current role of state and local government may increasingly act as a brake on the regional economy. There are two basic forces at work, one on the side of economic spin-offs from government spending, the second working to erode the tax base.

First, the employment and income multiplier in the private sector derived from government spending declines over time, because the mix of spending tends to shift from highly productive and complementary investments in public infrastructure (roads, harbors, sewers, etc.) to less-productive programs that simply redistribute income, such as public services (including welfare) and the regulation and control of existing institutions.

Second, growth in state and local government spending depends on a dynamic private sector that provides a growing tax base. However, in an economically mature region, with manufacturing consistently seeking to reduce operating costs in the low-wage regions, there is always the problem of an erosion of the tax base. To compensate, government may raise tax rates, thus putting further burdens on the remaining firms in the private sector.

The muted power of government multipliers, coupled with the reduced ability of government to raise its rate of spending without substantial increase in the tax rates, poses a serious dilemma. Herein, we see the crucial importance of maintaining a balance between the private and government sectors. We also see clearly that the traditional role of government—especially at the state level—cannot long continue its old time-tested ways of essentially transferring income from one group to another, while simultaneously failing to take into account the business sector's needs. Otherwise, it is painfully obvious that there will be a continuation of high unemployment, business exodus, and more stagnant growth.

Managing Economic Maturity: Choices and Costs

In the concluding section of the paper we are left with the nagging question: "Why grow, and if so, by how much?" The answer to this question goes considerably beyond the view that if the economically mature Northeast could only return to the sustained and rapid growth rates of years ago, then our economy's current ills would be solved. Unquestionably, this is far too simplistic, but it does have its element of truth. When there is growth there is an expanding economic and industrial base that provides a steady stream of tax receipts to pay for expanding state and local programs. But the bind seems to come when one argues—as the planners and environmentalists so often do—that the region must have qualitatively improved public services and less, or controlled, economic growth. These may be mutually exclusive and they represent the current and future choices and costs for the Northeastern region.

In the years ahead, the Northeast will continue to be an important debating ground for the economists (who are generally for growth) and environmentalists (who are for no growth or qualitatively controlled growth). Some of this debate is worthwhile, but too much discussion of the differences can only divert attention from the substantive issues. I submit that the issue is not really growth *per se* or no growth, but really how much growth can the region afford—financially as well as environmentally—and how much planning must be used to achieve any one of a number of generally acceptable growth scenarios.

This planning dimension to the growth issues is vitally important because it is here that we see one of the real, critical choices facing the Northeast. Historically, planning, any kind of planning, was considered antithetical to the fierce independence of most northeasterners. Their view has consistently been to let the market mechanism solve the problem. Today, it is obvious that the most appropriate policy option in an economically mature region is more planning. But to achieve this end, there must be a fundamental restructuring of the traditional role of state and local government. Before we discuss the elements in this restructuring, let's document the various dimensions of the problem.

At the present time, neither the Congress nor the executive branch of the federal government has been able to establish mechanisms that are capable of analyzing, understanding, and coordinating the thousands of discrete decisions and actions which impact on national growth and development. Within this context, much of this uncertainty, much of the responsibility and authority to deal with our nation's urban and rural, social and economic problems has been transferred to the states. In the face of this transferred management responsibility, it is not an exaggeration to say that no state has completely solved its intertwined social and economic problems to produce an improved quality of life in the community of choice. To some observers, this is more than to be expected, but I doubt it. The key to a better future rests heavily on being able to develop a consensus as to what must be solved first. As previously indicated, I believe that this is a qualitative improvement in state and local government capability to solve problems.

Toward this end, there are a number of encouraging signs. In 1974, the Congressional Budget and Impoundment Control Act was passed. Its broad objectives are well known, but one of its lesser provisions is particularly relevant to our discussion. The Budget Act also requires that, where practicable, budget information be supplied to state and local governments. The precise form this information will take has not yet been established, but under the Act, congressional committees are directed to include an intergovernmental impact statement in their committee reports. This is potentially significant, but the states must become better prepared to understand the impact of federal spending on their own economies, and this will require a change in one's perception of the role of state government and the local economy.

Historically, most regional economists have assumed that regional growth could be stimulated by increased spending by state and local governments, just as national growth can be stimulated by increased spending at the federal level. This analogy is not only imprecise, but it is wholly inaccurate. Studies by Mike Evans of Chase Econometrics show that most of the income received by individuals and businesses is spent on goods and services which originate outside the state.[3] Furthermore, most industrial production is sold on a nationwide basis with relatively little of the total product remaining in the state. Thus a national tax cut which stimulated auto sales would benefit Detroit, but a state tax cut which also stimulated auto sales would benefit the local region only in a very few cases. As self-evident as this conclusion may be, it is far from being trivial.

It is the principal hypothesis of this paper that the restoration of a functional balance between a viable private sector and a responsive public sector rests on the creation of state and local economic policies that increase the amount of private sector capital spending for new plant and equipment. This is not a new recommendation, but it is different in that it clearly suggests that the principal thrust of state and local government business and economic policy should concentrate on a single policy option: new private sector capital spending. This conclusion is not widely held, and even today far too many national as well as state programs are aimed solely at providing additional jobs—the CETA program is an outstanding example—at an extraordinarily great public-tax cost.

This line of reasoning argues simply that state and local government should evaluate the entire spectrum of state governmental policy alternatives and should select those policies that lower the cost of doing business because they will have the greatest long-run positive effect on investment and growth. To be more specific, state governmental policy options that favorably affect private sector investment should be selected over those policies that raise the cost of doing business, even if the investment policies have a much smaller short-term effect on employment and income.

Planning to achieve this policy end, while complex, is not beyond our ability to conceptualize and implement. Indeed, it is interesting to note that a number of the studies on the uses of revenue sharing show that it has been used to hold down the rise in local taxes. For instance, the April 1974 General Accounting Office (GAO) second report to this Congress on revenue sharing concluded that "about three-fourths of the 250 governments were using their funds in some manner expected to reduce local tax pressures." That's encouraging, but I suspect that the rationale for this decision was more a disaffection for higher taxation, rather than the deliberate selection of this policy alternative because it stimulates private capital spending. Nonetheless, it is significant that the intuitive policy option supports, rather than thwarts, the goal of increasing private capital spending.

What's left to be covered is essentially the introduction of a special planning model, or mechanism, to judge the economic and social consequences of alternative policy options. Again, we are back in the lap of more and better economic planning but, I submit, a radically different kind than we have become accustomed to in the past. Historically, planning has come to mean the rearrangement of various governmental functions—both operationally as well as spatially—to provide a more equitable delivery of public services to the citizenry. This is what I call "allocation planning." Implicit in this kind of planning is the assumption of a viable private sector standing ready to be taxed to pay for this planning exercise and subsequent income redistribution. I'm not opposed to more and better planning. Quite to the contrary, time and time again our analyses show that prudent economic planning is the most efficient—if not the only— way to manage our affairs within the context of economic maturity. I am, however, opposed to the variety of economic planning that ignores the essential need to stimulate private sector capital spending. Looking backward, I believe that one of our principal failings is the excess concentration solely on allocation planning at the expense of allocation and investment planning.

I define "investment planning" as the judicious selection of those state and local government policies that maximize the likelihood of increasing private sector capital spending. In my opinion, the conclusions made earlier on the region's cumulative capital spending lag certainly support the view that little attention is paid to the impact of state economic policy on the environment and costs to encourage new private sector capital spending. Thus, we are left with the specific recommendation that the path to a viable northeastern economy rests on the successful integration of investment planning into allocation planning. The doctrine of fiscal federalism provides the appropriate departure point. Fiscal federalism has done much to shift discretionary economic power to state and local governments during the past five years. While federal purchases of goods and services have increased 34 percent over this period, state and local government purchases have risen by a much more rapid 73 percent, and federal grants-in-aid have more than doubled from $24 to $52 billion. This substantial increase in funds has had a marked impact on regional economic development and growth. Yet unlike the federal government, where large policy staffs and sophisticated econometric models are used to evaluate the economic effects of alternative fiscal policies, state governors do not have any mechanism which they can use for determining the effect of alternative policy decisions at the state level. Whether justified or not, this has often led federal agencies to withhold funds which might otherwise be available on the grounds that the plans for spending these funds were not clearly formulated.

Regional econometric modeling is not exactly a new art. Yet the existing models of state and local economies are completely unequipped to handle the emerging problems mentioned above. Conceived in an earlier day, they are designed to predict tax receipts and controllable state expenditures during the next year. Such an undertaking, if done correctly, is clearly not without merit. However, such models contain two fundamental flaws. First, they are essentially short-run models which assume that the capital stock remains fixed and ignore the inflow and outflow of capital and jobs. Second, they provide no tools which would permit a governor, or state legislature, to determine which of a number of given expenditures, each of the same dollar amount and each initially creating the same number of jobs, would be of greatest long-lasting benefit to the state. Some expenditures encourage industry, since they improve the infrastructure of the state economy and hence lower the costs of doing business. Some expenditures discourage industry, since they require more government employees and hence an eventual rise in tax rates. Yet the simpler models of an earlier day, many of which are still in use, do not distinguish between these two cases, since they are designed to capture only the short-run effects on employment and tax revenues.

In a recent collaborative effort with our Bank, Mike Evans and

Dennis Paranzino of Chase Econometrics have conceptualized a broad planning model that integrates private sector investment planning into the more traditional allocation planning. The results are a significantly improved trade-off planning model that we have named "The Governor's Economic Policy Model."

Broad planning models at the state level, such as the Governor's Economic Policy Model, allow planners to trace the increases in government spending or decreases in tax rates over a three- to five-year time frame. The model is structured in a way that permits investment to respond to positive or negative stimuli that are instituted by the public sector. A model which is designed to forecast over this time period will allow the planner to determine whether an initial cut in tax receipts might attract enough additional business to pay for itself over the next five years.

Another reason for the importance of the Governor's Economic Policy Model is the recent large increases in unrestricted grants to state and local governments. This now gives governors, the legislative branches, and their key policy advisors the needed flexibility which they previously were lacking in the apportionment of funds for the maximum state economic and social benefit. A specific grant for aid to dependent children, while welcome, could not be spent for other purposes; nor could funds for highway construction be diverted to other forms of public transportation. The loosening of restrictions by the federal government will require state governments to make many additional decisions about the uses of the federal funds which they will now receive. In particular, the governor, or for that matter the legislative branch of state government, may want to determine how best to spend a given amount of funds in order to achieve the maximum effect on output and employment and root out the causes of chronic structural unemployment.

The Governor's Economic Policy Model, then, is designed to present the state investment planner with a large number of option throttles. The model is specifically structured to allow the user to examine the changes in output, employment, and tax revenues which would occur for different types of government policies. This includes several different types of construction expenditures, federal defense expenditures, federal or state and local government expenditures for other goods, services, employment, or transfer payments, and changes in tax rates on personal and corporate income taxes, property taxes, unemployment compensation, and sales and excise taxes. In particular, Evans and Paranzino stress that lowering tax rates to attract new business is in many cases a more effective use of policy alternatives than an equivalent increase in expenditures.

The Governor's Economic Policy Model includes all the necessary moving parts for prediction of the state economy and its principal sectors. It goes far beyond this task, however, in its ability to extend the forecasting framework for several years and its flexibility in allowing the state planner to discover the relative merits of alternative government policies at the state level. In view of the rapidly increasing pool of unrestricted federal funds being made available to state and local governments, coupled with increasing demands that these governments prepare plans indicating what results will come from spending these funds, the Governor's Economic Policy Model would seem to be a necessary adjunct to intelligent economic planning in the years to come.

There is little left to do but to attempt to put the various pieces together. The principal conclusion of this paper is pretty much inescapable; namely, within the context of economic maturity, the role of state and local government must be changed to integrate investment planning into allocation planning. Essentially, this recommendation means that there must be more policy attention given to those factors that stimulate private-sector growth—specifically new private capital spending. Otherwise, without this restructuring of policy directions, there will likely occur a cumulative public-private sector imbalance. In the final analysis, I submit that the various trade-offs between growth and the environment, as well as those between public and private production of goods and services, must be judged on some basis other than the present isolated ad hoc fashion. To achieve this goal, I have described the broad contours of a special kind of model— the Governor's Economic Policy Model. If this balance is achieved, I believe that there are a considerable number of reasons to believe that the Northeastern regional economy will overcome the current dilemma of our economic maturity. As we progress through these steps to a sounder economy with job and income growth, it is more than obvious that the balance of the United States will be carefully watching our experiences.

Notes

1. Throughout the paper, the author uses somewhat loosely the regional terms "New England" and "Northeast." The differences in these two areas are recognized, but this should not detract from the validity of the analyses. Finally, the paper has deliberately excluded any discussion of the special urban, or central city, problems of New York, Newark, Philadelphia, Boston, and the other large urban areas in the nine-state area.

2. The following table outlines the classification codes used by the Labor Department in characterizing labor market conditions in these areas:

Labor supply category	Description	Unemployment rate[a]
Group A	Overall labor shortage	Less than 1.5%
Group B	Low unemployment	1.5 to 2.9%
Group C	Moderate unemployment	3.0 to 5.9%
Group D	Substantial unemployment	6.0 to 8.9%
Group E	Substantial unemployment	9.0 to 11.9%
Group F	Substantial unemployment	12.0% or more

a. Ratio of unemployment to area's total work force.

For additional details on this concept see *Area Trends in Employment and Unemployment,* a monthly publication of the Manpower Administration, U.S. Department of Labor.

3. For a technical discussion of this, see Michael K. Evans and Dennis H. Paranzino, "Governor's Economic Policy Model: Proposal and Outline," Chase Econometrics Associates, Inc., September 1975.

An Economic Development Program for Massachusetts

Michael S. Dukakis
Governor of Massachusetts
August 1976

When Michael Dukakis took office for his first term as governor in 1974, Massachusetts was staggering under the burden of high unemployment, a massive budget deficit, and out-of-control state spending. With the following 1976 document, the state formally embraced economic development as a key item on its agenda for the first time. The full plan was seventy pages long, presenting nearly one hundred specific proposals aimed at creating "more jobs and higher incomes for the residents and businesses of the Commonwealth." The excerpts reprinted here are from the introduction and the plan's list of priorities.

Dukakis' economic proposal focused on promoting a climate favorable to business and new investment. It included plans for controlling energy costs, improving the availability of capital, and updating the state's transportation infrastructure. In addition it called on the state to reform the property tax structure and institute more responsible fiscal management.

The document, which brought together a number of existing programs as well as some new proposals, was largely the effort of the governor's Development Cabinet, under the direction of state planning director Frank Keefe. In an attempt to win the support of the diverse parties affected, business and labor leaders were asked to comment on the draft. The final draft incorporated some suggestions that had been made by the business community for years.

Although Dukakis made an important overture to the business community with this document, it ultimately led to little specific action to relieve the pressures in the business environment. An irate business community that perceived his administration as unresponsive helped force him out of office in the 1978 election.

Economic Goals: More Jobs and Higher Incomes

The single most important task facing Massachusetts today is the revitalization of the state's economy.

For too long the critical importance of a healthy economy has gone unrecognized in Massachusetts, in spite of the simple truth that satisfaction of the basic needs and worthwhile aspirations of the Commonwealth's residents depends upon good jobs and growing incomes.

Massachusetts cannot afford to take a neutral or negative posture with regard to economic growth. Instead, we must aggressively seize opportunities for new economic activity and promote a better overall "climate" in which to do business and make investments.

Anything short of this would be irresponsible. Not only are far too many people unemployed right now, but the best available estimates show that the population should increase in Massachusetts by one million by the year 2000. Since the baby boom generation is now beginning to reach age 30, the rate of household formation over the next 20 years will be twice that of the previous two decades. As such,

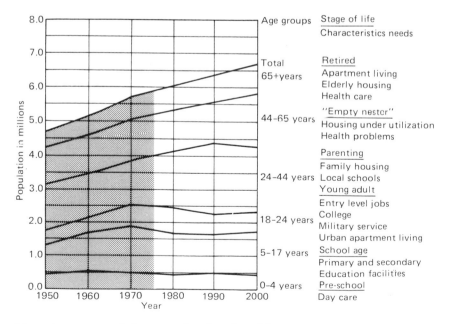

Massachusetts population, actual and projected by age, 1950–2000

significantly more young families will be in need of good, stable jobs in order to achieve an adequate standard of living. If new, well-paying jobs are not created in large numbers, the consequences for Massachusetts are clear: increased poverty, increased dependence on welfare, increased crime, increased urban deterioration, decreased capacity of state and local government to cope with all these problems, and increased migration out of state, perhaps at unprecedented levels.

What Massachusetts needs is a vigorous economic development program to bring balance to the social programs of the sixties and the environmental programs of the early seventies. We must acknowledge that more jobs and higher incomes are prerequisites to the improvement of public welfare and the enjoyment of our rich natural and man-made environment.

The ultimate goals of this program are clear and simple—more jobs and higher incomes for the residents and businesses of the Commonwealth.

Our Economic Condition

Due to years of indifference and neglect, the Massachusetts economy—together with the entire New England economy—has failed to keep pace with national economic trends. Until this year, important measures of our state's economic performance, including our rate of employment growth and rate of income growth, have deteriorated in comparison to national levels. Housing starts have fallen in relation to other sections of the country; state and local taxes have increased; and public assistance costs have escalated.

Yet these are symptoms, not the fundamental causes, of the Commonwealth's economic problems.

To a very large extent, these symptoms are a reflection of the two recessions experienced nationwide in 1970–71 and 1975. But these national recessions, as severe as they were, do not alone provide an adequate explanation of why Massachusetts has suffered more than the nation as a whole.

Since the Massachusetts economy is about average among the states in its sensitivity to the ups and downs of the nation's business cycle, we must look closer to home to find the causes of the state's relatively poor economic record. The true causes can be found in the character and structure of the state's complex economy, placing Massachusetts in a disadvantageous position relative to other states and sections of the country.

First, the high costs of energy—gas, oil, and electricity—and the costs of shipping products to and through Massachusetts make it difficult to sustain and expand the state's manufacturing base. Second, the rise of research and development firms has been both a salvation for and a weakness in the state's economy. While these firms helped to fill the void left by migrating textile and leather goods firms, their fragility became obvious in the late sixties and early seventies as defense and space program funds were reduced drastically, moving the Massachusetts unemployment rate beyond the national unemployment rate. Third, the increasing costs of state and local government have placed an added burden on firms wishing to expand in, relocate to, or simply continue operation in Massachusetts. And fourth, the demand for jobs in Massachusetts is much higher than the national average. The rate of participation in the Massachusetts labor force is 64.7 percent, a full 3.5 percent higher than the national average. If Massachusetts had a "labor force participation rate" equal to the nation's, the state's unemployment rate would have been closer to 6 percent than above 11 percent in 1975. This high labor force participation rate is the result of two factors. First, there is the higher cost of living in Massachusetts, which forces more people in the labor force. And second, while Massachusetts has led the country in the expansion of service-oriented jobs to replace its diminished manufacturing base, these new jobs quite often pay lower wages, which encourages households to send more than one member into the labor force in order to maintain an adequate standard of living.

Prospects for the Future

Reports of the impending demise of the Massachusetts economy, however, are greatly exaggerated. In spite of serious structural problems in our economy, there is reason for optimism.

Recently, the Massachusetts economy has picked up substantially—so much so that our rate of economic recovery, as measured by declining unemployment rates, is better than the nation as a whole. Thus, the Massachusetts economy has weathered the energy

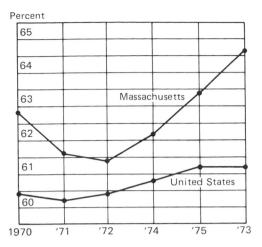

Percent

Labor force participation rate—total

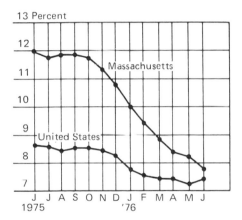

Unemployment rates

crisis of 1973–74 and the 1975 recession more successfully than was apparent a few short months ago.

Total employment of Massachusetts' residents has risen over 36,000 in the last year. Personal incomes are increasing. Moreover, state expenditures as a percentage of gross state product has leveled off and actually fallen for the first time in years. And many firms have announced in-state expansion plans.

In addition, Massachusetts has substantial attributes as a place in which to do business. Central among these are a skilled and productive labor force; educational and cultural resources that are difficult to

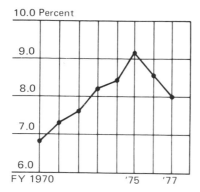

State expenditure as a percentage of gross state product

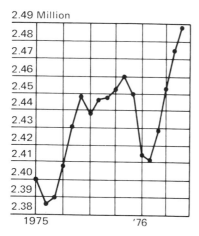

Employment

match; a natural and man-made environment which makes Massachusetts an attractive place in which to live and work; and an excellent highway, mass transit, and air and seaport system.

Perhaps most important of all, there is a new appreciation by state and local government, the media, and the business and labor communities that the state's economy will not and cannot attend to itself or be attended to by the Federal Government. Instead, a comprehensive economic development program for the state must be vigorously pursued as a major responsibility of both the public and private sectors within Massachusetts.

What State Government Can Do

Many observers point to the limited capacity of state government to improve its economic position. Before describing what a state can do, it is important to understand what it cannot do. Economic cycles, inflation, and long-term secular trends across the nation are beyond the capacity of state government to influence substantially. Natural advantages and disadvantages, such as climate, geographic location, and natural resources cannot be altered by state decision makers. The federal government exercises the most significant policy options over money supply, interest rates, taxes, and public works programs as well as exercising regulatory responsibilities over such things as energy prices and environmental standards. And, finally, the vast majority of new jobs will be generated by the private sector and not by government.

In the past, the awareness of these limitations has discouraged state government from undertaking a broader economic development program. It is clear today, however, that a handful of tax incentives and an advertising campaign will not suffice as the only components of the Commonwealth's economic development effort. Since most of the major decisions made every day by state government have economic consequences, and since the structural obstacles to economic expansion are complex, a more comprehensive approach to the state's economic revitalization is warranted.

There are three essential roles that state government can play to improve the Massachusetts economy. First, as *protector* of the state's competitive position relative to other states, state government can encourage federal policies which do not adversely affect the state's economic position and which minimize the state's natural and locational disadvantages, and can provide incentives for sound growth and development comparable to other states. Second, as a *catalyst* to development, state government can offer tax incentives for new, growth-oriented industries, flexible financing options for new and expanding firms, public improvements to accommodate development in key locations, and well-developed education and manpower training programs that provide a ready and willing labor force for anticipated jobs. And third, as *manager* of its own service delivery, facility development, and regulatory responsibilities, state government can create a climate in which there is a reasonable degree of confidence on the part of the private sector and the public-at-large in the fiscal stability and administrative capacity of state government.

In this context, much can be done within the full scope of state government's activities to put Massachusetts back on a firm economic foundation.

The economic development program that follows sets forth the basic problems and takes advantage of the most attractive opportunities within our state's economy. The policies and initiatives described in this program are directed at three objectives:

• State government must assist in the stabilization, and where possible, the reduction of the costs, and the increase of convenience of doing business relative to other states.

• State government must assist in the identification and encouragement of key investment opportunities in various areas and industries in the Commonwealth.

• State government must better manage its own activities and functions if an attractive climate for investment and expansion is to be provided.

Priorities

The economic development plan set forth in previous sections of this document represents a systematic attempt on the part of state government to address the underlying structural problems of the Massachusetts economy. Although virtually every action taken by state government has an economic consequence, this plan is built around those policy and program initiatives that attack the Commonwealth's economic problems most directly and thereby offer the people of Massachusetts their best hope for more jobs and higher incomes.

From among the hundred or so proposals advanced in this document, most of which already are at some stage of investigation or implementation, it was necessary to select a comparative few for priority attention. Selection of these priorities is not intended to suggest that state government will neglect the many other policy and program initiatives discussed in the body of this document. To the extent that resources allow, all will be pursued as potential stimulants to the state's economy.

Priority status was assigned to those proposals that scored best when measured against the following criteria:

• Will lead to the creation of a substantial number of new jobs.
• Will reduce or stabilize basic household and/or business costs.
• Will trigger substantial new private investment.
• Will have a short-term economic impact.

Not all of the priorities listed below scored well when measured against each criterion. It was clear, for instance, that support for OCS exploration and development would be of negligible short-term benefit to the Massachusetts economy. And yet, given a state commitment to plan and prepare now, the long-term economic benefits in terms of new jobs and increased private investment could be enormous. In this case, the possibility of substantial long-term rewards justified assigning priority status to Massachusetts' efforts to support the OCS exploration and development process. Although use of objective criteria helped to quantify the priority-setting process, trade-offs such as the one described above necessarily entailed an element of subjective judgment. In a very real sense, then, the priorities set forth below are those of the governor and his Development Cabinet.

Economic Development Priorities for Massachusetts

Energy

Priority: To Pursue an Aggressive Program to Increase Energy and Energy Efficiency Such a program can help to stabilize Massachusetts' overall energy costs by reducing the total amount of fuel consumed at the individual firm or household level, without adversely affecting comfort, productivity, or profitability. In addition, increased energy savings and energy efficiency can stimulate the state's economy by reducing expenditures on imported fuels, thereby retaining money within the state; by reducing the need for new energy facilities, thereby freeing capital and income for other needs; and by increasing jobs, especially among the building trades, through the installation of energy-efficient improvements such as insulation, storm windows, and weatherstripping. Under the Energy Policy and Conservation Act of 1975, the state will develop a comprehensive energy conservation plan to assist residential, commercial, industrial, and institutional consumers to achieve the twin goals of increased energy savings and energy efficiency.

Next Steps

A. Continue disseminating information on energy savings techniques to residential, commercial, and industrial users, and continue to provide technical assistance to municipal officials.

B. Follow up on Project Conserve to stimulate the purchase of energy efficiency improvements by homes and businesses.

C. Maintain the state's own energy conservation program to cut overall consumption within state government by 20 percent.

D. Incorporate strong incentives for energy conservation within future electric rate reforms.

E. Develop thermal efficiency standards for new construction; lighting standards for public buildings; car and van pooling programs; and new energy-sensitive government procurement practices.

F. Implement a statewide resource recovery program as recommended in the state's solid waste management plan. In converting solid waste to electricity under the state plan, the state could displace the consumption of some four million barrels of oil annually in Massachusetts, recapturing millions of dollars for the state's economy; stimulate approximately $500 million in private investment; and create 4,000 person-years of construction employment and 600 permanent jobs.

Priority: To Press for the Re-regulation of Natural Gas Massachusetts is heavily dependent on imported residual oil which is three times more expensive than the regulated natural gas used by competitors in the Southern and Midwestern states. The re-regulation of natural gas to allow a gradual increase in price, combined with adequate safeguards against pricing abuses will bring about closer parity between oil and gas prices. Re-regulation along these lines is the most significant step that can be taken to bring the overall energy costs of Massachusetts and New England into line with those of other states and regions across the country.

Next Steps

A. Support current congressional efforts to re-regulate the price of natural gas. Work toward this end must proceed in cooperation with the Massachusetts congressional delegation NERCOM and the New England and National Governors' Councils.

Priority: To Support Exploration for Oil and Gas on Georges Bank Active support for exploration and development of potential oil and gas reserves on Georges Bank necessarily entails a high degree of speculation. However, a significant find could produce substantial numbers of new jobs and private investment in Massachusetts' coastal communities as a result of OCS-related on-shore development. Moreover, discovery of commercially recoverable reserves of natural gas would improve the Commonwealth's access to this important fuel, the current cost of which includes an extremely high transportation component.

Next Steps

A. Render technical assistance to communities potentially affected by OCS exploration and development to help them determine ways to maximize the benefits and minimize any adverse impacts of future on-shore activity.

B. Render technical assistance to firms involved in the OCS exploration and development process to secure as many of the jobs and ancillary economic benefits for Massachusetts as possible.

C. Put Massachusetts on record nationally, through personal and media contacts, as being ready, willing, and able to host firms engaged in OCS exploration and development.

D. Continue to press for passage of federal OCS legislation which would guarantee Massachusetts and other coastal states a greater role in the off-shore oil and gas leasing process and enable the Commonwealth better to protect vital environmental, fishing, and tourism interests; and under recent amendments to the CZM Act, utilize federal funds to assist any Massachusetts communities adversely affected by OCS exploration and development.

Priority: To Establish Massachusetts as a Home Base for Innovative Energy Industries, Especially the Solar Industry The solar energy industry is but one of a number of innovative energy industries that are establishing themselves in response to national and international needs. If Massachusetts can become a major home-base for these new industries, at least some of which are likely to experience high growth over the next decade, the benefits in terms of increased employment alone could be significant. The state's primary responsibilities in this area are to increase the flow of federal energy research and development dollars to Massachusetts firms and to assist in the promotion and demonstration of existing technology in order to bolster the market for new energy equipment and devices.

Next Steps

A. Establish a close working relationship with the U.S. Energy Research and Development Administration and push for the speedy creation of a New England regional office for ERDA in Massachusetts. A regional ERDA office will better be able to service the specific energy needs of New England and should improve the ability of Massachusetts firms to secure federal energy R&D dollars.

B. In conjunction with the Capital Formation Task Force, explore the possibility of new, improved state finance mechanisms to provide start-up capital to high technology firms engaged in the production of new energy devices.

C. Push for the demonstration of alternative energy systems in public buildings through the institution of life-cycle costing measures.

D. Continue to work to have New England designated as the site for the nation's Solar Energy Research Institute.

Capital

Priority: To Activate Existing State Development Finance Programs Such as the Community Development Finance Corporation (CDFC) and the Massachusetts Industrial Mortgage Insurance Agency (MIMIA) CDFC, enacted into law in 1975, is designed to serve as one vehicle for the provision of equity and debt capital to businesses in economically depressed areas of the Commonwealth. Although the CDFC entity has been statutorily established, it currently remains unfunded.

MIMIA, which is designed to stimulate the availability of mortgage financing to industrial firms, has received a $2 million appropriation for its insurance funds and $70,000 for staffing. The board of directors and staff of MIMIA have yet to be appointed.

Taken together, these two new financing vehicles will enable many Massachusetts firms to obtain lower cost capital for the expansion of economic activity in the Commonwealth.

Next Steps

A. Secure legislative authorization of a $10 million bonding authorization for CDFC.

B. Provide the newly appointed board of directors of CDFC wth the guidance and assistance necessary to engage in many development activities in key areas around the state.

C. Appoint a board of directors for the MIMIA and use its $2 million appropriation to begin insuring loans for industrial expansion as soon as possible.

Priority: To Develop and Implement a Comprehensive State Program of Financing Mechanisms for Economic Development through the Capital Formation Task Force The Capital Formation Task Force is now reviewing and refining a number of new initiatives that will build upon and complement the recently enacted CDFC and MIMIA mechanisms. Four subcommittees are preparing specific short-term proposals to remedy capital needs for new business development, expansions of existing industry, and development in depressed areas, and to revise the state's tax laws. All of these proposals are intended to make Massachusetts competitive with other states in the financing options and tax provisions offered to businesses. A larger objective is to provide Massachusetts with a comprehensive, well-integrated set of financing tools that will be unsurpassed by any state.

Next Steps

A. Through the task force, review the efficacy of existing tax incentives for business in Massachusetts with a view toward revising or repealing those which are not serving a useful, cost-effective purpose.

B. Complete the deliberations of the Capital Formation Task Force on the details of each of the proposals emanating from the four subcommittees.

C. Prepare draft legislation for each of the proposals approved by the task force.

D. Submit the task force's legislative proposals to the governor and legislature for final review, approval, and enactment.

Priority: To Establish a New England Capital Corporation, as Proposed by the New England Regional Commission A New England Capital Corporation (NECC), which would complement the programs recommended by the Capital Formation Task Force, currently is under consideration by the New England Regional Commission. With the approval of $133,000 for the further development of the proposal orginally drawn up by NERCOM's Task Force on Capital and Labor Markets, a full description and analysis of the means of establishing such an entity, including its organizational framework and operating procedures, should soon be available for review by the New England governors.

Next Steps

A. Actively assist in the preparation of NERCOM's implementation plan for the New England Capital Corporation.

B. Review and revise the plan to ensure consistency with the existing and proposed financing mechanisms in Massachusetts.

C. Approve and implement the NECC plan.

Transportation

Priority: To Award at Least $200 Million in Construction Contracts for Highway and Transit Projects in 1976, and to Sustain or Increase That Level of Effort in Future Years Massachusetts' 1976 Consolidated Construction Program includes some $200 million in highway and transit construction projects. Award of contracts for those projects will lead to construction that will expand and improve the state's transportation system, trigger substantial private investment, and create thousands of construction jobs.

Next Steps

A. Monitor and manage the transportation component of the 1976 Consolidated Construction Program to ensure that all contracts are awarded as expeditiously as possible.

B. Develop a steady stream of fundable highway and transit construction projects to sustain or increase Massachusetts' current level of effort in this area. On the highway side, special attention will be given to depressing Boston's Central Artery, potentially the largest public works project in Massachusetts' history, and completing I-190 in Central Massachusetts; the missing link of I-495; I-391 north of

Springfield; I-95 north from Route 128; and Route 25 south to Cape Cod. On the transit side, emphasis will be placed on major corridor improvements, including extension of the Red Line to South Braintree and the construction of the South Quincy Red Line Station; extension of the Red Line from Harvard Square to Arlington Heights; a variety of Southwest Corridor projects, including rebuilding of the Orange Line to Forest Hills; and the extension of the Blue Line to Lynn. The state's construction program in transit should average $150 million annually over the next five years.

C. Work with NERCOM, AMTRAK, and ConRail to ensure that roadbeds for railroads in Massachusetts and throughout New England are reconstructed.

D. Lobby the federal government for increased levels of transportation funding and for increased flexibility in expending those funds. This step is essential if Massachusetts is to have the money it needs to construct vitally needed highway and transit improvements in the future.

Priority: To Increase the Amount of General Cargo Flowing through Massachusetts' Port Facilities While Developing Those Facilities to Their Maximum Potential Every ton of general cargo that passes through a Massachusetts port generates between $30–$70 in direct and indirect revenues for that port and the surrounding local economy. A significant increase in the amount of general cargo handled by Massachusetts' ports will lead to more jobs and higher incomes for the state's citizens. It also will lead to more productive domestic and international economic relationships for the Commonwealth.

Next Steps

A. Lobby Washington to have Boston's rail freight rates for containerized cargo equalized with those for other major East Coast ports.

B. Lobby Washington, and the state department in particular, to have Boston designated as a "favored port," thereby removing a significant impediment to Soviet shipping trade.

C. Secure foreign trade zone designations for the ports of Boston and New Bedford.

D. Continue to emphasize better service to shippers through MassPort as an important means to increase the amount of general cargo handled by the Port of Boston.

E. Utilize the overseas offices of MassPort and NERCOM, and NERCOM's World Trade Center office to attract foreign trade and investment to Massachusetts.

F. Provide technical assistance to Massachusetts' ports in order to enable them to determine and secure needed physical improvements to their harbors and related facilities.

Areas

Priority: To Foster the Full Realization of Growth Opportunities in Particularly Suitable Areas within the Commonwealth Massachusetts contains a wide variety of redevelopment and new development opportunities. Many town and city centers with distinctive features are ripe for revitalization through a combination of public and private investments. Abandoned federal military installations can be developed privately with assistance from the Government Land Bank. The underutilized or empty industrial mills of so many Massachusetts communities provide low-cost, business start-up possibilities. The thousands of acres of industrially zoned land across the Commonwealth and the fully serviced industrial parks in our cities and towns can easily accommodate major new industrial expansions for years to come. Coastal communities with underutilized port facilities, such as Gloucester, Lynn, New Bedford, Fall River, and Boston provide exciting development possibilities, as does the Southwest Corridor of Boston. All of the initiatives of this program will encourage development either directly or indirectly in these critical growth potential areas. Particular steps that also can be taken are described below.

Next Steps

A. Complete the new regulations for Chapter 121A Urban Development Corporations, as amended in 1975, to provide for more flexibility in the financial arrangements and kinds of redevelopment activity undertaken. This attractive vehicle for urban revitalization should be promoted to municipalities and the private development community.

B. Flexibly administer and coordinate federal and state public investment programs for roads, sewers, parks, and housing to advance sound local development plans and proposals that will trigger private investment and substantially increase local economic activity.

C. Press for passage of proposed amendments to the state's Government Land Bank to give it the longer-term financing capability that will enable it to assist communities more substantially in their base conversion programs.

D. Expedite and complete state public investment programs for the Lowell Heritage State Park, the state transportation building for Park Plaza, the Charlestown Navy Yard, Revere Beach, and the Southwest Corridor, as well as in many other locations throughout the Commonwealth.

E. Complete the statewide growth policy development process, as mandated by Chapter 807 of the Acts of 1975, through submission of a summary on local attitudes toward growth to the Special Commission on Growth, the governor, and the legislature.

Industries

Priority: To Encourage the Maximum Growth of New Jobs in Those Industries Which Are Best Able to Take Advantage of Massachusetts' Economic Assets All of the initiatives advanced in this program to constrain the costs and increase the convenience of doing business in Massachusetts will serve to encourage the creation of new jobs, especially in those industries that have natural growth potential. State government cannot create these new jobs directly. Instead, it must proceed by fostering an improved general climate for operating businesses and undertaking investments. More directly, the state can attract new corporate headquarters and encourage the expansion of technology and natural resource-based industries, as well as the exploitation of import-substitution opportunities, by pursuing the steps set forth below.

Next Steps
A. Enact a loss carry-forward tax provision for all new and expanding companies in Massachusetts.

B. Implement the Capital Formation Task Force financing mechanisms that receive gubernatorial and legislative approval.

C. Evaluate the cost-effectiveness of a variety of tax incentive proposals for such new growth potential industries as solar energy and fishing.

D. Continue the work of the "200-Mile Work Group" in assessing specific ways to expand the Massachusetts fishing industry.

E. Improve the capacity of state government to identify industrial development opportunities and to provide information and assistance to prospective entrepreneurs and investors, with specific regard to taking advantage of import-substitution opportunities. State government will work with private sector and academic economists to identify those products that are heavily imported to Massachusetts and to assess the opportunities for local production of these products and the potential consumer savings resulting from such local production. Most important, state government will distribute this information and provide follow-up assistance to those who might want to take advantage of these import-substitution opportunities.

Labor

Priority: To Pursue a Comprehensive Program to Accelerate the Implementation of a Full Array of Public Sector Construction Projects Through improved management and monitoring, state government can maximize the number of public construction projects initiated within any given year. This is a worthwhile objective not only for the immediate jobs that are provided for the hard-pressed construction industry but also for the spin-off jobs created throughout the state's economy, and for the private investment that is stimulated through public improvements in roads, sewers, parks, and housing.

Next Steps
A. Monitor the performance of all state agencies participating in the 1976 Accelerated Construction Program to ensure that they keep pace with the commitments made in January, and to ensure that at least $321 million in construction contracts are awarded by December 31 of this year. Public reports on the progress made by each agency will be submitted monthly, and special attention will be directed to the expeditious review of all applications for the construction of wastewater treatment facilities.

Priority: To Secure Legislative Approval and Quick Implementation of Proposed Reforms in the Unemployment Insurance Program The proposed reforms are aimed at restoring solvency to the unemployment insurance fund and at repaying the fund's debt to the federal government. A number of factors have combined to cause this condition: recent high unemployment; a taxable wage base which is only modestly higher than it was when first introduced in the 1930s; and eligibility criteria and benefits which are not competitive with those of other states.

Key items in the governor's proposal are: increase the taxable wage base, tighten up certain criteria where we are out of line with competing states, provide a greater degree of employer merit-rating within the tax schedule, and improve the administration of the appeals process.

Next Steps

A. Continue to work with the legislature's leadership and the Joint Committee on Commerce and Labor to get the full bill reported out favorably as soon as possible.

B. Press for enactment by the legislature.

C. Implement the act through the Division of Employment Security.

Priority: To Bring about a Better Match between Training Programs and Reasonable Projections of Job Opportunities Every year millions of dollars are spent on a variety of manpower training programs. It is vital that these funds be used to upgrade the skills of our labor force for good jobs that are likely to be made available by the state's employers. Used well, these funds can benefit job seekers, and can serve to encourage job expansion in the Commonwealth by offering employers a skilled and highly motivated labor force. This objective can be fulfilled primarily through better management of training programs and increased cooperation with prospective employers.

Next Steps

A. Continue to improve the capacity of the State Manpower Services Council to coordinate and manage Massachusetts' many manpower training programs. This includes the development of a close and effective working relationship between the CETA program, vocational education programs under the Executive Office of Educational Affairs, and the many skill centers and other manpower training efforts throughout the public and private sectors.

B. Improve coordination between the state's manpower training programs, the job referral service of the state's Division of Employment Security, and the job banks of other New England states.

C. Expand the Customized Manpower Training Program for employers with clearly defined skill and job requirements.

State and Local Government

Priority: To Practice Responsible Fiscal Management Within State Government The financial crisis that burdened state government throughout 1975 was precipitated by poor financial management and overspending in previous years. Having weathered that crisis by bringing state programs into line with realistic revenue projections, Massachusetts must consolidate its recent gains and create a stable state fiscal environment.

Next Steps

A. Maintain a modest budget surplus through fiscal year 1976, and plan for a third consecutive surplus in FY 1978.

B. Using the agency-by-agency implementation plans drawn up by each cabinet secretary, implement the recommendations of the governor's Management Task Force.

C. Work with the governor's Local Government Advisory Committee to formulate necessary administrative and legislative initiatives that can be taken to enhance the capacity of local government to control expenditures and practice responsible fiscal management at its level.

Priority: To Stabilize the Overall Tax Burden on Individuals and Businesses in Massachusetts The most notable feature of Massachusetts' current system of taxation is the heavy overall burden that it places on individuals and businesses in the Commonwealth as compared to other states. Stabilizing that burden will help to stabilize the cost of living and doing business in Massachusetts, a key step toward improving the condition of the state's economy.

Next Steps

A. Carefully control the level of state and local government expenditures in Massachusetts.

B. Work to develop new local aid formulae that will distribute the existing property tax burden more equitably.

C. Press for fundamental federal reforms including welfare reform, a full-employment program, nationalized health insurance, and a basic restructuring of federal grant-in-aid programs. Properly executed, these reforms would result in hundreds of millions of dollars of savings for state government that can be passed along in the form of property tax relief.

Priority: To Streamline the State's Development Permitting Process The state development permitting process is one area where government regulation directly affects not only the quality of economic development but the cost and convenience associated with initiating that development as well. Thus, there is a dual responsibility to protect public standards concerning the location and quality of economic growth while doing everything possible to ensure that legitimate development opportunities are not stifled. Systematically streamlining the state's development permitting process can reduce the cost and improve the convenience of doing business in Massachusetts without compromising established development standards.

Next Steps
A. Complete an administrative overhaul of all development permits administered by the Massachusetts Department of Environmental Quality Engineering. Since about half of the state's development-related permits are administered by DEQE, this step constitutes a substantial effort toward improving the state's overall permitting process. DEQE plans to produce both a guide to all the permits within this domain and a consolidated permit application that should simplify and expedite its review and approval proceedings considerably. In addition, the DEQE overhaul will produce a permit tracking office that will monitor and manage the progress of all the permits that it is handling.

B. Undertake similar administrative overhauls within other state agencies with significant development permitting responsibilities.

C. Review the Massachusetts Environmental Policy Act regulations with a view toward establishing a better defined scope and time frame for the entire MEPA process. The intent here is not to dilute the statutory authority of MEPA but to provide a set of guidelines that will enable prospective developers to fulfill their responsibilities in as timely and inexpensive a manner as possible.

D. Work with the governor's Local Government Advisory Committee to determine administrative and legislative initiatives that may be required to streamline the development-permitting process at the local level.

Federal-State Relations

Priority: To Push for National Full-Employment and Health Insurance Programs, and for Basic Welfare Reform at the Federal Level Massachusetts, like most other mature, industrialized states, is plagued by high public sector costs, which translate into higher costs of living and doing business. Currently, Massachusetts bears the financial burden of providing essential human services for the basic health, welfare, and employment needs of its citizens. The federal government, relying as it does on a progressive income tax, is far better equipped to provide for these basic needs. If national full-employment and health insurance programs, and fundamental federal welfare reforms were enacted, the cost of state government in Massachusetts would be reduced by hundreds of millions of dollars. Those savings then could be passed along in the form of property tax relief, a step that would stabilize the costs of living and doing business in the Commonwealth.

Next Steps

A. Press for full employment as a national goal and federal responsibility. A combination of tools such as countercyclical revenue sharing, labor-intensive public works projects, public service employment, and the targeting of federal investments toward areas of chronically high unemployment must become a permanent feature of federal economic policy.

B. Press for a national health insurance program. Waste, duplication, inaccessibility, and uncontrollable costs are all characteristics of the present national health delivery system. With the advent of a national health insurance program, these problems could be addressed in a concerted fashion, and state governments could concentrate on effective delivery and cost control systems as part of a total national health effort.

C. Press for fundamental welfare reform at the federal level. Our current welfare system is an administrative nightmare that often fails to help those most in need of assistance. Massachusetts must support a simplified system of income maintenance that does not penalize the working poor and that requires persons on welfare who are able to work to accept appropriate jobs or job training.

Priority: To Join with Other New England States in Working toward Solutions for Common Economic Problems and in Lobbying for Federal Policies More Responsive to the Region's Needs A growing recognition among New England states that they share a number of common social and economic problems makes a "regional" approach to those problems both necessary and much more likely than it has been in past years. The governor, the lieutenant governor and his Office of Federal-State Relations, the Massachusetts congressional delegation, and their analogs in other New England states, together with major groups such as NERCOM, the New England Governors' Council, and the New England Congressional Caucus are the basic building blocks for a powerful regional presence in a New England coalition that will aggressively pursue the region's best interests at all levels of government.

Next Steps

A. Actively resort to cooperative regional approaches to solving the problems and capitalizing on the opportunities presented by:

• OCS exploration and development.

• The proposed New England Capital Corporation.

• The NERCOM foreign trade and investment program.

• The proposed Solar Energy Research Institute.

• A New England regional office for the Energy Research and Development Agency.

B. Develop a regional plan to push for the restructuring of federal grant-in-aid programs so that Massachusetts and New England receive their fair share of federal funds.

C. Follow up on the organizational meetings already held by the governors of the New England states to identify specific economic development issues that can be addressed jointly through a unified regional presence in Washington.

A Four-Point Program
for the Northeast

Diane Fulman and James M. Howell
The First National Bank of Boston
March 1977

Regional economists have long been concerned about the specific effects of national economic policy on a particular area. The mature economy of the Northeast, for example, has needs that are fundamentally different from those of growing areas such as the South and West. One of the roles of state and local government is to find ways to take the best advantage of national economic policy within a particular region. In this 1977 paper Howell and Diane Fulman, a consultant to the bank, focused on this key aspect of economic development.

As it became clear that the region's cities were suffering from prolonged economic stagnation in the 1974–75 recession, the need to shift federal aid to cities became a pressing regional issue. Moreover the nation's cities were a particular cause of concern in the 1970s as the continuing urban exodus of manufacturing eroded the job base. One study reported here notes that for the thirty largest urban areas in the Northeast, the aggregate employment growth in the period from 1972 to 1975 came solely from growth in the government sector, reflecting a serious imbalance between the public and private sectors.

This imbalance, the authors maintained, was just one consequence of "governmental maturity," which they defined as the "archaic structure and outmoded practices" of a government designed to deal with growth patterns of the previous century. Such governmental stagnation, coupled with economic maturity, they claimed, was stifling economic growth in the Northeast, particularly in New England's cities—areas where nearly four out of five of the region's 12 million people resided and worked.

After identifying the regional problems associated with various proposed national approaches to economic programs, the authors presented a specific set of four recommendations aimed at revitalizing the Northeast. In so doing, the paper puts the concerns of the business community in the context of regional and federal aspects of economic development.

Introduction

Over the past fifteen years, we have had the opportunity to spend a considerable amount of time analyzing the manner in which economic growth takes place in the national economy and among the various regions. This work has led us down many paths—some old, others new—but it has always led us back to one virtually inescapable conclusion: national policy has different impacts on the various regions of the country. Economic hardship is not randomly distributed around the country, and the paradoxical fact is that past and currently proposed federal initiatives may have proportionately less impact in the very regions with the greatest need for them. As obvious as this may seem, national economic policymakers consistently overlook these regional dimensions when devising new policies.

From an economic point of view, there are major structural variations among the regions of the country that can facilitate or inhibit the capability of state and municipal governments to successfully implement new or expanded federal programs. And, of equal importance are the regional variations in the stage of industrialization that make it exceedingly difficult for the older industrialized parts of the country to create adequate job opportunities for the people who choose to live in them. These phenomena are clearly reflected in the economic difficulties of the Northeast.

In analyses conducted by the Economics Department of The First National Bank of Boston, we have repeatedly reached the conclusion that municipal governments in the Northeast are ill-equipped to play a role in solving the region's complex economic problems. Governmental structures still largely reflect growth patterns of the nineteenth century; local boundaries have simply not been changed to be more functionally compatible with changing economic patterns. Moreover, age-old management practices seriously undermine the ability of municipal governments to deal with modern world issues, let alone implement a wide range of new federal programs with skill and success. We have termed this dual problem of archaic structure and outmoded practices "governmental maturity," and the term is intended to describe the current condition of northeastern municipal governments.

To be more specific, our governments in the Northeast seem to be unusually characterized by outdated management control and accounting and personnel systems that must somehow attempt to deliver public services to a citizenry with a virtually insatiable appetite for more social services, and to a business community that has become increasingly discontented because it cannot cut through governmental red tape. Throughout all of this, these governments rest on a physical infrastructure that is simply worn out and a financial structure that simply will not balance. These aspects of governmental maturity provide an intellectually defensible box into which we may justly lay blame for many of the Northeast's current problems and which limits the region's ability to absorb the financial blessings from Washington.

The other part of the region's structural problem relates to its stage of industrialization. Over the past five years we have conducted a number of special studies in an attempt to isolate the characteristics of the process of industrial aging in a region. Once industrial maturity is reached, a wide range of new economic problems begin to manifest themselves: lagging capital spending, structural adjustment problems in labor markets, and a reluctance on the part of business management to expand in the region. Taken together, these factors produce regional economic stagnation—that is, the private sector stops making a net contribution to the region's growth. We usually refer to this unhappy state of affairs as "economic maturity."

Either of these problems alone would be enough to cause a considerable amount of regional difficulty, but when combined, they introduce into the northeastern states a significant structural drag on the region's economic and social progress. Yet it would be faulty economic reasoning to argue that the entire Northeast region is on the brink of economic stagnation: our empirical analyses of the Northeast's spatial dynamics show that there is much evidence to the contrary. Indeed, we find ourselves in complete agreement with a recent statement by an aide to President Carter expressing his views of regionalism: "Every region has both economically healthy and depressed communities within it, so aid programs must be aimed at pockets of distress, not entire regions." This view is implicit in the concept of targeting, a potentially significant approach to regional problem solving, to which we will shortly return.

Last fall, The First National Bank of Boston and the Boston University Geography Department carried out a joint project to determine the spatial dynamics of national economic growth, and in the first two attached maps one can clearly see juxtaposed growing and declining areas—much like grandma's patchwork quilt. However, in the third map, the structural economic problems contained within the Northeast are revealed. Northeast counties form a solid block of relative stagnation in manufacturing shares and in many counties there is, in fact, a decline in the absolute share.

An important conclusion: the manufacturing quilt of the Northeast does not follow a random pattern. Although there are growing as well as declining subregions in terms of population and personal income, the declining counties in the manufacturing employment share are consistently concentrated in the urban areas of the northeastern states. The erosion of the manufacturing base in the region's urban areas is a development that merits special attention, for our empirical analyses show that manufacturing investment is the key swing variable in a region's economic base.

The economic plight of the cities is similarly reflected in debt market perceptions of their financial condition. Shown in table 1 are the changes in bond ratings covering the period 1970–76 for the twenty-five largest central cities in the Northeast. Note that nearly one half of the twenty-five central cities recently experienced a downgrading in their municipal bond ratings. A downgrading of such a significant number of the municipal bond ratings of the central cities in the highly urbanized Northeast can have protracted negative growth implications on their contiguous suburbs. Furthermore, inas-

Table 1
Change in Moody rating, 1970–76

Direction of change in municipal bond rating	Number of central cities	Percentage distribution
Upgraded	4	16%
Unchanged	10	40
Downgraded	11	44
	25	100%

much as economic development of the region is inextricably bound up in the economic health of its cities, the consequences are even more pervasive.

Understanding the Northeast's Urban Problems

Unquestionably, to conclude that the northeastern states face an urban economic problem is hardly earthshaking. Nonetheless, we are still surprised to find how little serious analysis has been completed on the economic characteristics of the Northeast's urban areas vis-à-vis those in the more rapidly growing states.[1] This shortcoming badly needs correction, and the Council for Northeast Economic Action—an organization which we will describe more fully in a moment—has undertaken a substantial portion of this research. Today, we would like to share with you a number of our tentative conclusions.

Over the past year, we have begun to analyze empirically the 100 largest urban areas in the country. We have chosen these areas not only because of their size and geographical diversity but also because it is in urban America that much of the economic and social interaction takes place which is so critical to the stability of our country. The data contained in table 2 summarize one of the most important con-

Table 2

Region and number of urban areas analyzed	Percentage change in nonagricultural employment		
	1966–69	1969–72	1972–75
Northeast (30 largest urban areas)	7.7%	2.1%	1.3%
Net employment contribution from the following sectors			
Private	5.9	0.5	−0.8
Government	1.8	1.6	2.1
New South (35 largest urban areas)	15.9%	19.2%	7.8%
Net employment contribution from the following sectors			
Private	12.5	14.8	4.9
Government	3.4	4.4	2.9

clusions from our analysis. Of the 100 urban areas studied, we have provided data on those that contrast our region with the New South.

A number of conclusions may be derived from these data:

• Note specifically that during the period 1966–69, there was generally vigorous economic growth in urban areas in both regions, even though the rate of job increase in the New South urban areas was about twice that of northeastern urban areas. Overall increases in new private sector job growth accounted for approximately 77 percent of the 7.7 percent in Northeast urban areas, and approximately 79 percent in the New South urban areas. As economists know, this is the way orderly economic growth should take place, that is, a structural balance between the public and private sectors with the latter contributing anywhere from two-thirds to three-fourths of the overall growth rate.

• In the two subsequent periods, this equilibrium economic growth pattern continued to prevail in thirty-five New South urban areas. For instance, during the period 1969–72, the private sector contributed 77 percent of the total job increase and during the most recent period, 1972–75, it contributed 63 percent.

• For the thirty largest urban areas in the Northeast, this important economic relationship was broken and a perverse development resulted. In a sense, the public-private sector job balance that had previously prevailed came unstuck. Note specifically that during 1969–72 the net private sector job contribution slipped dramatically to 24 percent, and in the subsequent period it actually became negative. *In other words, during the period 1972–75, whatever aggregate employment growth took place was stimulated solely by the growth in the government sector.* To those of us who worry about the viability of the private sector, this is a disturbing finding.

Together, these three observations vividly depict the Northeast's structural imbalance between the public and private sectors, which we believe may be explained by the presence of both governmental and economic maturity.

In the months ahead, we will continue to analyze the dynamic interaction of these two phenomena in the 100 largest urban areas. In an attempt to better understand the interactions between the growth in the government sector and the urban areas as a whole, we recently ran a number of dynamic cross-sectional regressions. The results are critical to the development of a better understanding of the stages of governmental and economic growth, and we will summarize their key conclusions.

Among the thirty Northeast urban areas, in the first period (1966–69) a 1 percent increase in government employment contributed an additional 1 percent increase in total employment, but this relationship declined continuously in the two subsequent periods to the point where increases in government employment produced virtually no additional employment growth. The basis for this is, of course, the dramatic impact of government maturity on the private sector. The result pushed the private sector from a positive to a negative net contribution to total employment growth during the preceding decade. Among the thirty-five New South urban areas, changes in governmental employment in the first two periods are virtually insignificant, but in the final period (1972–75), a 1 percent increase in governmental employment contributed an additional 0.42 percent increase in total employment.

Specifically, these results imply that the urban areas in the New South are just younger variants of those in the Northeast. This is in itself not particularly surprising, but it carries with it an important policy implication. Many of the Northeast's current economic problems in urban areas are the direct result of a cumulative inattention to the process of governmental and economic aging, underscoring the causal relationship between governmental maturity and economic stagnation.

Now that we have finally begun to address this problem it will probably be more difficult to resolve than had we worked to minimize these consequences before the state of maturity was reached. By contrast, our colleagues in the New South are attempting to deal with the problem before it occurs. The Southern Growth Policies Board was recently created to put into place a wide range of policies to continue to stimulate private sector investment in order to avoid the problems of governmental and economic maturity.

At this point, it will be helpful to summarize. Clearly, a great deal more serious economic research needs to be undertaken in this area, but at least we, along with a few others, have begun the task. Furthermore, our analysis thus far provides a sound basis for believing that the dual problem of governmental and economic maturity lies close to, or at the very core of, the cause of these urban growth disparities in the Northeast. Finally, the fact that regions are in different stages of growth results in the differential impact of Washington's economic policies to stimulate orderly national growth and lower unemployment. Given the magnitude of existing regional differences, it is not surprising that macroeconomic policies will have different impacts in different areas.

Assessing Current Economic Policies in Light of Governmental and Economic Maturity

Before we examine the interaction of our region's dual maturities and national economic policies, it is critical to make absolutely certain that we understand where this line of reasoning is taking us. We are not arguing that the Carter economic policies are bad *per se* for our country. Quite to the contrary, in an aggregative sense, they are both consistent and sound in terms of what we have grown to accept as Keynesian economic policy. They are not, however, free of problems. First, current national economic policymakers in Washington fail to take into account the Northeast's structural maturities. If they did, they would understand why the Northeast will not fully benefit from a national growth strategy. Second, regional economic policymakers have generally not perceived the connection between the problems of governmental and economic maturity. This means that the potentially favorable regional impact resulting from national growth policies will be reduced considerably.

At this juncture, it would undoubtedly be helpful to cite three approaches to current national economic programming initiatives in order to judge their impact against the two critical dimensions of regional maturity.

1. *Stimulate growth and lower unemployment through expansionary fiscal policies.* For more than three decades, Democratic and Republican administrations have attempted to build their economic future on Keynesian economic policies. Although some economists—notably Milton Friedman—have strong views to the contrary, most would have to agree that the aggregative results of these policies have been good. In the post–World War II period there has been a generally acceptable 4 to 5 percent growth rate and an average unemployment rate of approximately 5 percent. But when one examines the per-

formance by individual states and regions it is evident that a 5 percent national unemployment rate necessarily means that the unemployment rate in many states will be well above or below this average figure. Yet national policymakers have consistently taken a great deal of pride in achieving the 5 percent national average unemployment rate. Presumably, one could allow this self-congratulatory response if economic hardship were randomly distributed through the economy, but as we stated at the outset, it is not.

The economic fallacies in this political reasoning are obvious to economists and noneconomists alike. Most significantly, Keynesian economics is exclusively demand oriented and as such fails to take into account both supply and regional factors—the very factors that are causing the slower growth and economic hardship in the Northeastern states. In straightforward language, governmental and economic maturity simply get in the way of orderly regional economic progress. One need not agree completely with Harvard's distinguished economist, Joseph Schumpeter, to sympathize with an observation he made in concluding his December 1936 *Journal of the American Statistical Association* book review of Keynes' *General Theory:* "The less said about the book the better."

2. *Reduce unemployment and stimulate private sector investment through specifically tailored federal programs.* This refers, of course, to President Carter's special economic stimulus package with its heavy reliance on public service employment and investment tax incentives. Again, to the national policymaker these new programs will undoubtedly appear sound, but regional maturity hampers their effectiveness in the Northeast. To implement a relatively large public service employment program, there must be effective government—not "mature" ones immersed in bureaucratic inefficiencies. As our empirical analysis indicates, employment increases in mature government structures have already reached the stage of rapidly declining returns to the overall economy.

Similarly, for federal investment tax credits to stimulate private sector capital spending in the Northeast, the cost-price structure in our region must be reduced relative to other competing regions, especially the New South. But again, national policies fail to hit the regional target because a national investment tax credit overlooks regional cost differences. Relative cost-price differentials are simply left unchanged. To emphasize a critical point: selective national economic policies such as public service employment and investment tax credits most likely will have a less significant impact in the regions that require the greatest assistance because of governmental and economic maturity. Seemingly paradoxical, but it is not.

3. *Revitalize the Northeast economy through a massive federal program of Marshall Plan dimensions.* A recommendation of this magnitude is, unmistakably, large, and most likely reflects a response based on the simplistic reasoning that a big problem (presumably such as New York City's) can only be solved by an equally big solution. Frankly, we do not find this line of reasoning very convincing. Any substantial increase in programming funds—let alone the quantum leap envisioned by those who advocate a northeastern Marshall Plan—could not be efficiently absorbed in the region. Municipal governments will simply not be able to digest such an increase in programming demands. Thus, we may conclude that large-scale programming would not improve our region's economic situation unless complementary policies were put into place to overcome governmental maturity.

Although we would discount a Marshall Plan for the cities as an unrealistic policy alternative, we do believe that more federal funds should be directed toward our older urban centers and this leads us to a fuller discussion of the concept known as targeting. Currently, much of the discussion over allocating federal resources among regions ends up as a debate over targeting to the areas of greatest need. But the recent controversy over the distribution of $2 billion in Counter-Cyclical Public Works funds shows just how difficult "targeting" can be. An equally timely example is the Community Development Block Grant program, which constitutes an important source of funds for the rebuilding of America's cities. Ironically, the present formula is an excellent example of how *not* to target.

The Economics Department of The First National Bank of Boston recently prepared an analysis for the Council for Northeast Economic Action to determine how the cities of the Northeast would fare under the Community Development Block Grant formula, as of fiscal 1980, when a significant alteration is scheduled to occur—the phasing-out of the "hold-harmless" provision. The results, as you can see in table 3, are startling. Nineteen of these twenty large central cities will receive $128 million less in 1980 than they received in 1975, even at a 20 percent higher appropriation level.

Table 3
The financial impact of changes in the community development block grants:
twenty selected cities (in thousands $)

City	FY 1975	FY 1980	Percent change
New York City, NY	$101,083	$156,537	+54.86%
Philadelphia, PA	54,522	34,076	−37.50
Boston, MA	30,307	11,840	−60.93
Pittsburgh, PA	16,429	9,150	−44.31
Buffalo, NY	11,716	7,445	−36.45
Newark, NJ	20,565	10,009	−51.33
Rochester, NY	14,366	4,505	−68.64
Jersey City, NJ	6,481	4,941	−23.76
Syracuse NY	11,652	3,070	−73.65
Worcester, MA	6,038	2,429	−59.77
Providence, RI	9,074	3,407	−62.45
Springfield, MA	9,109	2,571	−71.78
Hartford, CT	10,275	3,283	−68.05
Bridgeport, CT	4,107	2,613	−36.38
Paterson, NJ	4,266	3,058	−28.32
New Haven, CT	17,078	2,646	−84.51
Albany, NY	2,090	1,791	−14.31
Allentown, PA	2,426	1,338	−44.85
Trenton, NJ	5,075	1,985	−60.89
Camden, NJ	5,502	2,283	−58.51
Total	$342,161	$268,977	−21.39%

Our research, as well as an analysis conducted by the Brookings Institute, and the efforts of mayors and others who were distressed by the prospect of a significant loss in program funds has been welcomed by federal policymakers. Secretary Harris of the Department of Housing and Urban Development has proposed both an increase in program funds and a restructuring of the formula to favor older industrialized cities. Our initial analysis of this formula leads us to conclude that it goes a long way toward addressing the inequities which otherwise would have occurred.

Again, it would be helpful to summarize briefly. Washington's current economic policies have specified national means and ends, while the regional ends are omitted altogether. Although it may not be a popular view, we strongly believe that the development of the regional means is primarily our own responsibility, not that of Washington officials. Unquestionably, a part of the solution to this asymmetrical problem is increasingly to take into account the regional implications in the design of national economic policies. But within our own region, this means facing up to the problems of governmental and economic maturity.

Identifying the Ingredients of a New Four-Point Program

As we move toward regional policy initiatives based on a better understanding of the Northeast economy, it is apparent that we know (in theory) the answers and much of what is needed to translate this into real world solutions. Perhaps, then, the essential ingredient for rebuilding the lagging Northeast economy is the firm conviction to change a handful of fundamentals, specifically, building better government and overcoming economic maturity. Siegfried Hohn, manager of the Financial and Planning Department of Volkswagen Werk, and Governor Milton Shapp indirectly made this point in a recent presentation concerning VW's decision to establish a major production facility in New Stanton, Pennsylvania. The Pennsylvania site won out over more than 200 U.S. competitors because Governor Shapp was, in the end, able to make state and municipal government responsive to VW's needs with a bold and positive response. The payoff for this is impressive—approximately 5,000 prime manufacturing jobs, with another 25,000 supporting jobs scattered throughout the region—and the lesson is clear. Governor Shapp momentarily overcame the problem of governmental maturity and thereby provided an attractive opportunity for private sector investment.

There are numerous other examples that drive home the problems posed by governmental maturity—and the possibilities for overcoming them. At a recent Council for Northeast Economic Action conference in Trenton, on the future of the region's older, industrialized cities, we surveyed the more than 100 participants—most of them Northeastern mayors and business and labor leaders—concerning their attitudes on conditions or policies hindering regional growth, as well as suggestions for improving regional development. We were not at all surprised with the results. Out of a list of thirty options, the number one problem inhibiting regional growth was the substantially higher costs of living and costs of business operations (largely the consequences of economic maturity), whereas the fifth most significant factor was singled out to be bureaucratic delays and rigidities at all levels of government (the effects of governmental maturity). Interestingly, what impressed us in our conversations with the mayors is that although they demonstrated an appreciation for the problem of governmental maturity, they were unsure of how to develop new policies and programs to overcome it, and even here many expressed doubt they possessed the staff depth to implement these changes.

To begin to address these specific regional problems, we would like to propose four important courses of action, and in doing so, we cannot avoid the temptation of thinking back to an earlier four-point program which literally altered the course of economic progress in the third world countries. Our specific reference is to Harry Truman's inauguration day (January 20, 1949) address in which he proposed his now well-known four-point program. Unquestionably, the more frequently remembered point is Point Four because it launched a major program in the international exchange of technical knowledge and resources to, in Truman's own words, "help them (the third world countries) realize their aspirations for a better life. And, in cooperation with other nations . . . foster capital investment in areas needing development." Certainly, the Northeast is not an emerging, third world country, but one of us served in Latin America for two years in the Point Four Program, and we are increasingly reminded of the similarities among the problems in emerging nations and the problems of governmental and economic maturity in the Northeast. Yet this is not a symmetrical relationship, so the analogy must not be pushed too far.

At this juncture, we would like to set down the four points that our analyses, surveys, and meetings consistently single out as uniquely relevant to revitalizing the northeastern economy:

Point 1. The resolution of the Northeast's economic problems must take place within a national context, not in terms of greater sectionalism. In our opinion, the political rhetoric of assertion and counter-assertion between the North and South can in the end prove to be highly dysfunctional to our nation. Similarly, the aggressive pursuit of state and regional beggar-thy-neighbor economic policies will be most unwise. Economic poverty and hardship is a national problem, not one that is uniquely limited to the Northeast.

In our opinion, an excellent forum to begin to deal with these issues would be the long awaited White House Conference on Balanced Regional Growth. This concept is not new—indeed, the 1976 renewal legislation for the Economic Development Administration stipulated that just such a conference be held. We strongly believe that the present time is most propitious for President Carter to call this conference; it would help ease the current debate over purely sectional issues and give the issue of regional growth disparities the attention it deserves.

Point 2. The regional economic consequences of proposed federal programming and budgetary considerations should become a regular part of all presidential recommendations. Similarly, Congressional Budget Office analyses of these proposals/programs should include regional economic impact statements. Interestingly, the original legislation that created the Congressional Budget Office specified that its annual report on budget options should "take into account how alternative allocations will meet major national needs and affect balanced growth and development of the United States." We view that as an authorization—if not a direct command—for the kind of regional economic analysis we are calling for here. Yet, despite the extraordinary caliber of its overall work, we do not feel that the Congressional Budget Office has recognized the importance of the regional dimension to national economic policy. Let us quote to you from its latest report, entitled "Budget Options for Fiscal Year 1978." The report says:

The complex process of making decisions on the federal budget determines, in large measure, the answer to four key questions:

• What share of national output should be devoted to federal programs?

• How should federal resources be allocated among different activities?

• How should the federal government affect the distribution of resources among individuals and businesses?

• How much should the federal government stimulate or restrain the economy?

We strongly believe that a fifth question should be asked: "What are the regional implications of federal programs?"

Point 3. Just as federal programming initiatives should be predicated on regional variations, these initiatives should also take into account changing concepts of the proper allocation of functions among levels of government. Over the past decade, fundamental changes have been introduced (specifically New Federalism with revenue sharing and block grants) that have radically altered the spending and taxing responsibilities among levels of government. The full implications of these changes have yet to be addressed.

Welfare reform is an example of a new federal initiative that should take into account the changing functions and responsibilities at all levels of government. Although it is clear that we need a reform of the national welfare system, it is also clear that we cannot achieve reform without resolving key intergovernmental issues—which level should pay for the services, which should administer the services, and so forth.

Inasmuch as a critical reassessment of the respective roles of federal, state, and municipal structures is long overdue, it is encouraging that the Woodrow Wilson International Center for Scholars is launching a major conference on this subject in June.

Point 4. A broad private sector technical assistance program should be created to aid northeastern municipalities in overcoming the problems of governmental and economic maturity. This is a highly desirable objective because better government will mean qualitatively improved public services for all citizenry and will likely stimulate greater capital spending in central cities. Again, we do not dispute the need for greater federal funds targeted toward the cities which need them, but the increased aid must be matched by an increased ability to use it effectively.

Just as the United States used its industrial and scientific preeminence to launch the Point Four Program to facilitate world economic revival and progress nearly three decades ago, these very same skills must today be made available to municipal governments, especially in the Northeast. And it is worth remembering that substantial amounts of the technical skills that fulfilled the challenge then were from Northeastern academic and private sector institutions. Clearly, we can do no less than give to our own regional government that which we have so generously provided to the rest of the world for so long.

Steps have already been taken to develop a proper foundation for a major regional programming effort to transfer the technical skills of the private sector to the public sector. Robert Wood, President of the University of Massachusetts, first suggested in 1962 that academic and technical resources be brought to bear to solve the cities' problems—an idea that evolved into the Urban Observatory Program.

Three other initiatives—more recent ones—merit comment: The work of the New England Municipal Center, the public policy-research partnership between the Council for Northeast Economic Action and the University of Massachusetts, and finally, Martin Meyerson's recommendations to create a Northeast Regional Information System at the University of Pennsylvania. Unquestionably, these and other similarly directed efforts are important, but what is needed is a bold programming initiative that will integrate them into a northeastern Point Four Program to overcome governmental maturity. As members of the private sector, we find this possibility exciting and practical, and look forward to exploring it with our colleagues in both sectors.

The Next Step

In this paper, we have emphasized the special problems of governmental and economic maturity. We have deliberately concentrated our remarks on the Northeast's urban areas—especially the central cities—because this is where the obstacles posed by governmental and economic maturity are concentrated and it is, of course, where most of the population resides.

During this past fall, we had the opportunity to work with approximately twenty distinguished public and private sector leaders to create the Council for Northeast Economic Action. The council is funded by grants from the Department of Commerce's Economic Development Administration and the Department of Housing and Urban Development, and its purpose is to begin to build a broad regional collaborative process to solve our urban problems. Quite understandably, there are other northeastern institutions working toward an improved regional economy—and there should be, inasmuch as each group has a special expertise. The Council for Northeast Economic Action is focusing on the kind of technical economic research that we have presented to you today with an emphasis on the pressing economic and financial problems of the Northeast's cities. The Northeast–Midwest Economic Advancement Coalition, the Council of Northeast Governors (CONEG), and the Council of State Legislators have different emphases and the sum total is an important and encouraging plus for the region. The members of the Council for Northeast Economic Action look forward to working with these organizations as the council begins to put into place the elements of the Four Point Program outlined above.

Although we will strive to achieve simultaneously all four parts of the program, we nonetheless have a distinct preference for Point Four. Unquestionably, it is Point Four that will really make the difference over the long run, and ironically it is the only one that we have the power within our own resources to implement completely. What appears to be holding us back is simply our reluctance to act. Thus the overriding goal of the Council for Northeast Economic Action is to get urban matters off dead center and moving again in a positive direction.

Our Point Four Program would begin to put to rest the regional belief that we are suffering from a southern conspiracy that is condemning the Northeast to slower growth and higher unemployment. This is sheer nonsense, and to paraphrase one of my favorite poets: "If the Giver would only give us the power to see ourselves as others see us." Perhaps as a midwesterner and a sixth-generation southerner who have adopted the New England area for our home, we can at least partially see both sides; and especially clear are the economic and social consequences of governmental and economic maturity. Washington may be part of the solution, but a self-initiated Point Four Program may well be more than just enough to overcome our special maturities.

Note

1. Two important studies that have clearly not missed this point are *The Urban Predicament,* edited by William Gorham and Nathan Glazer; and *Growing and Declining Urban Areas: A Fiscal Comparison,* Thomas Muller. Both are published by the Urban Institute.

A New Social Contract for Massachusetts

Massachusetts High Technology Council
February 1979

Historically Massachusetts' industries had shown little interest in public polit-ical involvement. The lobbying efforts of the Associated Industries of Massa-chusetts (AIM), for example, one of the nation's oldest industrial lobbying groups, were typically low key and were conducted behind the scenes.

But by the late 1970s the high tech sector was ready for aggressive action. Believing that the concerns of the dynamic, high-growth technology-based businesses were different than those of the older, more established com-panies, some of the members of the emerging sector banded together in October 1977 to form a new lobbying group, the Massachusetts High Technology Council (MHTC).

The driving force behind the new council was Ray Stata, president of Analog Devices, Inc., an electronics firm he had founded in 1965. By 1979 the council's membership, restricted to chief executive officers of high technol-ogy companies, had grown to include eighty-nine companies, employing more than 140,000 worldwide.

Dissatisfied with Dukakis' efforts to improve the business climate in the Commonwealth, Stata wanted to produce another Look Out, Massachu-setts!!! *to shake the next governor—no matter who it was—into action. In an August 1978 meeting Stata, James Howell, and MHTC executive direc-tor Howard P. Foley, came up with the idea of drafting a "social contract." The concept, borrowed from an idea developed by British philosophers Thomas Hobbs and John Locke, held that as individuals must surrender personal liberties in order to enjoy the benefits of an organized state, the government must, in return, be responsive to the will of the people.*

The MHTC's social contract was a nonbinding agreement in which the companies promised to provide 60,000 new high technology jobs, and an additional 90,000 jobs in manufacturing and support services, if the state would cut taxes and work to improve the business climate. The target was to lower the Massachusetts tax burden to the average rate of seventeen states in direct competition with the Commonwealth. An important fact not stated in the document was that the MHTC's member companies had already planned to add that many jobs before the idea of a "contract" came up.

Governor Edward King, who had recently been elected on an overtly pro-business platform, signed the agreement with great fanfare on February 8, 1979. Although it was largely symbolic, this public agreement went a long way toward breaking down the barriers which had long existed between state government and the business community.

The importance of the contract even extended beyond the King administration. Although Dukakis defeated King easily in the next gubernatorial election in 1982, the legacy of this agreement has continued to affect policy decisions throughout Dukakis' subsequent administrations.

The Problem: The Loss of a Competitive Environment

In recent years it has become painfully clear that the climate for the successful growth of high technology industries in Massachusetts has deteriorated. This is a matter of great concern because of the present and future significance of high technology industries to the economic health and well-being of the Commonwealth.

For the Massachusetts economy as a whole, one manufacturing job in three is in the high technology industry. In the period 1970–77, a 29,000 employment increase in high technology manufacturing was the principal economic driving force behind the increase in more than 200,000 jobs in Massachusetts' private economy. During the same period, employment in non-high technology manufacturing decreased by 58,000. Today, Massachusetts' high technology industry employment stands at about 195,000. Approximately one-third of this employment is concentrated among the 89 firms that make up the Massachusetts High Technology Council.

It is increasingly clear that high technology jobs are drifting away because of the emergence of intense regional competition—especially from Sunbelt states such as Texas, North Carolina, and Arizona—and the deterioration of the business climate in Massachusetts. The principal cause of this deterioration has been the rapidly rising tax burden in the Commonwealth, particularly as it impacts individual taxpayers.

Managers and engineers required to stimulate and support growth in the high technology industry are in critically short supply across the nation. As the tax burden in Massachusetts rises relative to other states, this scarce pool of professional resources is being drawn to other parts of the country which offer a comparable quality of life at a substantially lower cost of living. With these professionals go thousands of other skilled and unskilled jobs in high technology companies as well as in other manufacturing and support services.

The purpose of this position paper is to identify the specific causes and consequences of the Commonwealth's unfavorable business environment as it relates to the high technology industry and to recommend steps that must be taken to restore and sustain our economic vitality.

An Important First Step toward the Solution—Real Tax Relief for the Individual Taxpayer

The single most important step to stimulate the growth of the high technology industry in Massachusetts is real tax relief for its citizens. Real tax relief will help the high technology companies to attract and retain professional workers on terms that are more competitive with the rest of the nation. We are proposing what we call a *Social Contract* between state government and the high technology business—an implicit understanding by which the state would reduce the total state and local tax burden to competitive levels which in turn would create more jobs and economic growth.

Council member companies would prefer to stay in Massachusetts because, all other things being equal, it is less costly and less disruptive to expand an existing base of operations than to move elsewhere. But some tangible evidence that property and income tax rates will be reduced is needed now to help them get the people they need in order to grow.

The Council believes that if decisive actions are taken by state and local government to reduce the total tax burden, then over the next four years Council member companies alone will create as many as 60,000 new jobs in the Commonwealth which, together with 90,000 other manufacturing and support service jobs, will create annually by 1982 $2 billion in additional personal income and a $300 million annual increase in additional state and local revenues.

In other words, if tax rates are reduced, jobs and hence tax revenues in Massachusetts will over time actually increase so that the Commonwealth will have greater financial resources to address its social problems and public responsibilities.

High Technology Industries Are Vitally Important to a Strong Regional Economy

The importance of the high technology industries to national economic growth has been well documented in a special report by the Massachusetts economic forecasting firm, Data Resources, Inc. The report, entitled *Technology, Labor and Economic Potential,* states:

Real growth: *High technology industries expanded at a 6.7% compound rate from 1950 to 1974, versus 2.3% for low technology industries and a 3.5% for all manufacturing industries.*

Productivity: *Output per employee increased 4.0% in advanced industries, only 2.0% or less in traditional activities, and 2.3% for total manufacturing.*

Inflation: *The favorable labor productivity record is mirrored in the price record—0.5% annual inflation in high technology versus 3.0% in low technology firms and 2.4% for all manufacturing.*

Employment: *The gains in output per worker were not at the expense of employment. The job gains of rapidly modernizing industries surpassed their conservative counterparts by a substantial margin—2.6% versus 0.3% and 1.2% for all manufacturing. The enhanced domestic and international competitive posture generated more than enough demand to expand employment at a fast pace.*

The relevant statistical comparisons for the high technology and all manufacturing industries on a national basis are shown on the accompanying chart. Although corresponding regional data are not available, it is clear that this area's high technology industries have outpaced our more mature industries by at least as wide a margin. Further, the last four years' aggregate economic indicators, when

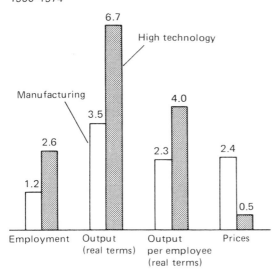

Compound annual growth rates
1950–1974

6.7

High technology

Manufacturing

4.0

3.5

2.6

2.3

2.4

1.2

0.5

Employment   Output   Output   Prices
              (real terms)   per employee
                              (real terms)

Economic performance of total manufacturing industries and high technology industries

they become available, will tell an even more convincing story about why this industry has become so important to Massachusetts.

Apart from the economic aspects, the high technology industry is a desirable one for Massachusetts for other reasons. High technology companies do not pollute the environment nor mar the landscape, but they do generate exciting, interesting jobs that pay on average 20 percent more than other manufacturing industries.

Massachusetts' High Technology Industries Are Facing Stiff Competition from the Sunbelt States—High Living Costs and Personal Taxation in Massachusetts Are a Major Cause

As the national economy has become more decentralized through expanding transportation and communications networks, the high technology entrepreneur and investor is increasingly looking for the most cost-effective location for his start-up and growth. The higher cost of living and doing business in Massachusetts can no longer be offset by the proximity of MIT or Boston's active venture capital market, or the cultural and environmental amenities of this region. R&D centers in Palo Alto, Phoenix, the North Carolina Research Triangle, and Houston now offer many of the same advantages in addition to a better business climate and a lower cost of living.

The spatial redistribution of the high technology industry away from Massachusetts was not recognized as a serious problem during the 1960s, probably because of the many new business start-ups during that period (nearly 600 new and rapidly expanding companies located along Route 128 alone from 1955 to 1965). In recent years, however, the start-up rate of new high technology businesses has fallen sharply and Massachusetts' position as an exporter of jobs and capital investment to other states is beginning to surface.

It has also become increasingly apparent that labor market conditions have begun to deteriorate in Massachusetts. A critical labor shortage has developed among professional engineers and managers who demand pay differentials of as much as 20 to 30 percent to work in Massachusetts to offset the higher cost of living and the higher state and local tax burdens relative to competing states in the Sunbelt as well as just over our borders.

The dramatic disparities among relative living costs and personal state and local taxation may be easily seen in the data shown in the accompanying chart. Note specifically that in Massachusetts the unadjusted personal income per capita at $7,258 is reduced to $4,857 as the result of higher taxes and other cost of living factors—a reduction in real purchasing power of about 35 percent. But note that the differential between the unadjusted $6,803 and the adjusted $6,064 income per capita in Texas amounts to only 11 percent. Moreover, at the same time note the significant tax burden disparities across the sample of competing states.

The Higher Costs of Living and Doing Business Together with Taxes Have Contributed Significantly to the Collapse of the High Technology Investment Climate in Massachusetts versus the Sunbelt

The full economic weight of these higher costs and taxes has a significant and adverse effect on high technology industry start-ups

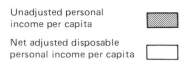

Unadjusted personal
income per capita

Net adjusted disposable
personal income per capita

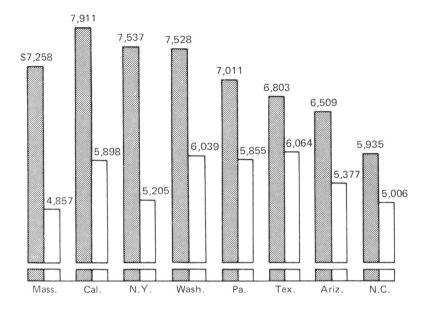

State and local taxes per capita

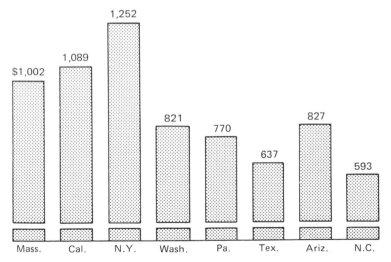

High living costs and high personal taxes—factors that harm the Massachusetts
investment climate, 1977

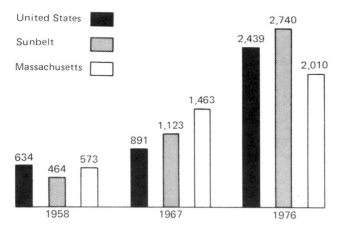

Capital spending for high technology industries per production worker (in dollars)

and expansions in Massachusetts. The impact of these forces can be clearly seen in the accompanying chart. These data show the ratio of high technology industry capital spending per production worker.

Professional workers are the raw materials that feed the growth of high technology companies. The availability of these workers is a primary factor in plant location and long-term capital investment decisions. The decline of capital spending in Massachusetts relative to Sunbelt states is an ominous sign that the Commonwealth is losing its position in the most promising growth industry in the nation today.

Cost and Tax Considerations Mean That Fewer High Technology Industry Jobs Will Be Created in Massachusetts

The accompanying chart shows the past and anticipated job increases among the firms in the Massachusetts High Technology Council. The 89-member firms increased their overall employment—in Massachusetts as well as elsewhere in the United States and abroad—by threefold from 1970 to 1977. Another 100,000 jobs is anticipated worldwide for the period 1979 through 1982.

The recent trend has been for an increasing percentage of total jobs created by high technology companies to go outside Massachusetts. The goal of the *Social Contract* is to reverse this trend by a

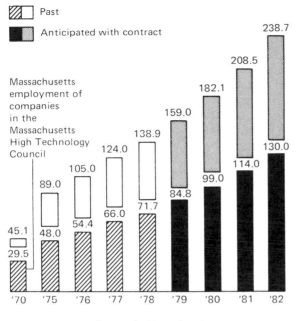

Total number of jobs worldwide (in thousands)

Past

Anticipated with contract

Massachusetts
employment of
companies
in the
Massachusetts
High Technology
Council

Percent in Massachusetts

Past

Anticipated with contract

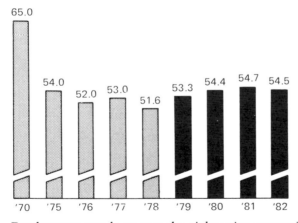

Employment trends among the eighty-nine companies in the Massachusetts High Technology Council, 1970–1982

cooperative effort between government and industry that will over time capture not all but certainly a higher percentage of high technology jobs being created by this industry.

The First National Bank of Boston's national economic forecast for total industrial production and for a specially created composite output index of high technology industries points clearly to a continuation of the rapid output growth and job creation in the high technology industries. Over the next four years, the national rates of increase in output among the high technology industries will average above 20 percent, while total national industrial production will advance at 14 percent.

This means that those states that are the most successful in attracting high technology industries will reap the greatest rewards—in jobs, in general economic development, and in tax revenues available for the common good.

Economics Work: History Shows That State Tax Policy Can Help or Hinder Economic Growth

Implicit in the *Social Contract* and MHTC's proposed policy for tax relief is the assumption that there is a correlation between state and local tax burden and economic growth.[1] The accompanying graph demonstrates that there is, in fact, a strong relationship. Following is a quote from the Harris Bank study:

Above average increases in a state's tax burden can lead to below average economic growth, while below average increases in a state's tax burden can lead to above average growth.

No one can prove that the *Social Contract* will work, but this historic experience suggests that lower personal tax rates will indeed create more high technology jobs for Massachusetts.

Restoration of a Competitive Tax Structure Will Halt the Erosion of High Technology Industrial Base in Massachusetts

As illustrated in the accompanying graph, in recent years the tax burden in Massachusetts has grown more than twice as fast as it has in

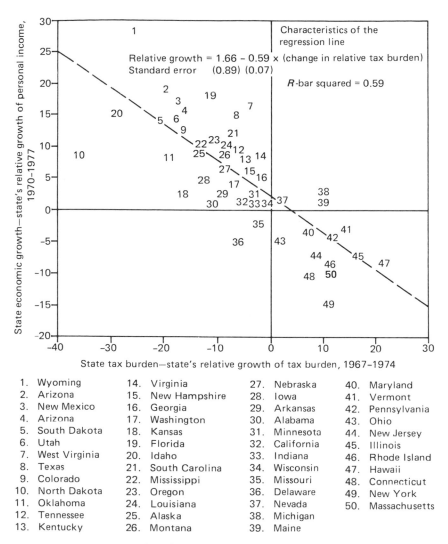

Characteristics of the regression line

Relative growth = 1.66 – 0.59 x (change in relative tax burden)
Standard error   (0.89) (0.07)

R-bar squared = 0.59

1.	Wyoming	14.	Virginia	27.	Nebraska	40.	Maryland
2.	Arizona	15.	New Hampshire	28.	Iowa	41.	Vermont
3.	New Mexico	16.	Georgia	29.	Arkansas	42.	Pennsylvania
4.	Arizona	17.	Washington	30.	Alabama	43.	Ohio
5.	South Dakota	18.	Kansas	31.	Minnesota	44.	New Jersey
6.	Utah	19.	Florida	32.	California	45.	Illinois
7.	West Virginia	20.	Idaho	33.	Indiana	46.	Rhode Island
8.	Texas	21.	South Carolina	34.	Wisconsin	47.	Hawaii
9.	Colorado	22.	Mississippi	35.	Missouri	48.	Connecticut
10.	North Dakota	23.	Oregon	36.	Delaware	49.	New York
11.	Oklahoma	24.	Louisiana	37.	Nevada	50.	Massachusetts
12.	Tennessee	25.	Alaska	38.	Michigan		
13.	Kentucky	26.	Montana	39.	Maine		

Relative economic growth and *changes* in state tax burdens (with three-year time lag to allow for the full effect of a tax burden change on personal income)

seventeen[2] industrial states with which Massachusetts competes for high technology business and for the scarce human resources needed by this industry. The Council believes strongly that in order to regain its competitive edge in high technology, Massachusetts must reduce the tax burden on its human and capital resources to a level more closely in line with that of competing states.

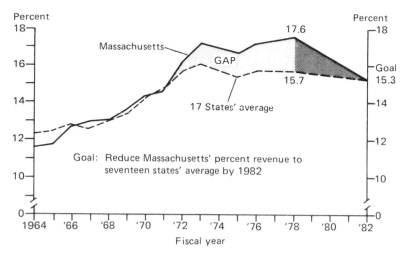

State and local general revenue from own sources as percent of personal income

Specifically, as part of the *Social Contract,* the Council proposes that the financial burden, as measured by total state and local government revenues collected from Massachusetts' citizens and businesses as a percentage of personal income, be reduced to the average level prevailing in the seventeen competing states. The Council's proposal calls for this equalization to be accomplished over a four-year period.

The Council supports the priority given by the new administration to the reduction in real property tax rates. But, in addition, the Council advocates that legislation be enacted in this legislative session to phase out the surtax on wages and salaries and to reduce, over the next four years, the tax on earnings from dividends, interest, and capital gains as required steps to meet the proposed goal of tax parity with competing states.

The Citizens of Massachusetts Will Be the Beneficiaries of the Proposed Social Contract

The Contract
Council member firms believe they can create as many as 60,000 new jobs in Massachusetts over the next four years if the Commonwealth takes substantive steps to restore competitive conditions and to estab-

lish a healthy climate for the growth of the high technology industry here. The proposed *Social Contract* is not a binding agreement; it is an implicit understanding between government and business that there are important benefits to be derived by working together toward the common goal of job creation.

The Benefits

The beneficiaries of positive action by both government and industry will be all the citizens of Massachusetts. The benefits to be derived by 1982 are:

• 60,000 new high technology jobs, plus an additional 90,000 new jobs in manufacturing and support services.

• A $2 billion annual increase in personal income by 1982 and $300 million annual increase in state and local revenues to fund state and local tax rate reductions and to support worthy social goals.

Council Members

Accutest Corp.
Adams-Russell Co., Inc.
Adar Associates, Inc.
Advent Corp.
Aerovox Industries, Inc.
Alpha Industries, Inc.
American Pacemaker Corp.
Amicon Corp.
Analog Devices, Inc.
The Analytic Sciences Corp.
Applicon, Inc.
Aritech Corp.
Arthur D. Little, Inc.
ATEX, Inc.
Augat, Inc.
Avco Everett Research Lab., Inc.
Baird Corp.
BASF Systems, Inc.
BBF, Inc.
Bolt Beranek & Newman
BTU Engineering Corp.
Codex Corp.
Compugraphic Corp.
Computek, Inc.
Computer Devices, Inc.

Computervision Corp.
Concord Computing Corp.
Control Logic, Inc.
Controlonics Corp.
Cooper Scientific Corp.
Corning Medical
Data General Corp.
Data Terminal Systems
Daymarc Corp.
dbx, Inc.
Digital Equipment Corp.
Dynamics Research Corp.
Dynatech Corp.
Foxboro Co.
Frequency Sources, Inc.
GCA Corp.
General Scanning, Inc.
GenRad, Inc.
Germanium Power Devices
Haemonetics Corp.
Hewlett-Packard Co.
Honeywell Information Systems
Hybrid Systems Corp.
Hy-Sil Manufacturing Co.
Incoterm Corp.

Inforex, Inc.
Instrumentation Laboratory, Inc.
Intronics, Inc.
Ionics, Inc.
Itek Corp.
Kalba Bowen Associates, Inc.
Keane Associates, Inc.
Kurzweil Computer Products, Inc.
Kybe Corp.
LFE Corp.
M/A COM, Inc.
Megapulse, Inc.
Metal Bellows, Inc.
Micro Communications Corp.
Microfab, Inc.
Micro Networks Corp.
Millipore Corp.
Minnesota Mining & Manufacturing Co.
Modicon Div./Gould, Inc.
National Medical Care, Inc.

New England Nuclear Co.
Nixdorf Computer Corp.
Nypro, Inc.
Omni Spectra, Inc.
Orion Research, Inc.
Prime Computer Corp.
Printed Circuit Corp.
Semicon, Inc.
Sigma Instruments, Inc.
Sippican Corp.
SofTech, Inc.
Sperry Research Center
Sprague Electric Co.
Technical Operations, Inc.
Teradyne, Inc.
Thermo Electron Corp.
Unitrode Corp.
Valtec Corp.
Wang Laboratories
Waters Associates, Inc.

Associate Members

Arthur Andersen & Co.
Arthur Young & Co.
Coopers & Lybrand
Deloitte, Haskins & Sells
Ernst & Ernst
Peat, Marwick, Mitchell & Co.
Price Waterhouse & Co.
Touche Ross & Co.

Notes

1. Based on a study by Robert Genetski, economist for Harris Bank, showing relationship between state's economic growth of personal income and the state's relative growth of tax burden for the period 1967–74. Data allowed for a three-year period of adjustment to tax changes.

2. Arizona, California, Connecticut, Illinois, Maine, Maryland, Michigan, New Hampshire, New Jersey, New York, North Carolina, Ohio, Pennsylvania, Rhode Island, Texas, Vermont, Washington.

New England's Economy in the 1980s

Lynn E. Browne and John S. Hekman
Federal Reserve Bank of Boston
January 1981

As New England's economy—led by Massachusetts—gradually pulled out of its downward spiral with unexpected strength and resilience, several senior regional economists of the Federal Reserve Bank of Boston, including Richard Syron, began to study the remarkable transition, not only to explain what had happened but also to see if the upturn could be sustained. Lynn Browne, an economist at the Federal Reserve Bank, and John Hekman, an economics professor at Boston College then on leave as an economist at the Fed, collaborated in 1981 to identify many of the critical changes the regional economy underwent in the 1970s and to set them in a broader historical context.

Browne and Hekman reached some important conclusions about the revitalized region. For example, they noted that the turnaround did not result from a rejuvenation of existing mature industries but from their replacement by new ones, in particular companies based on such emerging technologies as the computer. The traditional industries that were left behind continued to experience problems in adjusting to out-of-state competition.

Moreover the two economists concluded that New England is unlike most other regions whose economies rely on such traditional characteristics as geographic location, natural resources, or low production costs. New England's most valuable economic resource had become the knowledge and expertise represented by the area's concentration of research and educational institutions. Maintaining the ability to retain skilled workers and to attract professional workers should therefore be a key aspect of economic development policies for the area.

New England's image is rapidly changing in the public mind. It was formerly looked on as "old," or more graciously as "mature." Its basic industries had shrunk to mere vestiges of their earlier size, its cities were stagnant, and unemployment in some areas was alarmingly high. Today New England has a healthy manufacturing base which is growing at a higher rate than the national average, an unemployment rate which is lower than most other regions, and many cities which are rejuvenating themselves. A comprehensive picture of the region today would show that there is some of the old as well as some of the new in this economy. This article provides an analysis of the strengths and weaknesses of New England's economy in the 1980s. It attempts to sort out both the potential problem areas and the industries and occupations that are likely to prosper.

How should we think of New England? The often-used term "mature economy" has widely varied overtones. It has been used to mean an economy which is aged, with an antiquated capital stock that cannot compete with newer regions. This was true to a certain extent in the 1960s, but it does not apply today. Nevertheless, New England is mature in several other senses. It is especially mature in the sense that the region is no longer in a growth stage like that of the South, the West, or a developing nation. The population and labor force have been growing at a slow, fairly steady pace for the past 40 years; net inmigration has been modest. New England has had substantial numbers of women in its labor force far longer than other regions, so the increase in female participation in recent decades has been smaller here than elsewhere in the United States.

New England is also mature with respect to the utilization of its resources and land area. There will probably not be large moves to develop coal, oil shale, ores, or hydroelectric power which would change the nature of the region's economy. And there are no large undeveloped areas which can experience rapid growth or industrialization on the order of that in the South, the West, and the Northwest.

There are many ways in which a mature economy can change, however, even if its population growth is steady and its industrial potential is well developed. Structural changes in the form of outside competition or altered demand for industrial output can greatly disrupt a mature region, creating the need for large-scale reinvestment of capital and reallocation of labor. Such changes have been particularly great for New England, with the result that the region is "developing" today in that its industrial mix is being substantially transformed by these pressures. One question for the eighties is whether the region will move smoothly along its present path or whether additional structural changes will require further shifts in direction. To answer this question, it will help to look at the factors involved in the decline of the region's economy in the fifties and sixties as well as the forces behind the growth of recent years.

Economic Performance in the 1970s

While the changes in a mature region may seem modest in relation to those taking place in rapidly growing areas, they can mean the difference between a prosperous, vital economy and stagnation. This was clearly evident in New England's experience in the seventies.

From the early fifties through 1970 New England's per capita income was 7–10 percent above the national average. However, the 1970 recession, which for much of the nation represented only a slowing in growth, affected the region severely. Employment fell more sharply than in the nation and remained depressed long after the national recovery had begun. The region's unemployment rate increased relative to that elsewhere and remained a percentage point above the national rate throughout the early seventies. Wage rates, responding to the pressure of unemployment, grew more slowly than in the country as a whole. New England's per capita income fell from 109 percent of the national average in 1970 to 104 percent in 1974.

The region was only just beginning to recover fully from the earlier recession when the 1973–75 downturn began. Again New England suffered a sharper employment decline than the nation and in 1975 New England's unemployment rate of 10.2 percent was the highest of the major regions. The region's per capita income continued to fall relative to the nation.

New England's fortunes reached a low in 1975. In retrospect, however, the year seems to have been a turning point. In contrast to the experience in 1970–71 the New England economy began to recover at the same time as the nation. Employment growth in the region closely tracked the national pattern both during the recovery period and in the ensuing expansion. From the trough of the recession in early 1975 through the end of 1979 nonagricultural employment in New England grew 16 percent, while nationally 14 percent. Not only was New England's employment growth much stronger, both absolutely and relative to the rest of the country, than in the first half of the decade, but relative to the nation it was stronger than at any time since World War II. The growth in manufacturing is particularly striking when one considers that there was no increase in the number employed in manufacturing in New England over the preceding 25 years. The recent strength has been concentrated in durable goods manufacturing. However, employment in nondurables, which had been declining for many years, also increased.

This vigorous employment growth has occurred at a time when the region as a whole has experienced very modest population growth. The labor force—the number of people employed or seeking work—has grown much more rapidly because of increasing participation rates and changing age structures. However, because population growth has been limited, the labor force in New England has not grown as rapidly as in the nation. This combination of vigorous employment growth and moderate population growth has brought about a dramatic improvement in New England's unemployment rate. In 1979 the unemployment rate in the region averaged 5.4 percent, compared to a national rate of 5.8 percent. As yet there is no indication that the tighter labor market has caused an increase in wages relative to those elsewhere; however the decline in relative per capita incomes has been arrested.

Underlying Trends

Why was the second half of the seventies so different from the first? More importantly, are the eighties likely to be a continuation of New England's recent experience or will there be a return to earlier doldrums?

The period 1975–79 was a time of unusual prosperity for New England. However, the region's poor performance in the early seventies was also unusual. Although employment growth in New England lagged that in the nation throughout the fifties and sixties, the disparities were never as great as in the early seventies. Unfavorable trends dating back at least 30 years were reinforced by developments peculiar to the first half of the seventies.

Throughout the postwar period New England has faced continued employment losses in its older industries—particularly textiles and, more recently, leather goods. New England's prosperity was built on textiles and shoes, but the technology of large segments of these industries is such that, today, low wage costs are the primary locational consideration. New England is not a high wage area but manufacturing wages are not as low as in the South and in many parts of the world. Consequently, there has been a steady loss of jobs in these industries to the South and abroad. In 1950 there were 264,000 textile jobs in New England, in 1979 63,000.

Despite the employment losses in these industries, New England's unemployment rates and per capita income growth were comparable to those of the nation through most of the fifties and sixties. The region's population growth was less than that of the nation, so that the need for new jobs was correspondingly less. Also, total employment did increase in New England: opportunities in nonmanufacturing activities, especially in services, grew vigorously and at times the durable goods sector showed considerable strength. In particular, during the mid to late sixties there was a large expansion in aircraft and shipbuilding and in the manufacture of electrical and electronic equipment to serve the needs of the aerospace program and the Vietnam war.

Then came the early seventies, a period marked by two national recessions—the second commonly characterized as the worst since the Great Depression—and sharp cutbacks in defense expenditures. New England was severely impacted by the recessions. New England still has a high proportion of its employment in manufacturing which is more vulnerable to cyclical downturns than nonmanufacturing. There were large employment losses in the older textiles and leather goods industries. From 1969 to 1971 employment in these industries fell more than 30,000; from 1973 to 1975, another 17,000. These losses have not been made up to any extent. The demand for textiles and leather goods is not as cyclical as that for many other manufacturing industries. However, both industries face severe competitive pressures from other parts of the country and from abroad, and marginal operations are more vulnerable in recessionary periods than in expansions.

The defense cutbacks in the early seventies also fell particularly heavily on New England. Although New England has only 6 percent of the nation's population, it typically receives 10 percent or more of the nation's prime defense contracts. Between FY67 and FY71 defense contracts fell roughly 40 percent in real terms and then remained flat for the next five years. In 1973 and 1974 the federal government pulled its fleet out of Newport and closed down the Quonset Airbase and repair facility in Rhode Island as well as the South Boston Naval Annex. Finally, 1974 was also the year in which oil prices rose 2½ times. New England, with 80 percent of its energy coming from oil, was again more severely affected than the country as a whole. Thus, for New England the first half of the seventies brought one economic shock after another.

The unfavorable character of the early seventies obscured the fact that some firms, especially in the instrument and computer areas, were growing very rapidly. Indeed, the growth of these firms may actually have been enhanced by the difficulties elsewhere in the region as manpower, particularly with scientific and engineering skills, could be obtained very readily. The seventies saw a tremendous expansion in computer applications. It was also a time of considerable change. Not all firms were successful. However, New England was fortunate to be at the most scientific end of the computer spectrum and to be the home of some of the most innovative firms. Thus not only did New England benefit from the national expansion in computer use but the region's share of the computer market increased. Instruments also fared well, with increased emphasis on pollution control and, after 1974, on energy conservation, fostering a demand for precise measuring and control devices.

The key factor of production for such industries is professional labor—scientists, engineers, computer programmers. New England has long been a center for research and development and has had a relatively abundant supply of scientific and professional personnel. This resource has in turn fostered the growth of industries heavily reliant on research and innovation, so that competition for highly trained manpower is keen. In the early seventies, however, the defense and aerospace cutbacks released many engineers and scientists making them available to the young computer and instrument firms. Search costs were minimal.

It also seems likely, although the evidence is anecdotal, that the difficulties of the times forced some of the more established industries to seek out new and growing markets. They found these markets, frequently in the export area. In 1972, 5.2 percent of the shipments of New England manufacturers went abroad; in 1976, 9.2 percent. (For the United States as a whole the increase was from 4.8 percent to 7.0.) It is not easy to penetrate export markets. One must learn new government regulations, new customs, new ways of doing business. Therefore, such an expansion in New England's export business suggests an aggressiveness which may not have been present before. The high cost of energy may also have served as a catalyst, forcing firms to take a hard look at their operations to see what cost-cutting measures were available. Even the textile industry seems to have recognized that its future in New England is dependent upon cost saving investments and developing new markets.

The second half of the seventies also brought a turnaround in defense spending. From FY76 to FY79 the real value of prime defense contracts awarded to New England plants increased 42 percent. This increase reflected both an increase in the value of national defense contracts and an expansion in New England's share of these contracts.

Fortunately, too, after the dramatic increase in 1974, real oil prices remained fairly stable until 1979. In the intervening years the price of natural gas, which is the most important industrial fuel nationally, rose sharply.

This combination of favorable developments produced the vigorous expansion of the second half of the seventies, particularly the strong growth in manufacturing. Most of the new manufacturing jobs in this period came in the instrument, electrical equipment, and computer industries. However, traditional industries held their own. The decline in textile and leather goods employment slowed dramatically. Employment in primary metals, paper, and jewelry actually increased from 1976 to 1979. The duration of the expansion was of course a benefit—not only to the older, more troubled industries but also to the high technology firms, since many of their products are capital goods and therefore sensitive to economic downturns.

Looking Ahead

The future appears to hold considerable opportunity for New England's continued growth, led by the rapid expansion of high technology manufacturing and professional services, many of which, such as consulting firms in business, economics, engineering, and architecture, are export oriented. It is possible to argue that the recent growth of these industries cannot be maintained in the long run. These pitfalls will be noted first, and then the basic strengths of New England's industry will be examined.

The problems experienced by the region's industry in the past have come either from the demand for particular industrial products or from the strength of outside competition. To illustrate, it was a sudden drop in the national demand for defense goods that produced a severe slump in several defense-related industries in the early seventies and created a large oversupply of engineering personnel, while it was mainly outside competition which nearly wiped out New England's textile and footwear industries since World War II.

It is one thing to say that "high tech" has a bright future, but the picture becomes less clear when one looks at any particular industry. New England produces a wide variety of industrial process controls, testing equipment, and sophisticated instruments for manufacturers. One factor in the growth of these products has been the need to reduce industrial pollution and energy consumption. Once these demands have been met, the market may not continue to grow as rapidly. Similarly, the demand for defense equipment may be going through a temporary upward adjustment rather than a long-run upswing.

In electronics, New England has helped to create and has profited enormously from the move from large mainframe computers to smaller, less expensive minicomputers and more recently from the "microprocessor revolution." The broad applicability of these machines virtually assures a long period of growth for this industry. However, New England's share of this growth is less certain. Presently many New England firms have a technological edge over their competitors in other regions, but this could be lost either through increased investment in research in other areas or through a lessening of the importance of technological ability, through the standardization of design, for example. Other regions could turn out to be more favorable locations for computer manufacturing as the industry increases in its scale of operation. At the very least, major portions of the production process, such as peripheral equipment and subassemblies, will tend to be increasingly located outside New England, with the design and development work staying here. Thus the growth of computer-related employment in this region may be at a lower rate than that for the nation or the world.

These speculations regarding instruments, controls, and computers are intended to suggest that the presence of high technology industry does not guarantee a high rate of growth in the economy for a long period. With this reservation in mind, however, New England's technological and knowledge-based industries do appear to have good prospects, not so much because the demand for individual products will grow as because the demand for New England's particular skills will remain strong.

New England's advantage in manufacturing does not derive from any natural resources, from its location or from a low cost of production. Rather, the region has long specialized in products which have a large component of skilled labor and which often utilize relatively new technologies that have not found their way into general use. The fundamental reason for the emergence of New England's particular group of industries is the common needs that they share. In the nineteenth century the machine tool industry which was concentrated in the region created the critical metalworking machinery which in turn allowed other industries to develop high-speed, sophisticated machinery for textiles, shoes, paper, rubber, clocks, bicycles, and other products. The final goods producers were more productive in New England than elsewhere because of their connection with the toolmakers and machinery builders. Thus, developments in the early years of this century laid the foundation for the high technology industries we have today. The combined skills from metalworking, machine tools, instrument making, and, increasingly, industrial and scientific research from the region's universities helped give New England a head start in industries such as electric and electronic equipment, industrial controls and specialized machinery. These fields began growing rapidly after World War II and passed the traditional industries in importance in the 1960s.

The presence of a large base of skilled engineers, metalworkers and designers is both an asset and a liability. Being the incubator for new products has produced periods of rapid growth for New England, primarily from textiles in the nineteenth century and from electronics-related firms at present. But many industries in the region have experienced a product life cycle in which rapid growth resulting from technological development is followed by a more stable maturity during which standardization of production and labor-cost orientation have made other regions more attractive to producers. Even within the newer industries there has been considerable change in the particular products made in the region. Hand-held calculators were produced here for a time, but their production moved to other regions and overseas very quickly as mass production methods became available. Similarly, the manufacture of certain electronic components like circuit boards has largely moved overseas. The future strength of high technology industry in New England is related more to the pool of skills residing here than to the prospects for any individual group of products.

A technologically oriented industrial structure requires a more technically trained labor force. More people must be engaged in research and in developing commercial applications for this research—more scientists and engineers. The need does not stop, however, with scientists and engineers or with computer programmers. There is a need for managers who understand and can take maximum advantage of the skills of their specialized staffs; for technical writers to make new developments and products readily comprehensible to those who would use them; and for technicians who can use new, more complicated processes in the workplace. Thus in addition to the need for particular professions, there is a need at all levels for a broader understanding of the fundamentals of technology—an understanding of mathematics; a familiarity with computers; and, most importantly, an innovative outlook and an acceptance of change.

New England's position as a technological center owes much to the quality of its labor force. The average educational attainment of people in New England is above that of the country as a whole. The difference is due in part to a lower proportion of the population with very little education, but more so to the high percentage of New England residents who have completed at least four years of college. The region's advantage is even greater for those who have had some graduate education.

New England's educational system has a strong scientific orientation. The number of scientists and engineers who graduate from New England colleges and universities is greater than would be expected, based on the region's population. Students are attracted from all over the country and many choose to stay in New England. The availability of such professionals clearly fosters the growth of industries with large research requirements. At the same time, the existence of a cluster of high technology firms attracts scientific and technical personnel because of the diversity of opportunities and greater employment security it offers.

The rapid growth in New England's high technology firms over the past several years has greatly expanded the demand for scientists, engineers, and people trained in computer applications. The surplus of personnel created by the defense cutbacks in the late sixties and early seventies has been absorbed. With defense spending now rising in real terms, competition for scientists, engineers, and technicians is keen.

As firms compete for personnel, salaries will be bid up and firms will be forced to recruit from more distant locations. Rising costs may slow the growth in employment. Moreover, if firms cannot obtain the necessary labor within New England, they may eventually look to other locations in which to expand their operations. For every professional who is hired, technicians, production workers, and office staff will also be needed. Thus a critical question for New England is whether the growth in the technical component of the region's labor force will sustain a continuation of the recent expansion in high technology employment.

Young people are responding to the strong demand for electrical engineers and computer programmers. College enrollments in these subjects are up. However, universities and colleges are limited in how rapidly they can respond to changing market demands. Financial constraints prevent them from simply adding personnel in the new fields, while the tenure system restricts the extent to which resources can be diverted from one area to another. Moreover, universities are understandably reluctant to make major changes until the nature of the new direction is clear. The demand for engineers has been volatile in the past; no school wants to expand its engineering program only to find that the emphasis has shifted again.

Changes in the age structure of the population make this problem more severe. From 1980 to 1990 the number of people aged 16–24 will fall more than 15 percent at the national level. This will mean sharp declines in what has traditionally been considered the college age population. Educational institutions, particularly four-year resident colleges, will face severe financial pressures. Funds for new programs will be scarce. Colleges and universities will be forced to reach out more and more to older adults who already have a college degree. Presumably many institutions will find that the way to attract such students is by offering training in the skills which are in so much demand today. However, the transition will be difficult; not all institutions will survive.

The decline in the number of young adults also means that it will be more difficult for society to respond to new industry requirements. A young labor force is flexible. The eighties will undoubtedly see an increased emphasis on retraining. However, it is still easier to teach new skills to young people who have not yet made a career commitment, than to persuade someone who has invested considerable time and money in one career path to shift to another.

The changing age structure has positive implications as well. Young people tend to have higher unemployment rates; they lack experience. Consequently, the decline in the number of new entrants to the labor force will have a favorable impact on unemployment; the greater maturity of the labor force is likely to mean greater stability and therefore higher productivity for a given technology. Nevertheless, fewer new entrants mean less flexibility. And this lack of flexibility may limit the application of new technologies. This is a problem for the country as a whole but certainly for New England as the region's recent growth has been so tied to the expansion in high technology industries.

Several trends at the national level have beneficial implications for this region's industry. Reindustrialization is being used as a catch-all term for attempts by business and government to revitalize America's industry. In the private sector this is taken to mean more emphasis on research and development and on investment in more sophisticated equipment and production processes. In the public sector it also means the encouragement of research and (according to some, at least) the promotion of fast-growing "new" industries rather than noncompetitive "old" ones. These trends indicate that New England has the industry mix, and more importantly the skill mix, that is right for the 1980s. Revitalization of industry will mean more robots, more microprocessor-controlled machines, more sophisticated process controls, and more consulting services demanded from this region.

Manufacturing increased its share of New England's employment between 1975 and 1979, reversing a downward trend that started at least as long ago as 1947. Looking ahead, it is quite possible that manufacturing will continue to grow as rapidly as the economy as a whole. The employment categories which have had the largest increase in the past have been services and retail trade. However, these areas will probably not continue to expand so rapidly in the future; this would mean an increase in the relative importance of manufacturing. For example, the medical services area has increased its employment by over 200,000 since 1967; this has been by far the biggest factor in total services growth. But much of the growth over this period was an adjustment to the Medicare and Medicaid programs. Considering that the facilities for these programs are now largely in place and that the current drive is to contain overall medical costs, it is doubtful that medical services will continue to expand as rapidly as in the past.

In retail trade, over half the employment increase of 225,000 since 1967 was in eating and drinking establishments. Much of this was in fast food restaurants and a good deal of this employment is part-time, so that it overstates the economy's expansion in comparison with areas like manufacturing. Again, there is probably a limit to further expansion here, as meals purchased outside the home are not expected to sustain recent growth rates.

Other nonmanufacturing areas of the region's economy are similarly unlikely to grow as rapidly as they have of late. Federal, state, and local government employment increased rapidly from 1967 to 1973 but growth then leveled off to about one-third of that rate of increase from 1973 to 1979. The outlook for private education is for no growth or a reduction in size because of demographic trends.

New England's strong performance in the late seventies was attributable, in part, to increases in defense contracts and expanding export markets. Both defense and exports hold considerable promise for New England in the eighties. The mood of the country now favors a stronger defense and calls for fiscal restraint generally exclude defense spending. Thus it would seem that the nation can expect a significant increase in defense expenditures over the next several years. Since New England typically captures such a large share of prime contracts, this expansion should work to the region's particular advantage.

Between 1972 and 1976 New England's exports almost doubled. This growth reflects both increasing penetration of world markets by New England manufacturers and the rapid growth of some of the nation's major trading partners. Manufacturing is not, however, the only sector which has developed ties to other countries. New England management and economic consulting firms advise firms in many countries; New England engineering firms help build power plants and other large installations around the world. Yet some markets are still largely untapped. The United States still has very limited trade with much of the developing world. There are also opportunities in the industrial countries: recent tariff cuts negotiated in the Multilateral Trade Negotiations open up interesting export possibilities in Japan, particularly for high technology products. The Commerce Department has identified computers and peripheral equipment, electronic components, and communications equipment as areas where exports to Japan might increase substantially because of tariff reductions.[1]

While defense spending and exports offer opportunities to New England firms, there are pitfalls as well. As the experience of the early seventies so painfully taught, attitudes about defense spending can change. While public sentiment is strongly for more defense today, what will be the situation five or ten years from now? Because the government is such a large purchaser any cutback can have severe effects. Thus New England firms must take care not to become so dependent on defense contracts that private sector markets are not developed.

In the export area the problem is also one of changing attitudes and the federal response to these attitudes. There appears to be a growing protectionist sentiment in the country brought on by the difficulties of U.S. auto and steel companies in competing with imports. The auto companies are now actively lobbying for quotas on auto imports and the federal government has just agreed to increase the trigger price at which imports of steel are restricted. One must sympathize with the difficulties of these industries. However, restrictions on imports will most certainly lead to retaliatory measures which will then limit the growth in U.S. exports. The issue is not simply the United States vs. Japan or the United States vs. West Germany. If American firms are to penetrate foreign markets, particularly those of the developing nations, the United States must be prepared to let the products of these countries into our own markets. Export markets hold considerable potential for New England firms; but these markets will not be developed if other countries are not allowed to compete for a share of the U.S. market. And it would be foolish to deny that such competition may create difficulties for some industries, including some in New England.

Federal efforts to promote "reindustrialization" through increased expenditures on research and development and greater incentives for capital formation will also affect New England's future. Because of its concentration of prestigious universities and because of the technological orientation of its industry, New England should benefit from more emphasis on research. The effects of accelerated depreciation and other incentives to investment are less clear. On the one hand, New England industries—both the new high technology and the more traditional ones—tend to be labor intensive. Therefore, the region can probably not expect to get a share of federal investment incentives corresponding to its share of economic activity. Even if the percentage increase in investment in New England is comparable to that elsewhere, the dollar increase will be relatively small because of the low capital intensity of its industry. However, if New England does not benefit directly, it will gain indirectly from the expansion in the demand for capital goods. New England's manufacturing industries today are oriented to the production of producer durables; many high technology products are investment goods. The region is an important supplier of architectural and engineering services. Consequently, national efforts to stimulate capital investment will expand the demand for New England products.

What of energy? One cannot talk about the future without some discussion of the energy situation. New England still derives roughly 80 percent of its energy from oil; nationally oil accounts for just under 50 percent of energy use. And the Iran-Iraq war has made clear once again that world oil supplies are not secure. A number of efforts and initiatives are underway that could reduce New England's dependence on oil: the conversion of some oil-fired power plants to coal; the possibility of significant purchases of hydroelectric power and natural gas from Canada; numerous small scale efforts to tap renewable energy sources in the region—wood, low-head hydro, solid waste, and solar power. Eventually aggressive pursuit of such options may leave New England in a relatively favorable energy situation. However, for the eighties New England remains vulnerable to energy supply disruptions.

New England will also continue to face an energy cost disadvantage. The average cost of energy in New England in 1979 was about 24 percent above the country as a whole.[2] This disparity is due, in large measure, to New England's dependence on oil. Elsewhere natural gas is the primary fuel for industrial and commercial purposes and, for much of the country, natural gas prices have been held artificially low by federal regulation. These controls on gas prices are being relaxed, and in 1985 controls on new natural gas will be completely eliminated. These increases plus the replacement of old, low cost supplies with newly discovered gas subject to today's higher ceilings are causing sharp increases in the cost of gas to the end-user. It will be some time, however, before oil and gas costs are comparable. New gas prices will not be fully deregulated until 1985. Other categories of gas will be deregulated still later, while gas from wells already committed to interstate markets will not be fully deregulated. And meantime, of course, the price of oil is not standing still.

Thus for most of the eighties and perhaps beyond, New England will continue to pay more for its energy. The region has, however, adapted to high energy costs. The most important manufacturing industries in New England—nonelectrical machinery, electrical equipment, and instruments—all use relatively little energy per dollar of value added. With the exception of paper, those industries which use energy intensively—primary metals, chemicals, glassmaking— are substantially less important in New England than nationally. New England's industrial structure is, therefore, less sensitive to energy costs than that in other regions; so the effects of future energy cost increases may prove less disruptive here than elsewhere.

Finally, even adversity offers opportunities. Emphasis on energy saving has increased the demand for measuring and controlling instruments and has spawned numerous manufacturing and consulting enterprises dedicated to developing alternative energy resources.

Conclusion

The picture that emerges for New England in the 1980s is one with good growth prospects for the important durable goods industries and the professional services related to them. The lack of natural resources and poor geographical location which have worked against the region in the past are becoming less important liabilities as New England's economic activity turns more and more to durable goods with very high value-to-weight ratios and to export-oriented services in which the region has a sharp comparative advantage.

Manufacturing employment may increase in size relative to government, trade, and services, since analysts see favorable growth prospects for high technology goods, while the other major employment areas may experience a leveling off of their growth. It is important to note in this regard that manufacturing is becoming increasingly specialized in the production of capital goods. Consumer goods such as apparel, textiles, and shoes will probably see little or no growth in the eighties, nor will durable consumer goods such as autos or appliances have many opportunities for employment. Most of New England's industrial output is now in the capital goods category—computers, instruments, control devices, aircraft parts, and defense equipment. This specialization may make the region highly sensitive to cyclical swings in investment spending; when the country catches a cold, New England will have pneumonia, as the saying goes. At present many of our capital goods are cost-saving products that are in steady demand, but as this market is saturated, demand will be dependent on replacement decisions by users, and this will put us squarely in the investment cycle. Fortunately there is at present such a diversity of uses for these products that this problem may never materialize.

Defense employment is another area which experiences erratic cycles. New England is almost certain to see an expansion of defense jobs in the early eighties. The negative side of this is that substantial unemployment will result if a defense cutback subsequently occurs; the positive side is that new product spin-offs for the private sector may be created as has been the case before. These spin-offs could soften the blow from a loss of defense jobs.

The growth of the newer industries and services in New England in the 1970s has underscored the importance of small business in creating employment. Many of the products produced in the region today did not exist 20 years ago, and of these a large proportion were developed by small firms, whether as a result of university research, government projects, or subcontracts from larger firms. *The "reindustrialization" of New England has come about not through reinvestment by existing industries but by their replacement with new ones.* It is well to keep this in mind when formulating economic development strategies. So often such strategies tend to pay the most attention to large, established businesses.

The other ingredient in New England's growth formula has been its unique labor force. To a large extent the region's industry mix is a result of its labor mix and not the other way around. Thus development policies should be aware of the fact that New England attracts *people,* not industry. The availability of skilled and professional workers is currently one of the factors constraining growth in some industries. While this is widely understood, there is disagreement over what can and should be done to make the region competitive in this national labor market. There will undoubtedly be much discussion in the next few years regarding the proper balance of social and cost considerations in developing a favorable economic climate.

One way to attract workers is to provide facilities available for their education. New England is being called on to make difficult decisions at the public and private levels to determine what kinds of professional and technical training programs should be established or expanded. Today we have a surplus of teachers and a shortage of computer programmers. The challenge will be to remove this imbalance without reversing it.

Finally, one must look outside the region to see what national policies will affect the region. New England's industry is highly dependent on exports to sustain its growth. In the nineteenth century our textiles competed with imported goods in the domestic market, causing New England to favor tariff protection, while the South wanted free trade policies to help their exports of cotton. Today the situation is reversed, as New England produces export goods, and the South struggles to compete with imported textiles. New England's interest clearly lies with free trade in the eighties.

Notes

Lynn E. Browne is Assistant Vice-President and Economist of the Federal Reserve Bank of Boston; John S. Hekman is Assistant Professor of Economics, Boston College, on leave as Economist at the Federal Reserve Bank of Boston. The authors would like to thank John S. Strong and Heinz Muehlman for their valuable insights.

1. Alan O. Maurer, "MTN Agreement on Tariff Cuts Opens Opportunities in Japan," *Business America* 22 September 1980.

2. New England Congressional Caucus, *New England Energy Fact Book,* July 1980.

The Massachusetts Economy in the 1980s

Economics Department
The First National Bank of Boston
November 1981

By 1981, just ten years after the first warning appeared in The New England Letter, *it was clear that the Massachusetts economy was well on the road to a remarkable recovery. During the brief recessions of the early 1980s, manufacturing employment in the state managed to inch upward 2.2 percent at the same time that national employment slipped by 2.3 percent. And from 1978 to 1980 nonagricultural employment in the Commonwealth rose by 5.6 percent, compared to just 3.4 percent nationally.*

With a major bond issue about to go to the market, Governor King wanted to get the word out to security dealers and investors throughout the country that the state's outlook had changed. He therefore asked The First National Bank of Boston, which had sounded such a sour note a decade before, to prepare an analysis of the current prospects for the state's economy. The report was released at a breakfast press conference held jointly by King, Bank Chairman William L. Brown, and James Howell on November 13.

In addition to documenting a considerably brighter outlook for the economy overall, the report noted one unexpected development. The service sector, which economists had largely ignored in their concern for revitalizing manufacturing, turned out to have played a surprisingly large role in providing new jobs, as well as in drawing wealth into the state.

Overview

The Massachusetts economy has outperformed expectations of many observers over the past year during difficult economic times nationally. In part, the good showing of Massachusetts has been tied to an absence of negatives—particularly to the underrepresentation of residential construction and auto production in the state's economy. Yet, more significantly, Massachusetts did well recently because it has revitalized and realigned its industrial base, while supplementing it with an expanding and competitive service sector. As a result, Massachusetts has not only ridden out the 1980 recession well but is poised for future growth when the national economy recovers.

The Manufacturing Sector in Perspective

The fortunes of the Massachusetts economy have swung widely over the past thirty years. Historically, the performance of the Massachusetts economy has been most closely linked to its manufacturing sector. Dating from the nineteenth century, the traditional industrial base was centered in textiles, apparel, and leather goods, and these industries dominated Massachusetts' manufacturing well into this century. However, the Great Depression removed many of these firms, and most of the survivors chose to close or relocate early in the post-World War II period. By the late 1950s, however, Massachusetts began to assemble a new industrial base centered on what would become known as high technology. The pressure of the Cold War and heavy military spending, combined with the achievements of the Soviets in space, made federal research and development funds available at a time of significant scientific advancement. The development of high technology manufacturing held sway during most of the 1960s, and the relative disadvantage of Massachusetts' manufacturing sector eased. Late in the 1960s, a cutback in NASA spending and the winding down of the Vietnam War signaled less federal support for development of new technologies, and growth ended. In the last two years of the 1960s, and over the six-year period bounded by the 1970 and 1975 recessions, Massachusetts' employment in manufacturing fell, much as it had done during the 1950s. Since 1975, the Massachusetts economy has undergone a significant revitalization. High technology industries have resumed their rapid increase of earlier years, this time, though, less dependent on federal support. Total manufacturing employment during these years rose 95,000, or by 16 percent, of which 76,000—or four-fifths of the new jobs—were located in high tech occupations. Employment in all durable goods manufactur-

Table 1
Percentage changes in employment in Massachusetts and United States, 1950–1980

	1950–1960		1960–1970		1970–1975		1975–1980	
	Massachusetts[a]	United States[b]	Massachusetts[a]	United States	Massachusetts[a]	United States	Massachusetts	United States
Manufacturing	-2.4	10.0	7.1	15.3	-8.3	-5.4	16.4	10.8
Durable goods	21.0	16.7	3.0	18.5	-1.7	-4.6	28.4	14.0
Nondurable goods	-16.6	2.5	-15.9	11.2	-15.5	-6.4	1.8	6.3
Nonmanufacturing	15.4	24.1	33.7	37.8	7.3	13.8	16.6	19.9
Total nonagricultural	8.2	19.4	18.7	30.8	2.8	8.6	16.6	17.7

a. Data based on pre-1972 Standard Industrial Classification codes.
b. Excludes Alaska and Hawaii.

Table 2
Employment by industry in Massachusetts and United States, 1975–1980 (in thousands)

	1975		1980		Percent growth		1980 distribution of employment	
	Massachusetts	United States	Massachusetts	United States	Massachusetts	United States	Massachusetts	United States
Manufacturing	577.8	18,323	673.1	20,299	16.5%	10.8%	25.4%	22.4%
Durable goods	319.0	10,688	409.7	12,181	28.4	14.0	15.5	13.5
High technology	200.6	4,309	276.6	5,309	37.9	23.2	10.4	5.9
Nondurable goods	258.8	7,635	263.4	8,118	1.8	6.4	9.9	9.0
Nonmanufacturing	1,694.6	58,622	1,974.7	70,265	16.5	19.9	74.6	77.6
Construction	79.8	3,525	73.2	4,399	−8.3	24.8	2.8	4.9
Transportation	113.7	4,542	122.3	5,143	7.6	13.2	4.6	5.7
Wholesale and retail trade	511.8	17,060	571.3	20,386	11.6	19.5	21.6	22.5
Finance, insurance, and real estate	135.1	4,165	159.0	5,168	17.7	24.1	6.0	5.7
Services and mining	489.1	14,644	638.6	18,921	30.6	29.2	24.1	20.9
Government	365.1	14,685	410.3	16,249	12.4	10.7	15.5	17.9
Federal	58.0	2,748	58.3	2,866	0.5	4.3	2.2	3.2
State and local	307.1	11,937	352.0	13,383	14.6	12.1	13.3	14.8
Total nonagricultural	2,272.4	76,945	2,647.8	90,564	16.5	17.7	100.0	100.0

Table 3
Employment by industry in Massachusetts and United States, January 1980–August 1981 (in thousands)

	January 1980		August 1981		Percent change	
	Massachusetts	United States	Massachusetts	United States	Massachusetts	United States
Manufacturing	683	20,836	669	20,517	-2.0	-1.5
Durable goods	413	12,591	411	12,336	-0.5	-2.0
High technology	275	5,384	282	5,436	2.5	1.0
Nondurable goods	270	8,245	258	8,181	-4.4	-0.8
Nonmanufacturing	1,961	69,851	1,989	71,412	1.4	2.2
Construction	79	4,556	66	4,272	-16.5	-6.2
Transportation	121	5,185	126	5,168	4.1	-0.3
Wholesale and retail trade	570	20,337	584	20,871	2.5	2.6
Finance, insurance, and real estate	156	5,090	166	5,354	6.4	5.2
Services and mining	620	18,575	671	19,825	8.2	6.7
Government	415	16,108	376	15,922	-9.4	-1.2
Federal	59	2,790	57	2,770	-3.4	-0.8
State and local	356	13,318	319	13,152	-10.4	-1.2
Total nonagricultural	2,644	90,687	2,658	91,929	0.5	1.4

Note: Data are seasonally adjusted by component.

ing in Massachusetts gained 91,000 jobs and the growth was twice as fast as that of the nation. Employment in nondurables increased only slowly, by 5,000, but these gains reversed the downward trend plaguing these industries over many years. More recently, employment in Massachusetts' manufacturing has declined, owing to the national recession in 1980 and the economic slowdown in 1981. Measured on a monthly basis after seasonal adjustments, manufacturing employment fell 14,000, or 2 percent, from the peak in the business expansion in January 1980 through August 1981. Most of the reductions occurred in nondurable manufacturing, which experienced a loss of 12,000 jobs. For high tech industries, employment growth slowed appreciably, but 7,000 new positions were gained.

The Vitality of Services

The structural adjustments within Massachusetts' manufacturing underscore the adaptability that characterizes the state's economy. The Massachusetts economy is diverse, with a significant segment devoted to high-value, high–skill industries. The educational institutions provide the basic resources for these "knowledge" industries and determine their location in Massachusetts. Massachusetts in particular, and New England more generally, has been described as "the most knowledge-intensive region in the world."

Outside of high technology manufacturing, service employment is a major contributor to the state's well-being—both in terms of providing employment opportunities and providing an inflow of dollars from outside the state. Many service sector jobs depend either directly or indirectly on the educational facilities. Its research position in educational and medical fields supplements other activities, and together education and health service comprise almost one-half of employment in services within the state. Many other service sector jobs not in the educational and medical fields are heavily education dependent, particularly in consulting positions and engineering.

Following the 1974–1975 recession, the growth in the service sector was spectacular. From 1975 to 1980, service employment gained 149,000 jobs, or 31 percent. These increases outpaced all other major sectors in Massachusetts, including total manufacturing, although high tech manufacturing employment growth separately was faster at 38 percent. The 1980 recession and subsequent economic slowdown in 1981 have further demonstrated the benefits of having a strong and diverse service sector in Massachusetts. Since January 1980 service sector employment has gained 51,000 even as other sectors in Massachusetts showed little growth or were in decline. Much of the vitality has been the growth in services outside of education and medicine, particularly in services provided to businesses.

Other Nonmanufacturing Industries

Nonmanufacturing employment (excluding the service industry sector) grew moderately during the late 1970s, accounting for 131,000 new jobs in the aggregate, or a growth of 11 percent. The largest gains, both in absolute changes and as a percentage, occurred in wholesale and retail trade, state and local government employment, and in the financial sector. From 1975–1980, employment in wholesale and retail trade expanded by 60,000 jobs, or 12 percent, while employment of state and local government workers expanded by 45,000 jobs, or 12 percent. Finance, insurance, and real estate added 24,000 jobs, an 18 percent rate of expansion. The only other sector showing growth was in transportation and public utilities, where employment rose 9,000. The number of federal employees held virtually constant over the period, while the number of construction workers fell 7,000.

The trends established in nonmanufacturing during the latter half of the 1970s have continued, with one major exception, during 1980 and 1981. Since January 1980 employment in trade, finance, and transportation industries has risen by 29,000 jobs, while the numbers of federal employees have declined by 2,000. The number of construction workers dropped 13,000 from a temporary, sharp peak reached early in 1980. The contraction has been particularly acute in recent months as spending curtailments occasioned by Proposition 2½ have had dramatic effects. The major exception has been employment in state and local government, which from January 1980 through August fell 37,000.

Proposition 2½

Proposition 2½ is a statute adopted by public referendum in November 1980 designed to reduce the state's property tax burden and, ultimately, to make the state's economy more competitive. The chief provision of the statute is to limit local property taxes to 2½ percent of full market value. Communities exceeding this limit are required to reduce property taxes by 15 percent annually until the 2½ percent limit is reached. After reaching the 2½ percent limit, communities are allowed to raise tax levies by 2½ percent annually. No expenditure items have been excluded under Proposition 2½, and the limit is subject to override only upon two-thirds vote in individual localities. The law also more than halves automobile excise taxes, repeals compulsory binding arbitration for police and fire personnel, eliminates fiscal autonomy for local school boards, permits a state income tax deduction for apartment dwellers equal to half of rent payments, and limits annual increases in county and authority assessments to 4 percent.

The imposition of Proposition 2½ on Massachusetts' cities and towns has been uneven in its impact, but in the aggregate has required substantial layoffs of personnel, even with higher state aid to cities and towns. Current estimates suggest 20,000 state and local workers have been laid off because of Proposition 2½, with most of the layoffs occurring on the local level. State aid to localities has been increased in order to mitigate some of the harsher effects of Proposition 2½, but the increase in state aid also has led to layoffs of state workers.

Many of those laid off have been public schoolteachers who have been terminated not only due to loss of financial support but also to declining enrollment in the Commonwealth's public schools.

As significant as Proposition 2½ has been, reduction in state and local government employees predated Proposition 2½ by several years. Massachusetts' reputation as a high tax, high public service state was a major issue in the 1978 gubernatorial campaign, and the outcome of the election set Massachusetts on a new course. Under the King administration, a Social Contract with the private sector—and particularly with the high technology industries—was adopted to make Massachusetts more competitive with other states. In exchange for lower taxes, Massachusetts' High Technology Council pledged to expand within the state and create 150,000 new jobs by 1983. Preliminary estimates to date support the view that both sides of this important contract are going to be met.

As a part of the broader King administration initiatives, the growth in state and local payrolls has been curtailed. State and local government employment peaked in 1978 at 372,000, fell to 359,000 in 1979, and to 352,000 in 1980. More recently, employment at the state and local government level after Proposition 2½ has dropped to 319,000, or about the same level as of 1976. The proportion of state and local government workers to private nonagricultural employment dropped from one state and local government worker for every 5.6 in private employment in 1978 to one for every 6.4 private sector worker in 1980. Most recently, the ratio has fallen to one to 7.1, and Massachusetts now has fewer public workers relative to the private sector than the national average.

Under Proposition 2½ further employee cutbacks lie in store. Some of these are already budgeted on the state and local government level for fiscal year 1982, and still others will be required over the next two fiscal years. The major cities in Massachusetts, without exception, are facing multiyear adjustments in their local funding, of which fiscal year 1981 contains only the first installment. Major downward adjustments will be required in fiscal year 1982 if Proposition 2½ is not amended, and moderate adjustments in fiscal year 1983. Unquestionably, the consequences of these adjustments on some of Massachusetts older, larger cities could become fiscally troublesome unless additional state aid is forthcoming.

Transition for Growth

The realignment in Massachusetts' public sector occasioned by Proposition 2½ and the public's support for reduced budgets reveals the difficulties as well as the economic rationale for such transition. Redirecting resources is expensive, both in human terms and in costs to the economy, and the benefits are often delayed. In 1981 and 1982, public sector layoffs will be swelling the state's level of unemployment as workers laid off are not absorbed immediately by the private sector. Even in the context of an expanding economy, retraining is necessary and the process of job placement often takes months. When the influx is as large as that occurring under Proposition 2½ and is as protracted, the state's level of joblessness may be expected to be higher for two or even three years. Other factors, though, are much more positive in the state, so that the overall level of unemployment is likely to remain comfortably below the national average.

Clearly, the retraining and reemployment of terminated public sector workers is a high priority goal of both the state and the private sector. This is not only to benefit workers but also to provide an adequate labor supply for high technology industries and other expanding sectors. Shortages of trained computer technicians, programmers, and engineers in Massachusetts already have proved to be bottlenecks, and can and should be alleviated by the establishment of second careers for many laid off public sector workers.

Service employment, as well, may undergo a significant transition in coming months, not so much owing to events within the state as withdrawal of federal support. Reaganomics, partly by design and partly by budgetary requirements, is forcing a cutback in funding for research in educational and medical institutions. Further redirections are scheduled at least until 1984. The reshuffling of federal priorities in favor of tax reductions and increases in defense expenditures puts the state's network of educational institutions in about the same position as the state's high tech industries were in during the late 1960s. Unless funding levels are increased significantly and soon, there will be few employment gains in health and education in coming years. In addition, demographics are diminishing the pool of college-bound high school students which will further slow growth in the state's institutions of higher learning.

These factors, combined with the likelihood of little economic growth nationally until mid-1982, suggest the unemployment rate in Massachusetts will remain near current levels. The unemployment rate is averaging 6.1 percent thus far in 1981 versus 5.5 percent in 1979 and 5.6 percent in 1980. However, this is a favorable situation relative to the national performance and is likely to continue. Also, personal income growth in Massachusetts in recent years has closed the gap that existed in the mid-1970s and is likely to about match national increases in personal income in 1981.

Table 4
Unemployment rates and personal income growth, 1975–1980

	Unemployment rate		Personal income growth (%)		Personal income growth per capita (percent)	
	Massachusetts	United States	Massachusetts	United States	Massachusetts	United States
1975	11.2	8.5	6.6%	8.4%	6.8%	7.3%
1976	9.5	7.7	7.6	10.1	7.8	9.1
1977	8.1	7.0	8.6	10.6	8.8	9.5
1978	6.1	6.0	9.8	12.0	9.8	10.8
1979	5.5	5.8	12.6	12.9	12.5	11.7
1980	5.6	7.1	12.6	11.5	12.5	10.2

Achieving Growth in the 1980s

The difficulties of transition, notwithstanding, Massachusetts is poised for substantial economic growth in the 1980s. What has been relinquished in terms of public sector employment and potentially in some parts of the service sector is more than compensated for by the favorable position of high technology and other growth industries in the years ahead. In part this is due to the structural adjustments that have already occurred. For example, nondurable goods employment, which has been chronically weak in the Commonwealth, now accounts for only 39 percent of total manufacturing employment in the state. Indeed, nondurable industries in the Commonwealth comprise only a slightly larger proportion of the state's nonagricultural employment than is true nationally. By contrast, high technology industries in Massachusetts account for more jobs than do all nondurables. The high technology industries not only represent a much larger share of employment in Massachusetts than is true nationally, but also the share for high technology continues to rise just as the share for nondurables continues to fall.

In addition, Massachusetts is not tied closely to interest-sensitive consumer goods industries or to construction. Autos and housing, which have been buffeted in 1980 and 1981, are far less significant in Massachusetts than nationally. Employment in construction and in the manufacture of transportation equipment in the Commonwealth accounts for 4.9 percent of total nonagricultural employment, while nationally the proportion is 10.3 percent.

A second part of the explanation for a positive outlook for Massachusetts lies in the redirections of federal dollars. The move to a more capitalistic economy with more economic freedom for individuals and businesses is designed not only to improve the public/private sector mix but also to boost productivity. Massachusetts' high technology firms and that part of the service sector tied to businesses are in a position to benefit greatly from the Reagan economic program. The earlier effort to make Massachusetts' economy more competitive internally now is being matched by similarly inspired programs at the national level which should serve the interest of Massachusetts.

The drive to upgrade the quality of the nation's military is of particular interest to Massachusetts. The technological requirements of such efforts favor the state, and Massachusetts historically has received a relatively large share of federal military contracts. In fiscal year 1979, Massachusetts received 4.6 percent of prime military contract awards, although it has only 2.6 percent of the nation's population.

Thus, Massachusetts has learned to adapt, putting less reliance on its traditional industries and more on its knowledge-based high technology and service sectors. In the years ahead, these sectoral adjustments bolster prospects for further growth and put off the ones of economic maturity.

High Technology and Business Services

Lynn E. Browne
Federal Reserve Bank of Boston
July 1983

One of the great surprises of the 1970s was not only the explosive growth of the service sector in Massachusetts but the ability of this emerging sector to strengthen the economy by bringing wealth into the region. In this 1983 paper economist Lynn Browne examined the critical role that high technology played in spurring the growth of service businesses in the state.

Many of the new services were in fact high technology businesses. Data processing operations, software companies, and consulting firms were all direct participants in the high tech boom. In addition the needs of the burgeoning high tech community both created and supported a network of related service businesses such as advertising, public relations, and law firms.

Browne's paper underscored the fact that economic development policies have tended to focus on how to stimulate growth in specific manufacturing industries, including high technology. Yet the service sector in New England provided similar opportunities for expansion, and may even have had certain advantages over manufacturing. Economic growth can come from unexpected quarters, Browne maintained, and policymakers must be open-minded and flexible enough to foster a variety of businesses with high-growth potential.

Since the mid-seventies employment has grown at the same rate in New England as the nation despite the region's substantially slower population growth. Manufacturing employment grew even faster in New England than in the nation during the expansion in the second half of the seventies and did not suffer as severe a decline in the recent recessions. After years in which the growth in New England's manufacturing industries had fallen short of the nation's and manufacturing had become a progressively smaller, although still important, part of the regional economy, this strong performance attracted considerable attention. One result has been extensive public admiration for the fastest growing of the region's manufacturers—the high technology industries, such as computers, electronics, and various forms of instrumentation.

However, high tech manufacturing has not been the sole source of new jobs in the region. Growth has been very rapid in the services industries; and within the services category, growth in New England business service employment has surpassed not only growth in business services nationally but also growth in most New England high technology manufacturing industries. But while it would be a mistake to look upon high technology as the only reason for New England's prosperity, it would also be a mistake to view these other developments as entirely independent of the developments in high tech manufacturing. In particular, the growth in some of the most rapidly expanding business services is, to some extent, a reflection of the growth in high tech manufacturing.

In some cases the high tech expansion has had a multiplier effect on local business services. According to the Massachusetts Division of Employment Security "30–40 percent of the increase in advertising payrolls [from 1975 to 1980] has been the result of expenditures by high technology firms."[1] In other industries, for example, computer and data processing services, the growth in services has been propelled by the same forces responsible for the growth in high technology. As computer technologies have advanced and computers have become more accessible, the demand for computer-based services has grown hand-in-hand with the demand for the computers themselves. Thus, one finds firms which do nothing but manufacture computers and accessory devices; firms which manufacture computers and also develop programs and applications to go with them; original equipment manufacturers (OEMs) which do not actually manufacture equipment so much as design packages of computers and peripherals to meet specialized needs; software houses which develop computer programs; time-sharing firms which sell access to computers and to computer programs; and computer-based consulting firms. The division between the manufacturers of computers and the computer-related services industries is far from clear. Time-sharing firms, which are in the service category, frequently compete directly with computer manufacturers—since a firm which has access to a computer through a time-sharing arrangement is less likely to need a device in-house. Computer-based consulting firms are again both customers of the computer companies and also their competitors. They themselves must have computers, but if their analysis substitutes for what client firms could otherwise do in-house, they compete with the computer makers hoping to sell to these client firms.

This article looks at two fast growing business services, (1) computer and data processing services and (2) management consulting and public relations services, and discusses their similarities and differences from high technology manufacturing. The article argues that the growth in these industries is due to many of the same factors responsible for the growth in New England's high technology manufacturing. One complication of this growth is that policymakers who wish to stimulate technological developments must not take a narrow view of what constitutes high technology.

What Are Service Industries?

What are service industries? Occasionally one hears the term "services" used to describe all industries other than manufacturing. However, most compilations of service employment, income, and other statistics are based on the definition of services in the 1972 Standard Industrial Classification (SIC); accordingly, services "includes establishments primarily engaged in providing a wide variety of services for individuals, business and government establishments, and other organizations." Excluded establishments are those engaged in wholesale and retail trade, and those providing transportation, communication and financial services, as well as those engaged in such goods-producing activities as agriculture, mining, construction and manufacturing. In addition, most of the data sources referenced in this article also exclude educational and other services provided by the government, treating them as part of a separate "government" category rather than as part of "services."

Even with these exclusions the services sector is very large. In 1982, 21 percent of the nation's nonagricultural wage and salary jobs were in services, the same percentage as were in manufacturing. In

Table 1
Growth in private payroll employment, 1975–1980 (percent change)

	United States	New England	Massa-chusetts
Private payroll	23.6	22.7	20.7
Manufacturing	15.1	18.3	15.8
Office and computing machines (357)	57.4	50.2	33.3
Electric and electronic equipment (36)	28.8	28.2	22.4
Instruments (38)	24.1	24.8	34.5
Nonmanufacturing	27.2	25.1	23.0
Services	35.9	37.9	40.1
Business services	53.1	73.7	72.7
Computer and data processing (737)	92.0	198.5	211.3
Management consulting and public relations (7392)	72.5	44.7	29.7

Source: U.S. Bureau of the Census, *County Business Patterns*, 1980, 1975.

New England services accounted for 23 percent of wage and salary jobs. (Manufacturing is still more important in New England, with 26 percent of the region's jobs.) The service sector is also very diverse. It appears to be a residual category consisting of all the service-type industries which are not large enough to justify separate classifications. Thus, services includes establishments providing laundering and beauty care services to individuals as well as establishments selling data processing services to businesses and government. Such diversity makes it very difficult to generalize about the service industry. However, one generalization seems justified: service industries were a major source of employment growth in both New England and the nation during the second half of the seventies and into the eighties (table 1).

Within the services sector one of the fastest growing categories has been business services, and within the business service category one of the fastest growing industries has been computer and data processing services. Since 1975 employment in the computer services industry has almost doubled in the country as a whole and more than doubled in New England. It is the expansion in computer services which is the focus of this article. Management consulting and public relations services, considered a miscellaneous business service, will also be discussed. It too has experienced rapid growth, although not so rapid in New England as in the nation, and it has close ties to computer and data processing services.

Are these services large enough to be of relevance for public policy? At the end of 1982 more than 350,000 people nationwide were employed in computer and data processing services. This amounts to more than 10 percent of all those employed in business services, but only 2 percent of total service employment and 0.5 percent of total nonagricultural employment. However, in a nation with as diverse an industrial base as the United States, few individual industries account for a large share of total employment. For example, the manufacture of office and computing machines, an industry in which policymakers now take a very active interest, employed under 500,000 people at the end of 1982, and as recently as four years ago it employed 350,000—the same as computer services today. Moreover, between 1975 and 1982 the numbers of new jobs created in the manufacture of office and computing machines were about the same as in computer and data processing services. The management consulting and public relations industry is about the same size as computer and data processing services.

Sources of Growth

Computer and data processing services consist of establishments engaged in providing "services in computer programming, systems design and analysis, and other computer 'software' "; establishments providing "data processing services to others" including such activities as keypunching, computer time-sharing, and the management of computer facilities; and establishments providing computer-related services which cannot be classified as either data processing or programming. Of the three categories, data processing is the largest, employing roughly 60 percent of those in this industry; computer programming and software follow, with 25 to 30 percent of total industry employment. However, it should be recognized that the distinctions among the categories are not clear-cut. For example, data processing centers frequently develop programs that they make available to clients on the data processing centers' own computers. Moreover, the line between computer and data processing services and other industries, particularly management consulting, is blurred by the existence of computer consultants who advise on the choice of a computer or office automation system; economic research firms that offer time-shared computer access to economic models; and data processing firms that sell computer packages designed to solve a variety of management problems.

The growth in computer and data processing services and related activities is a function of the growing demand for the services of computers, particularly for business applications. That a large part of this demand for the services of computers is being reflected in a demand for computer services as well as computers themselves stems from the decline in the cost of computers and two closely related and mutually supporting developments: (1) the increased accessibility of computing power to medium-sized and small users lacking expertise in computer science, and (2) the growth of computer applications and "a shift to provide complete solutions to users' needs."[2]

The driving force behind the development of the modern computer was the military requirements of World War II. However, the commercial opportunities were apparent from the beginning, and UNIVAC, the first computer designed to meet the needs of business, appeared in 1951. The early users of computers were very large—the Department of Defense, the Bureau of the Census, major corporations. Computers were very expensive, and a user had to be large in order to afford one and to have a computational or data processing task large enough to justify automation. The early user also had to have its own large staff of computer specialists to program the computer.

The programming limitation was eased to a significant extent in the late fifties and early sixties with the development of FORTRAN, COBOL, and other programming languages. These languages had a much stronger resemblance to English than the form of programming then in use and thus were easier to write and interpret.[3] Programming languages had a further advantage over existing programming methods in that they were not machine-specific and a program written in FORTRAN for use on one computer could be adapted relatively easily for use on others. Thus, the development of programming languages not only made computers more accessible to those without highly technical backgrounds but also opened the door to the development of computer programs for use by a number of different computer users.

The programming required for computers to perform large tasks such as payroll and inventory management is difficult and time-consuming. Consequently, a computer user, even a very large one, is likely to find that the number of problems to which it would like to apply its computer far exceeds the capacity of its computer staff to develop the necessary programs. However, there are economies of scale in programming. Other computer users are likely to have some of the same problems. If they could share in the costs of programming a solution, the cost to each one might be readily supportable. Not surprisingly businesses that write and sell computer software have appeared in order to take advantage of these economies of scale. By selling to many users, they can spread the initial costs of developing the programs over a broad base and they can offer their programs at attractive prices against which many internal computer operations cannot compete. They have been especially successful in addressing large problems facing many businesses and in specialized markets too small to be exploited by the computer manufacturers themselves. Computer manufacturers have been and still are among the most important developers of computer programs and for a long time they did not explicitly charge for their programs. Rather, software was part of the total "package" offered by the manufacturers and provided another competitive dimension. However, independent software houses still had a place: they were specialists; the manufacturers' first priority was computers not programs. In addition, IBM's decision in 1969 to charge separately for its software gave a boost to other software establishments.

By no means all of the programs developed and distributed to many users were the products of hardware manufacturers and firms selling software. Universities played an important role. Data processing centers were also major contributors. The development of data processing centers greatly increased the accessibility of computing services. Users too small for their own computers and too small for their own data processing operations can, with a data processing center, rent time on a computer and obtain the services of a trained data processing staff. However, data processing centers do not serve just small firms. Their clients include some of the nation's largest corporations, particularly divisions within large corporations that feel their computing needs are not accorded high enough priority by internal corporate data processing operations. Nor do data processing centers simply offer raw computing time, although raw time is an important product. Data processing centers were far ahead of most internal data processing operations in providing interactive or time-shared computer services, whereby a user sees results at once and can immediately go on to build upon these results or reformulate the problem. Data processing centers offer data bases consisting of economic information, stock market figures, and trade data. They have developed programs to deal with major business problems such as payrolls, taxes, and unemployment compensation, and they have tapped specialized markets—banking, health care, real estate.

The growing array of services offered by data processing centers is, in part, a response to a demand for new applications. As users become more familiar with computers and their capabilities, they see new ways in which to use computers to solve their problems. In part, however, it is a response to the decline in the cost of computers. The declines in recent years have been particularly significant, and users that previously could only afford computing services by using a data processing center can now obtain the same computing power through the purchase of a mini or even a micro computer. The data processing establishments have responded in many cases by lowering their own prices. As major purchasers of computers, they have seen their own costs affected by the decline in computer prices. Data processing operations have also bolstered their competitive position by offering their clients more data bases, developing applications for new markets, and becoming more like management consulting firms.

The decline in computer prices has also affected software sales. Computing power has become much more accessible. However, the new users of computers are much less familiar with computers than users in the past. Software must compensate for the lack of training and experience. Two of the forms in which we see this development are the growth in microcomputers and the increased feasibility of artificial intelligence. Microcomputers are very low cost computers. They are comparatively powerless, but for specific problems and with modest amounts of data they can perform functions previously handled by much more complex machines. They enable small businesses and even individuals to enjoy some of the computing advantages large corporations and financial institutions have had for 20 years. Many firms have entered the business of producing micros, and many of these have no software capabilities of their own. They or their customers must buy software from others, so that the rapid growth in micro sales has created a new market for sales of easy-to-use programs handling relatively simple tasks.

Artificial intelligence makes it possible for individuals with almost no programming knowledge and with no time or desire to acquire any to use computers. The more common form of artificial intelligence is the "natural language front-end," a program which translates commands given in English into a language to which the computer can respond. With a natural language front-end, the user can sit at a terminal and, subject to some limitations, give the computer directions in his own words. The second form of artificial intelligence is the computer which "thinks," or more precisely the computer which is programmed to respond to questions and interpret data as would a trained analyst. The computer functions as a consultant for a particular task, for example, financial asset and liability management, enabling a user with a very limited knowledge not only of computers but also of financial management to query the computer and obtain results. The programs for this type of artificial intelligence are elaborate for they attempt to replicate what is done by consultants, and the computers required are not small. However, the reduction in computer costs has meant that what was once only a subject for science fiction is now feasible in a few areas.

Data processing and computer services operations complement the manufacture of computers, they are customers of the computer manufacturers, and they compete with the manufacturers. The development and sale of computer programs make the purchase of a computer a more attractive investment because it increases the number of potential uses for the computer and reduces the need for an internal programming staff. However, programming can make a less powerful computer competitive with a larger one for specific functions. Data processing centers provide services which some users might be able to obtain from an in-house computing staff, and to this extent they compete with the manufacturers. However, for some users purchase of a computer has never been an option, and for others use of a data processing service can provide a period of familiarization which eventually leads to computer purchase. Interestingly, IBM set up some of the first data processing centers; this subsidiary was divested and sold to another computer manufacturer in the early 1970s. Management consulting firms are purchasers of computers and computer services, and they are sometimes competitors of these same industries. For a number of problems, the analysis of a consulting firm substitutes for the work an internal staff would do using a data processing firm or an in-house computer.

High Tech Services and High Tech Manufacturers Compared

Because the computer and data processing services industry is tied so closely to the computer industry, it should come as no surprise that computer services and also management consulting have a number of characteristics in common with high technology manufacturing. Rapid growth is one similarity that has already been noted. Other similarities include linkages with the Department of Defense and the universities. As a major purchaser of computer programming and other services, the Department of Defense has helped foster the growth of the computer service industry; the specialized needs of defense have resulted in new programming languages and have encouraged developments such as time-sharing and computer graphics. Universities have also contributed to these industries in many ways. Academics have written many important programming languages and have founded a number of computer service and management consulting firms.[4] In addition, universities have also been an essential source of labor, for the computer service and management consulting industries—like high technology manufacturing—depend upon professional and technical manpower.

Professional and technical occupations account for roughly 40 percent of employment in both computer and management services, compared to 15 percent of employment in all industries (table 2). The high technology manufacturers also have heavy professional and technical requirements, with some 40 percent of those in the computer industry and 24 percent of those in communications equipment employed in these occupations. The technical orientation of the high technology manufacturers leans more heavily toward engineers and engineering technicians than that of computer services and management consulting. While engineering occupations account for a larger fraction of computer and management services employment than of

Table 2

Occupational distribution 1978: selected high technology manufacturers and business services (percent)

	All Industries	Manufacturing	Nonelectric machinery			Electrical machinery			Services[a]	Business services			
			Total	Office accounting machines	Computers	Total	Radio, T.V. communications	Instruments		Total business	Business management	Computer programming	Research and development[b]
Professional and technical	15.1	9.9	13.4	18.6	39.5	17.4	23.5	17.0	35.3	19.5	42.8	39.4	55.9
Engineers	1.2	2.8	4.4	4.8	9.2	7.0	9.7	5.1	0.7	1.6	4.7	2.5	12.1
Scientists and mathematicians	0.4	0.5	0.2	0.4	0.5	0.3	0.3	0.8	0.4	0.5	0.5	0.3	8.4
Technicians: engineers, scientists	1.0	2.2	3.0	3.8	7.1	4.8	6.2	4.6	0.9	1.8	1.4	1.5	17.6
Computer specialists	0.5	0.7	2.1	3.3	13.7	1.0	1.5	1.0	0.5	2.9	2.4	29.4	4.1
Social scientists	0.3	0.2	0.3	0.8	1.3	0.4	0.4	0.5	0.5	1.0	6.2	1.0	1.3
Medical workers	2.5	0.1	0.1	0.1	0.1	0.1	0.1	0.9	8.1	0.1	0.1	0.0	0.8
Teachers	3.9	0.1	0.1	0.4	0.5	0.1	0.2	0.1	13.5	0.1	0.1	0.5	0.1
Accountants	1.1	1.0	1.1	1.6	1.8	1.2	1.4	1.2	1.4	2.0	12.0	1.2	1.0
Other	4.2	2.3	2.1	3.4	5.3	2.5	3.7	2.8	9.3	9.5	15.4	3.0	10.5
Managers, officials, proprietors	10.7	7.0	7.8	9.0	10.0	6.2	6.0	8.5	7.4	11.9	15.6	12.5	8.8
Sales	6.3	2.4	1.8	4.9	2.2	1.0	0.6	2.1	0.7	3.6	3.2	2.3	0.6
Clerical	17.9	12.1	14.0	18.3	17.8	13.8	16.0	16.9	18.6	30.8	32.0	33.9	19.5
Crafts	13.1	19.6	22.8	18.2	10.0	12.8	14.7	16.6	5.2	6.2	4.6	9.3	8.0
Operatives	15.3	42.3	35.9	28.5	18.9	44.8	36.1	35.6	3.5	5.2	0.9	1.9	3.7
Service	13.6	1.9	1.7	1.2	1.1	1.7	1.5	1.7	27.5	21.7	0.8	0.6	2.3
Laborers	5.0	4.8	2.6	1.5	0.6	2.4	1.7	1.7	1.9	1.2	0.1	0.2	1.3
Farm	3.0	—	—	—	—	—	—	—	—	—	—	—	—
Total	100.0	100.0	100.0	100.0	100.0	100.0	100.0	100.0	100.0	100.0	100.0	100.0	100.0

a. Includes public education and health services.
b. The category commercial research and development laboratories is included for comparison. It is smaller than the other two service industries.
Source: U.S. Bureau of Labor Statistics, National Industry-Occupation Employment Matrix, Vol. 1, 1981.

total employment, they are not the dominant professional group—as they are for the high tech manufacturers. Most of the professional and technical personnel in the computer services industry are computer specialists. Social scientists, particularly economists, and persons with accounting backgrounds are important in management consulting.

The average salary in computer and data processing and in management consulting and public relations is about 30 percent above the average for nonfarm private industry and about 50 percent above the average for the service sector alone (table 3). However, because professionals and technicians make up such a large proportion of the work force in computer and management services, one cannot say to what extent the high average salary reflects the high education and skill requirements of the industry and to what extent it reflects a generous pay scale. The same difficulty exists when one tries to compare wage rates in high technology manufacturing with other industries. For example, the average wage and salary in the office and computing machine industry is significantly above that for all of manufacturing; however, for production workers only, average hourly earnings in computing and office machines are below the manufacturing average. (Production worker wages in computers and other high tech industries are still well above those in most nondurable goods industries, but they fall well short of those in autos, steel, farm and construction machinery.)

Comparing wages and salaries in computer and data processing and management consulting with those in the manufacture of office and computing machines, one finds that wages and salaries are generally 12 to 15 percent lower in the service industries than in computer manufacturing. Since the proportions of employment in professional and technical occupations are similar for all three industries, it seems likely that at least part of this difference represents lower wage scales in the two service industries. This pattern of lower wages and salaries in computer and management services does not apply in all parts of the country, however. The most notable exception is Massachusetts. It is a high tech center and also a center for computer services and management consulting. In Massachusetts the average wage and salary in the two service industries exceed that in office and computer manufacturing. Moreover, in all states wages and salaries in computer and management services are much more similar to wages in high tech manufacturing than to wages in most other service indus-

Table 3

Average annual salaries for selected high technology and service industries, United States and leading states, 1980 (dollars)

	Private payroll employment	Manu-facturing	Office and computing machinery (357)	Electric and electronic equipment (36)	Instru-ments (38)	Nonmanu-facturing	Services	Business services	Computer and data processing (737)	Management consulting and public relations (7,392)
United States	13,886	16,868	19,839	16,246	17,233	12,711	11,489	11,935	17,490	17,052
States prominent in high technology manufacturing and management and computer services										
California	14,940	17,829	20,375	17,887	17,749	13,957	13,187	12,786	18,286	17,692
Illinois	15,174	18,164	19,497	15,217	15,679	13,828	12,332	13,391	16,164	19,169
Massachusetts	13,299	16,083	19,327	16,278	18,347	12,081	11,199	12,582	19,259	20,610
New Jersey	14,945	17,855	17,459	17,125	17,977	13,565	12,181	11,769	17,567	17,302
New York	15,341	17,598	21,402	17,660	21,218	14,572	13,123	14,251	19,387	20,026
States prominent in high technology manufacturing										
Indiana	14,021	18,286	10,811	17,350	15,049	11,405	9,867	9,438	15,208	10,369
New Hampshire	11,824	13,685	18,153	13,703	14,571	10,789	9,859	11,105	17,945	17,915
Vermont	11,529	15,031	15,170	NA	13,370	9,938	8,425	9,182	15,899	13,986
States prominent in management and computer services										
District of Columbia	15,258	20,746	NA	24,354	NA	14,922	15,224	13,995	17,447	23,628
Maryland	13,372	17,400	17,512	20,271	14,245	12,348	11,888	12,048	17,767	16,046
Virginia	12,373	14,415	NA	17,293	15,452	11,633	11,244	13,264	18,819	20,400

Source: U.S. Bureau of the Census, *County Business Patterns*, 1980.

tries. Service industries are commonly viewed as providing low-paying, dead-end jobs. For some industries this is an accurate perception, but it does not apply to computer and management services.

Location

Because computer and management services share the high tech manufacturers' dependence upon professional and technical manpower and their close ties to the academic community, one would expect both industry groups to be drawn to those locations offering a relative abundance of professional talent and proximity to major universities. Furthermore, the concentration in a particular geographic area of high tech manufacturing or computer and management services, in itself, provides a reservoir of talent which industries with similar professional and technical needs may draw upon. Although the competition for professional manpower in such an area may be intense, the cost of labor may still be lower than if one had to recruit from distant locations.

This suggests that we should find computer and data processing services and management consulting concentrated in those areas that are centers for high technology manufacturing. To some extent we do. The two states most closely identified with high technology manufacturing, California and Massachusetts, also account for a disproportionate share of the nation's employment in computer and data processing services and management consulting. According to the 1977 economic censuses, California with 11 percent of U.S. nonfarm wage and salary employment had 16 percent of the nation's high technology manufacturing employment and also about 16 percent of U.S. employment in computer and management consulting services. Massachusetts with less than 3 percent of nonfarm employment had about 5 percent of high tech employment and 4 percent of computer and management services employment. New Jersey and New York were also prominent in all three industries; and at the other end of the spectrum, the plains, mountain, and most of the southern states had very little employment in either high tech manufacturing or computer services and management consulting.

However, in spite of this evidence of a tie between centers of high technology manufacturing and centers of computer and management services, the correlations between states' shares of high tech employment, relative to their shares of total U.S. employment, and their relative shares of employment in computer and data processing services and management consulting are weak (see appendix). The correlations are positive but not statistically significant. While there is a general tendency for high tech manufacturing to be associated with both computer services and management consulting, there is one very large discrepancy. The District of Columbia and the states of Maryland and Virginia together account for 11 percent of the nation's employment in computer and data processing and 9 percent of employment in management consulting, but only 4 percent of total nonfarm employment and only 3 percent of U.S. employment in high tech manufacturing. If the District of Columbia and neighboring states are excluded from the analysis, the correlations between high tech and computer services and between high tech and management consulting are both statistically significant.

A second, less striking disparity between state shares of high tech manufacturing and their shares of these service industries occurs in New England. Here most states have relatively large shares of high tech manufacturing employment given their shares of computer and management services. All of the New England states except Maine and Rhode Island account for significantly larger shares of U.S. high tech employment than of total U.S. employment; but only Massachusetts also accounts for a larger share of employment in computer and data processing services and management consulting. Connecticut and Rhode Island's employment in these service industries reflects their share of total U.S. employment; the northern New England states have shares of service employment which are smaller than their shares of total employment. The situation in the Midwest is similar although less pronounced. Most midwestern states account for roughly the same proportion of the nation's high tech employment as they do of total employment, but their share of computer services and management consulting employment is smaller. The exception is Illinois, which has relatively high proportions of employment in high technology manufacturing and in management consulting. (The accompanying maps show the geographic distribution of high technology manufacturing and of the total of computer and data processing and management consulting and public relations.)

The most striking difference between the locational pattern of computer and management services and that of high technology manufacturing—the concentration of service industries in Washington, D.C., Virginia, and Maryland—can only be explained in terms of the consulting and computer software and data processing needs of the federal government. This suggests that computer and management services may be more market oriented than high tech manufacturing. The high proportions of service employment in New York, New Jersey, Illinois, and, to a lesser degree, California and Massachusetts are also consistent with a market orientation—although they can be explained equally well by ties to high technology manufacturing and the availability of scientific and technical personnel. Large financial institutions and corporate headquarters are major purchasers of consulting services, computer software, and data processing. New York City and Chicago are the financial and corporate centers of the nation. Los Angeles is also very important, and in the financial world so are Boston and San Francisco.

The difficulty in distinguishing the relative influences of the availability of professional labor and an orientation to a market dominated by the federal government and major financial and nonfinancial institutions arises from the fact that the nation's centers for government, finance, and business have an absolute abundance of professional talent. In part, this abundance is simply a function of the size and density of these metropolitan areas; in part, it is due to the attraction that cities like Washington, New York, and Boston hold for the well-educated.

The argument for a market orientation in management consulting is that the consultant must have frequent face-to-face contacts with his clients. In computer programming and data processing, there are also a number of circumstances requiring interactions with customers. It may be necessary for the designer of computer software to confer with potential clients on the problem to be solved. Purchasers of computer software must be instructed in its use and, on a continuing basis, assisted as unforeseen difficulties arise. Similarly, users of time-sharing and related data processing services require introductory instruction and continuing technical assistance. The importance of these face-to-face contacts may well have increased as use of computers and computer services has expanded to the less technically sophisticated. In this regard, it is significant that not only do

Washington, New York, and Chicago have large concentrations of potential users of computer services and management consulting; but in addition, they have excellent air connections with other parts of the country.

To the extent that there is a market orientation to the computer and management services industries, it is a very different orientation from that commonly associated with the service sector. Most service industries, for example, health care and personal services, serve the needs of local populations. Computer and management services serve the needs of large financial, corporate, and government entities. Since these customers are concentrated in particular areas, one finds computer and management service firms clustering in these same areas. However, a management consulting firm based in New York will probably have clients in Chicago and Washington as well as in smaller centers; and a firm located in Boston will almost certainly have clients located outside the Boston area.

Differences

Although computer and management services and high technology manufacturing have similar requirements for professional and technical personnel, similar client bases and to some degree, similar location patterns and although analysts sometimes speak of computer services, computers, and telecommunications as being part of a single "communications" industry, there are important differences between the two service industries and high tech manufacturing. Because of these differences economic developments and policy actions favorable to the growth of one will not necessarily help the other.

The most obvious difference is that between a manufacturing and a service establishment. In a manufacturing plant, materials and components are fabricated into products which typically are sold to many users. In services one sells the time of individuals with particular skills or knowledge. In management consulting it is the time of the consultant; in computer programming the time of systems analysts and computer programmers. One may be able to leverage the consultant's time by developing management philosophies applicable to a number of situations and the programmer's by selling the same program to a number of users; but the essence of these industries is

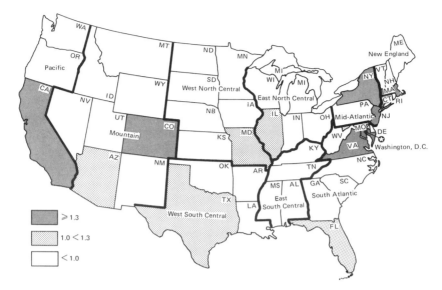

Share of U.S. computer and management services employment relative to share U.S. total employment, 1977

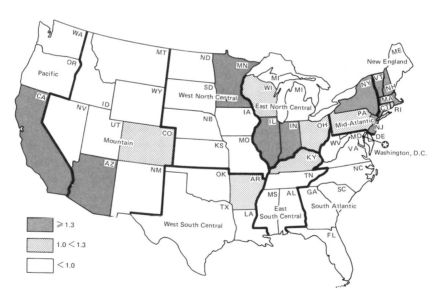

Share of U.S. high tech employment relative to share U.S. total employment, 1977

selling the time and talents of highly trained and experienced individuals. In data processing, the customer purchases time on a computer, but the support provided by the data processing center's computer operators, programmers, and consultants is an important part of the service—sometimes the most important part.

The distinction between manufacturing and services has a number of implications. Labor costs account for a much higher proportion of revenues in the service industries, as service establishments do not have to purchase large quantities of materials or maintain large physical plants. Payroll costs absorb roughly 40 percent of the revenues of management consulting and computer and data processing firms, compared to about 25 percent of the revenues of high tech manufacturers and 20 percent of all manufacturing revenues. Because labor is such an important cost element and the time of key personnel is such an important part of the service offered, the economies of scale tend to be much smaller for service firms than for manufacturers. One can see this most clearly for a pure management consulting firm, for which taking on additional clients generally requires hiring additional consultants and an increase in costs roughly proportional to the increase in revenues. This absence of large economies of scale is reflected in the size of computer and management services establishments. Not only is the average size much smaller than for high technology manufacturers, but within the computer and management services industries, the average size is smaller the more important the sales of pure unleveraged, unaugmented time. Thus, the average size of management consulting establishments is only 12 paid employees. The average size of computer software houses, which can achieve some economies of scale by selling the same programs to many users, is about 20, and the average size of data processing establishments is 30. The average size for electrical and electronic equipment establishments is 150 and for office and computing machinery more than 250. The size figures are skewed by the existence of a lot of very small management consulting and computer service firms; even so, roughly 65 percent of the employment in management consulting and 50 percent in computer and data processing is in firms with less than 100 employees, compared to 12 percent of employees in electrical and electronics equipment and about 5 percent in computers and office equipment.[5]

Not only is labor the most important cost element for the management and computer service firms, it is also their major asset. This can be a serious problem when service companies seek start-up or expansion financing, for investors fear with some justification that the company's major assets—its key personnel—can walk out the door. High technology manufacturers have at times encountered investor resistance for the same reason, as their dependence on professional manpower is greater and their physical assets are smaller than for most manufacturers. However, high tech manufacturers generally have more physical assets than management and computer services firms, and they also have patents and tangible products.

The relatively small size of most computer and management services firms gives them considerable flexibility in choosing a site for their operations. In addition, they do not have to worry about such problems as the transportation of large amounts of equipment and the disposal of wastes. It is not surprising, therefore, that computer and data processing and management consulting establishments are more likely to be found in the largest metropolitan areas within a state than are high technology manufacturers. For example, in Massachusetts 85 percent of those employed in computer and data processing services and 90 percent of those in management consulting work in the Boston metropolitan area (SMSA), whereas 36 percent of those employed in office and computing machinery and 52 percent of those in electrical and electronic equipment are in Boston.[6] A similar relationship exists between the New York City SMSA and the states of New York and New Jersey, as well as between the Los Angeles and San Francisco areas and the state of California. This tendency for the service establishments to be located in the larger metro areas may reflect individuals' locational preferences, and it is also consistent with the market orientation of computer and management services and their need for good airline service.[7]

Policy Implications

The development of computer software and data processing services and of management consulting is significant not so much because of the number of jobs involved—for although these industries have been growing and although their employment is now comparable to that in computer manufacturing, they still account for only a tiny fraction of the work force. Rather, it is significant because it illustrates how industrial evolution can take many forms; and for policymakers concerned about fostering the growth of new industries, this evidence of the varied nature of industrial development should be a powerful argument in favor of creating an environment conducive to innovation and entrepreneurial activity rather than targeting assistance to specific industries.

At the present time there is considerable interest in high technology manufacturing and a number of legislators at both federal and state levels have proposals to stimulate high technology. The thrust of most of these proposals is strengthening math and science teaching in the secondary schools or increasing the capacity of colleges and universities to train engineers and computer specialists. This emphasis on math and science and more rigorous education in general is very positive. Not only high technology manufacturing but also computer and management services depend upon professional and technical manpower. In addition, many "smokestack" industries, for example, motor vehicles and rubber, employ significant numbers of engineers, scientists, and technicians—although relative to size not so many as the high technology industries.

The danger in the current interest in industrial development is that it may eventually lead to policies to stimulate the growth of particular industries or particular groups of industries that are believed to have promising futures. However, a program which substantially reduces taxes or lowers the cost of capital for one set of industries necessarily raises taxes, relative to what they would have been, and increases the cost of capital for others. Moreover, it is very difficult to know which are the industries of the future, so that help for one industry runs the risk of retarding the development of another still more promising. In all the talk of high technology there has been little mention of computer and data processing services. Yet computer services offers attractive employment opportunities, is rapidly growing, and is now about two-thirds the size of the computer industry—the industry which for many typifies high technology. In addition, both computer services and management consulting are likely to be less vulnerable to foreign competition than many manufacturing activities, both because they are somewhat market oriented and because success in these industries requires a detailed knowledge of American business practice. The appropriate response to the development of these service industries is not to redraw the definition of high technology to include computer and data processing and management consulting but to recognize that growth can come from any number of sources—from high technology manufacturing, from the service sector, from many industries.

Appendix: High Technology, Data Processing, and Management Consulting Correlations

Location coefficients were calculated for high technology manufacturing, computer and data processing, and management consulting and public relations employment in each state. The coefficients consist of that state's share of U.S. total high technology (or computer and data processing or management consulting) employment divided by the state's share of U.S. total employment.

Correlations between the different location coefficients were run for all 50 states and the District of Columbia, and then for all states except Maryland, Virginia, and the District of Columbia. The results are shown in matrix form below:

	Correlation coefficients for all states (51 observations)			
	High technology manufacturing	Computer and data processing	Management consulting	Management and computer services
High technology manufacturing	1.00	0.19	0.20	0.22
Computer and data processing	0.19	1.00	0.73*	—
Management consulting and public relations	0.20	0.73*	1.00	—
Management and computer services combined	0.22	—	—	1.00

* Significant at 0.05 level

	Correlation coefficients for all states except Maryland, Virginia, District of Columbia (48 observations)			
	High technology manufacturing	Computer and data processing	Management consulting	Management and computer services combined
High technology manufacturing	1.00	0.39*	0.50*	0.49*
Computer and data processing	0.39*	1.00	0.71*	—
Management consulting and public relations	0.50*	0.71*	1.00	—
Management and computer services combined	0.49*	—	—	1.00

* Significant at the 0.05 level

Data Definitions and Sources

High technology employment is defined using the Massachusetts Division of Employment Security's definition, as found in *High Technology Employment, Massachusetts and Selected States, 1975–81,* which includes the following SIC codes:

283 Drugs

348 Ordnance and accessories

357 Office computing and accounting machines

36 Electrical and electronic machinery

376 Guided missiles and space vehicles and parts

379 Miscellaneous transportation equipment

38 Instruments

In order to ensure consistency among all states, the figures used to calculate the high technology location coefficients are not from the Massachusetts Division of Employment Security's publication which included only selected states but from the *Census of Manufactures,* 1977. Computer and data processing (SIC 737) and management consulting and public relations (SIC 7392) figures are from the *Census of Service Industries,* 1977. Location coefficients for management and computer services are composed of the state's share of the sum of data processing and management divided by that state's share of total employment.

Notes

Lynn E. Browne is Vice-President and Economist, Federal Reserve Bank of Boston. The author thanks Pamela S. Barr for her research assistance. This article owes much to the insights of Stephen J. Browne and to the work of John S. Hekman, "The Future of High Technology Industry in New England," *New England Economic Review*, January/February 1980.

1. Massachusetts Division of Employment Security, *Business Support Services Employment in Massachusetts 1975–1980*, p. 16.

2. Alfred R. Berkeley, "Millionaire Machine," *Datamation*, August 25, 1981.

3. In the early days programs were written in machine language to which the computer could respond directly or in symbolic representations of machine language. With programs written in FORTRAN and other programming languages, the computer still must receive instructions in machine language; however, previously written intermediate programs translate the FORTRAN expressions into a form the machine can understand. The portability of computer programs was reduced by manufacturers' efforts to ensure that programs written for their own computer-make could run only on their computers. As IBM came to dominate the market, most programs were written so as to be compatible with IBM computers.

4. Languages written by academics or in academic settings include ALGOL, BASIC and ATP. The last is used for numerically controlled machine tools. Firms in New England which were founded by academics or with very close academic connections include the economic consulting and time-sharing firm Data Resources Inc. (DRI), the management consulting firm Management Analysis Center (MAC), the software house and time-sharing operation Management Decisions Systems (MDS), and the artificial intelligence companies Artificial Intelligence and Cognitive Systems.

5. Size figures are from *County Business Patterns 1980*.

6. These figures are from the 1977 *Census of Service Industries* and the 1977 *Census of Manufactures*.

7. Good air service is also important for high tech manufacturers. The value to weight of their products is high and they frequently ship by air. However, more alternatives are available to the high tech manufacturer.

The Role of Small Business in New England

David L. Birch
Massachusetts Institute of Technology
November 1983

As Massachusetts' economy grew more and more robust, bankers, economists, and others became increasingly intrigued by what lay behind the state's new-found well-being. Of special interest was the exact makeup of the companies that were bringing such vitality to the formerly depressed state.

In 1983 physicist-turned-economist David Birch, an economist at MIT's Laboratory for Architecture and Planning, prepared a report, taking a close look at the dynamics of New England businesses. His research produced two key findings: small businesses were at the heart of the New England turnaround, and expansion in the service sector was the main factor in the generation of new jobs.

Birch's New England study followed a 1979 report called "The Job Generation Process" produced for the federal Commerce Department in which he showed that small businesses create most of the new jobs in the United States. Birch drew on a file of Dun and Bradstreet data dating from 1969 to track the evolution of 5.6 million business establishments which represent about 80 percent of all formal businesses in the United States. The file included such information as sales, age, industry, number of employees, and location for each establishment.

According to this paper, although small businesses have a far greater failure rate than large ones, the contractions of large companies since 1969 represented a greater share of lost jobs than small business failures. About 40 percent of replacement jobs came from independent businesses with fewer than twenty employees, he reported, and 60 percent were generated by all businesses with fifty or fewer employees. He concluded that "it is the willingness of small businesses to form and expand in New England that is keeping the New England economy as strong as it is."

Historically, it has been difficult to measure the contribution of small businesses to the New England economy, or to any other economy, for that matter. We know that there are a great number of small businesses, but we have had no accurate way of measuring their contribution.

The problem arises from the fact that small businesses do not sit still. They tend to grow or go out of business. In either case, they are no longer small businesses when we count them a second time. The only way out of this quandary is to measure *not* how many small business firms or jobs existed at different points in time but what happened to a particular group of small businesses over time.

In order to achieve this goal, a group of us at MIT have assembled a file of 5.6 million business establishments and have traced the evolution of each establishment from 1969 to 1972, 1974, and 1976. We know a fair amount about each establishment—its sales, number of employees, age, industry, corporate affiliation (if any), and location down to the street address.[1] With this information we can learn what small businesses (and other kinds of businesses) are contributing to the New England economy as they themselves evolve over time.

Position of Small Businesses in the New England Economy

Before delving into the dynamics of change, a brief profile of the small business sector and its relationship to the New England economy will be helpful.

The most obvious thing about small businesses[2] is their number. As table 1 shows very small (0–19 employees) businesses accounted for about 88 percent of all establishments, and small businesses (0–99 employees) about 98 percent. In this regard, New England is very similar to the United States as a whole (see table 1).

Because they are small, small businesses account for a much smaller percentage of jobs than firms. Again, turning to table 1, we find that the 88 percent of the firms that are very small account for

---

Table 1

Distribution of establishments and employment by size of establishment for New England and the United States in 1976

Employment	Establishments		Employment		Sales	
	Percent	Cumulative percent	Percent	Cumulative percent	Percent	Cumulative percent
New England						
0–4	56.4%	56.4%	7.9%	7.9%	7.6%	7.6%
5–19	31.1	87.5	16.3	24.2	16.5	24.1
20–99	10.0	97.5	23.5	47.7	25.7	49.8
100–249	1.6	99.1	14.2	61.9	15.3	65.1
250–499	0.5	99.6	9.8	71.7	9.6	74.7
500–999	0.2	99.9	9.3	81.0	10.0	84.8
1000+	0.1	100.0	19.0	100.0	15.2	100.0
United States						
0–5	56.7	56.7	8.7	8.7	8.8	8.8
5–19	31.6	88.3	17.7	26.4	20.4	29.1
20–99	9.5	97.8	23.3	49.7	25.7	54.8
100–249	1.4	99.2	13.4	63.1	14.6	69.4
250–499	0.4	99.7	9.4	72.6	9.4	78.8
500–999	0.2	99.9	8.3	80.9	8.1	86.9
1000+	0.1	100.0	19.1	100.0	13.1	100.0

only 24 percent of the work force. Similarly, the 98 percent of establishments classified as small employ only 48 percent of the work force. Said another way, 2 percent of the firms employ over half of the entire work force.

The sales picture is only slightly different, the difference being that small firms generate slightly more sales per employee than larger ones do. Part of this can be explained by the different industry mix within different size groups, and it does not necessarily reflect greater productivity.

In fact, as table 2 shows, different economic sectors tend to have quite different size mixes. Manufacturers tend to be larger, along with (to a lesser degree) transportation and wholesaling companies. Construction, retailing, and service firms, in contrast, tend to be smaller. This pattern holds up at the state level as well. Table 3 summarizes establishment sizes by industry for Massachusetts.

Ownership patterns also vary a great deal by size of firm. The great majority of smaller establishments tend to be independent, with

Table 2
Establishment size by industry for New England, 1976 (percent)

Industry	Employment size								Total employment
	0	1–4	5–19	20–99	100–249	250–499	500–999	1,000 +	
Agriculture	0.0	63.0	31.5	4.8	0.3	0.2	0.0	0.0	3,469
Mining	0.7	45.0	36.8	13.6	2.5	1.1	0.4	0.0	280
Construction	0.0	69.4	24.9	5.1	0.4	0.0	0.0	0.0	31,130
Manufacturing	0.1	32.2	34.1	23.3	6.3	2.4	1.1	0.6	27,422
Transportation	0.4	46.5	36.5	13.8	2.0	0.5	0.2	0.0	8,642
Wholesale	0.2	49.4	38.1	11.4	0.8	0.0	0.0	0.0	21,268
Retail	0.0	60.2	31.8	7.3	0.5	0.0	0.0	0.0	77,626
Finance	0.1	62.2	28.0	7.3	1.4	0.3	0.2	0.3	12,007
Services	0.2	58.1	28.7	9.7	2.2	0.6	0.3	0.2	39,168
Overall percentage	0.1	56.2	31.1	10.0	1.6	0.5	0.2	0.1	221,012

Table 3
Establishment size by industry for Massachusetts, 1976 (percent)

Industry	Employment size								Total employment
	0	1–4	5–19	20–99	100–249	250–499	500–999	1,000 +	
Agriculture	0.0	59.4	35.4	4.8	0.1	0.1	0.0	0.0	1,388
Mining	0.8	45.7	37.8	15.0	0.8	0.0	0.0	0.0	127
Construction	0.0	69.5	24.4	5.3	0.5	0.1	0.0	0.0	13,667
Manufacturing	0.1	32.1	33.7	24.0	6.2	2.3	1.0	0.6	12,857
Transportation	0.4	47.2	35.4	13.9	2.2	0.6	0.3	0.0	4,317
Wholesale	0.1	50.1	37.2	11.6	0.9	0.1	0.0	0.0	10,924
Retail	0.0	59.0	32.6	7.6	0.6	0.0	0.0	0.0	34,816
Finance	0.1	61.5	26.8	9.0	1.8	0.4	0.2	0.3	5,948
Services	0.1	56.5	29.2	10.3	2.5	0.6	0.4	0.3	18,578
Overall percentage	0.1	55.3	31.3	10.6	1.8	0.5	0.2	0.2	102,622

very small independent establishments accounting for over 75 percent of all establishments in New England (see table 4). Larger establishments, on the other hand, are more likely to be parts of larger firms than not. Looked at another way, although all forms of ownership tend toward the small end of the scale, independents are predominantly small.

Contribution of Small Businesses to Economic Growth

As indicated earlier, the descriptions of the small business sector just presented give us little feeling for the role small businesses play in bringing about economic change. Perhaps the easiest way to understand this predicament is with an example. Suppose that the 1970 small business sector (defined now as firms with 0–20 employees) in a town consisted of 10 firms each employing 15 people. Suppose further, that all 10 firms grew to be medium sized and employed 45 people each by 1980, while 10 new firms were formed during the 1970s and each of them had a 1980 employment of 10. The standard measure of the performance of the small business sector in that community would show a decline from 150 employees in 1970 to 100 employees in 1980—that is, a decline in the number of people employed in small businesses. But, in fact, small businesses created 400 new jobs in the process (300 through expansion and 100 through formation)—a rather remarkable accomplishment for a town of that size.

It is in the interest of tracing what small businesses do (not what the small business sector does) that we assembled our file of business establishments. By aggregating it, we can see how change takes place in any particular location.

There are six possible ways in which change in a place occurs between two points in time:

Birth	Formation of a new establishment.
Death	Dissolution of an existing establishment.
Expansion	Increase in the number of employees of an existing establishment.
Contraction	Decrease in the number of employees of an existing establishment.

Table 4
Types of establishments and employment by size of establishment for New England in 1976

Type of establishment	Employment size						Totals
	0–19	20–99	100–249	250–499	500–999	1,000+	
Number of establishments							
Independent	170,958	15,419	1,719	415	190	142	188,843
Parent/subsidiary	1,654	826	255	70	25	10	2,840
Headquarters	9,503	2,449	650	278	147	85	13,112
Branch	12,080	3,617	1,084	379	211	136	17,507
Total employment size	194,195	22,311	3,708	1,142	573	373	222,302
Percentage of total establishments by type							
Independent	90.5	8.2	0.9	0.2	0.1	0.0	188,843
Parent/subsidiary	58.2	29.1	9.0	2.5	0.9	0.4	2,840
Headquarters	72.5	18.7	5.0	2.1	1.1	0.6	13,112
Branch	69.0	20.7	6.2	2.2	1.2	0.8	17,507
Total percentage of employment size	87.4	10.0	1.7	0.5	0.3	0.2	222,302
Percentage of total establishments by employment size							
Independent	88.0	69.1	46.4	36.3	33.2	38.1	84.9
Parent/subsidiary	0.9	3.7	6.9 '	6.1	4.4	2.7	1.3
Headquarters	4.9	11.0	17.5	24.3	25.7	22.8	5.9
Branch	6.2	16.2	29.2	33.2	36.8	36.5	7.9
Total employment size	194,195	22,311	3,708	1,142	573	373	222,302

In-migration   Movement into the area of an existing firm previously located elsewhere.

Out-migration   Movement out of the area of an existing firm previously located there.

In the situation where an establishment moves and changes size, it is classified as a migrant rather than an expander or contractor. As will become obvious, this arbitrary decision has few practical implications since there are so few migrants.

Collectively, we refer to these six processes as the "components of change of an area." The tabulations of these components presented in this paper have not been adjusted for known underreporting of births and other phenomena that can be calibrated. They thus understate both births and aggregate net change. Based on our work to date, however, the adjustment is fairly consistent over space and time. The results therefore are comparable.

Since contribution to employment growth is our focus, our first step was to sort states across the country by their rate of employment change to see which components accounted for most of that change during different phases of the business cycle. Table 5 summarizes the results. The most obvious aspect of the table is the virtually negligible role played by migration of establishments from one state to another during all time intervals. Much attention has been given by the local and national presses to migrations when they do occur, and their symbolic effect may well be important. Their direct effect on the job base, however, is quite small, especially relative to the other processes at work.

Second, the death and contraction rates vary very little from one place to the next despite the rather large range of net change rates involved. Table 6 summarizes losses due to deaths and contractions and gains due to births and expansions from table 5. Practically all the variation in net change is due to variation in the rate of replacement, not the rate of loss. And an awesome rate of loss it is. In order to break even, a state must replace about 8 percent of its job base each year, or roughly 40 percent of its job base every five years. It is the extent of replacement that is remarkable, not the fact that a few states occasionally come up short in the process.

We note also that the rates of loss and replacement are somewhat sensitive to the business cycle. The period of 1969 to 1972 was an

Table 5
Annual rate of employment change for states by growth rate of state

State growth rate	Births	Deaths	Expansion	Contraction	In-migration	Out-migration
1969–1972						
Fast	7.5	5.6	6.2	2.7	0.1	0.03
Moderate	6.0	5.2	4.7	2.8	0.2	0.03
Slow	4.5	4.8	4.0	2.9	0.03	0.03
Decline	3.9	5.1	3.4	3.2	0.2	0.1
U.S. average	5.6	5.2	4.7	2.9	0.1	0.03
1972 to 1974						
Fast	6.5	4.6	5.8	2.5	0.1	0.05
Moderate	5.0	4.4	5.0	2.7	0.05	0.05
Slow	4.3	4.6	4.5	2.9	0.2	0.1
Decline	—	—	—	—	—	—
U.S. average	5.5	4.5	5.3	2.6	0.1	0.05
1974 to 1976						
Fast	9.5	5.7	5.4	3.1	0.2	0.05
Moderate	6.9	5.3	4.4	3.3	0.1	0.1
Slow	6.2	6.1	4.4	3.5	0.1	0.1
Decline	4.5	5.4	3.6	3.8	0.2	0.1
U.S. average	6.7	5.7	4.4	3.4	0.1	0.1

Note: The four classes of employment change are fast (over 4 percent per year), moderate (2 to 4 percent per year), slow (0 to 2 percent per year) and decline (less than 0 percent per year). On the average, this breakdown divides states into four roughly equal groups, although the size of each group in any particular year is sensitive to the business cycle.

Table 6
Sum of major loss and gain components by rate of state employment change

Period	State growth rate	Sum of annual percent job losses due to deaths and contractions	Sum of annual percent jobs replaced by births and expansions
1969 to 1972	Fast	8.3	13.7
	Moderate	8.0	10.7
	Slow	7.7	8.5
	Decline	8.3	7.3
	U.S. average	8.1	10.3
1972 to 1974	Fast	7.1	12.3
	Moderate	7.1	10.0
	Slow	7.5	8.8
	Decline	—	—
	U.S. average	7.1	10.8
1974 to 1976	Fast	8.8	14.9
	Moderate	8.6	11.3
	Slow	9.6	10.6
	Decline	9.2	8.1
	U.S. average	9.1	11.1

average period, by our measures, 1972 to 1974 was expansionary, and 1974 to 1976 was a recession. The loss and gain rates rise and fall as the cycle rises and falls in the expected directions with the exception that the rate of replacement actually increased during the recessionary 1974 to 1976 period. So too did the loss rate, and the net effect was a net decline. Nevertheless, replacement through births and expansions continued undaunted through the rather difficult 1974 to 1976 period.

The New England states, as exemplified by Massachusetts (table 7) exhibit much the same pattern. Particularly noticeable in New England is the decline in manufacturing and the important role played by the service sector, especially during recessionary periods. Without expansion in the services, the New England states would be facing acute job losses, even in good times.

The relative insignificance of migration (in the formal, moving-van sense) and the relative stability of the loss rate lead us to focus attention on replacement—through both births and expansions. Who generates these replacement jobs? What role do small businesses play?

Table 7
Components of employment changes in Massachusetts

Industry	Total base	Net change	Components of change (percent of base)					
			Births	Deaths	Expand	Contract	In-migration	Out-migration
1969 to 1972								
Farming	5,732	-2.7	5.5	-12.0	15.7	-11.9	0.0	0.0
Manufacturing	673,795	-11.5	10.7	-17.6	7.3	-11.9	0.2	-0.2
Other	173,103	1.9	13.5	-11.7	12.2	-11.9	0.2	-0.3
Trade	305,617	8.2	19.1	-19.1	15.3	-7.3	0.2	0.0
Service	79,463	5.3	16.9	-17.7	15.4	-9.2	0.1	-0.2
Totals	1,237,710	-3.6	13.6	-17.1	10.5	-10.6	0.2	-0.2
1972 to 1974								
Farming	6,040	5.7	5.6	-7.2	11.9	-4.5	0.0	0.0
Manufacturing	616,049	5.1	8.4	-7.5	9.9	-5.4	0.0	-0.3
Other	215,972	4.9	9.8	-8.5	9.8	-6.2	0.2	0.0
Trade	355,990	3.5	10.1	-10.7	9.2	-5.1	0.2	-0.1
Service	113,781	8.8	15.4	-9.8	9.0	-5.9	0.1	-0.0
Totals	1,307,832	5.0	9.7	-8.8	9.6	-5.5	0.1	-0.2
1974 to 1976								
Farming	7,754	-3.5	3.2	-18.7	12.0	-6.2	6.4	-0.3
Manufacturing	676,377	-6.0	4.3	-8.2	6.9	-9.0	0.3	-0.2
Other	353,797	-0.8	8.6	-8.7	7.9	-8.5	0.2	-0.1
Trade	395,530	-2.4	10.3	-14.2	8.1	-6.7	0.2	-0.1
Service	206,223	13.4	23.2	-15.5	10.5	-4.7	0.0	-0.2
Totals	1,639,681	-1.5	9.0	-10.8	7.9	-7.8	0.2	-0.2

What role do conglomerates play? These are the questions we began asking for New England.

A first step would be to examine the replacement rates by size and type of firm. Before we could do this, however, we had to assemble all the branches and subsidiaries into the corporate families to which they belong so that we could measure the sizes of whole firms, not just the individual establishments. For it is firms, not establishments, that for the most part make investment decisions. Table 8 reflects this aggregation into firms.

As we can see in table 8, half of the replacement jobs are being generated by very small businesses, and about 60 percent by businesses with 50 or fewer employees. About 40 percent of the replacement is being generated by independent, very small businesses.

Replacement is of course only half of the story. A gnawing question remains: Don't smaller businesses have higher failure rates, and hence isn't their role in replacement more than offset through losses? It turns out that smaller businesses do, in fact, have higher death rates but that the larger corporations are contributing even larger losses though the contraction of their New England facilities. On balance therefore, when the total losses are netted against the total gains, the small business sector accounts for a very large share of all net new jobs generated in New England (see table 9). In short, it is the willingness of small businesses to form and expand in New England that is keeping the New England economy as strong as it is.

Conclusion

When we look beneath the aggregates, we find a vital group of small businesses that are contributing more than their fair share of jobs to the New England economy and that are, in many cases, the sole creators of employment.

The easy conclusion from these findings is that we should focus most, if not all, of our economic development efforts on these job providers, making physical and business environments more attractive to them. There is something to be said for such a strategy, or at least for a strategy that does not focus most of its attention on wooing a few large plants—plants whose long-run loyalties to New England may be questionable.[3]

Table 8
Replacement of jobs through birth and expansion by employment size and type of firm, 1969–1976

Type of establishment	Employment size						Total
	0–20	21–50	51–250	251–500	500+		
Replacement jobs							
Independent	407,536	103,447	92,789	14,986	42,920		661,678
Headquarters/branch	60,518	41,149	76,188	33,367	67,588		278,810
Parent/laboratory	10,742	11,139	38,119	19,318	47,087		126,405
Total employment size	478,796	155,735	207,096	67,671	157,595		1,066,893
Percent of total							
Independent	38.2	9.7	8.7	1.4	4.0		62.0
Headquarters/branch	5.7	3.9	7.1	3.1	6.3		26.1
Parent/laboratory	1.0	1.0	3.6	1.8	4.4		11.8
Total percentage of employment size	44.9	14.6	19.4	6.3	14.8		100.0

Table 9

Percentage of net new jobs created by employment size and type of creating firm in New England, 1969–1976

Type of establishment	Employment size					
	0–20	21–50	51–250	251–500	500+	Total
Independent	69.8	2.2	−11.0	−3.0	12.6	70.6
Headquarters/branch	18.0	8.4	5.0	−5.0	−5.4	20.9
Parent/subsidiary	4.0	2.7	5.0	−0.5	−2.8	8.5
Total percentage of employment size	91.7	13.3	−1.0	−8.4	4.4	100.0

Implementing a strategy to focus on smaller businesses may be far more difficult than it at first sounds, however. Small businesses fail—often. There are literally millions of them in the United States, and almost 200,000 in New England. What institution is equipped and prepared to select a few small businesses from among thousands for assistance, and to fail 30 or 40 percent of the time in the process? Certainly not most government agencies—they are enormously averse to failure and the threat of scandal that comes with it. Certainly not commercial banks, who hold very low reserves against such losses and cannot afford the processing costs. Even venture capital firms like to see a firm in business for several years with a reasonably well-defined market before investing in it. Community development corporations offer some hope, but they are not totally divorced from political (rather than economic) considerations and are a relatively new and untested vehicle.

If we are to build on the vitality of small businesses, we must at the same time develop, test, and carefully evaluate vehicles that can identify productive needles in a large haystack and that can, even with improved selection techniques, be prepared to fail a high percentage of the time.

To make matters more complicated, we must also discover what to offer the needles once we have found them. Many have argued that small businesses need, use effectively, and cannot easily get capital. Improvements in capital markets are thus an obvious first step.

But capital availability, and economic factors generally, are only part of the picture. Recent interview data[4] suggest that quality-of-life considerations are at least as important as economic ones in determining which places businesses will choose to operate in. Business people (particularly small business people) are, after all, people as much as they are economic units. With interstate highways and improved telecommunications they are much freer to do business where they want to rather than where they have to. They thus express a great concern for schools, crime, ease of truck access (i.e., lack of congestion), adequate infrastructure, and a physically attractive environment. If New England (particularly its older cities) is going to foster small business growth, it is going to have to spruce up its buildings, roads, harbors, and schools as well as its capital markets if it is going to succeed. There is evidence in many places that the need for this kind of a dual strategy is now being recognized. But such a dual strategy is just in its embryonic stages relative to what might be possible and relative to what will probably have to be accomplished if it is to be at all successful on a nontrivial scale.

Notes

1. This file represents about 80 percent of all formal businesses in the economy. For a detailed description of its contents and characteristics, see Birch, *Using the Dun and Bradstreet Data* (MIT Program on Neighborhood and Regional Change, February, 1979).

2. Throughout this paper, reference will frequently be made to a four-way breakdown of businesses defined as follows:

Phrase	Size
Very small	0–19
Small	0–99
Medium	100–999
Large	1,000 +

3. In other research, we have found that a large share of births and expansions in the South are controlled from the Northeast. Although firms may not be moving in the moving-van sense, they appear to be moving capital through differential investment in the South (and abroad) while contracting in the North. See Birch, *The Job Generation Process* (MIT Program on Neighborhood and Regional Change, 1979).

4. See Matz, *Central City Businesses—Plans and Problems* (Joint Economic Committee, 1979).

Route 128: The Development of a Regional High Technology Economy

Nancy S. Dorfman
Massachusetts Institute of Technology
December 1983

As the number of Massachusetts high technology companies mushroomed in the decades following World War II, hundreds of fledgling firms settled along Route 128, a highway that describes a wide arc around Boston. The proliferation of these companies soon came to be known as the "Route 128 phenomenon." It was these firms, according to Nancy Dorfman, an economist at MIT's Center for Policy Alternatives, that spearheaded growth in the state, particularly in the late 1970s. In her 1983 study of Route 128, Dorfman explained why these businesses developed in Massachusetts and assessed the role of these new companies in the growth of the high tech sector.

In particular, Dorfman observed that the explosive growth in the high tech sector was fueled by advances in computers and electronics. Not only did these fields spawn start-ups from university laboratories but also from existing high tech companies. And the tendency of these spin-offs to remain near the source that engendered them fostered the extraordinary concentration of firms along Route 128.

Dorfman's study drew another important conclusion. The Boston area's high technology community did not arise from any effort by state or local government to attract industry. It developed spontaneously as a result of entrepreneurial efforts of individuals building on the existing technological infrastructure, and drawing on the network of universities and related research laboratories in the area.

Introduction

In the last two decades, concentrations of high technology (or high tech) firms in the United States have emerged in a relatively few geographical regions. The most notable of these are California's Santa Clara County, better known as Silicon Valley, and a small corner of Massachusetts close to Boston's Route 128. Much smaller high tech clusters have sprouted in six or eight other states, but none compares in size with the two mentioned. The conditions that stimulate such growth in a location bear looking into, not only from the point of view of a state or region that wishes to replicate the experiences of Massachusetts and California but in the interest of a nation that is striving to maintain its competitive position in world markets for new products.

This paper reports on a study of the Massachusetts high tech economy, conducted at the Center for Policy Alternatives (CPA) at MIT [10]. The study focuses particularly on the very rapid growth in the state's high tech sector toward the end of the 1970s and its relationship to earlier trends. Its purpose is to discover the characteristics of industries that caused a proliferation of new firms, clustering together in a relatively few geographical regions, and what caused them to cluster where they did.

Massachusetts' high tech boom in the late 1970s pulled it out of a recession that had seen unemployment average 11 percent of the labor force in 1975, compared with a national average of 8.5 percent. The decline of the state's traditional nondurable industries after World War II, led by the steady closing of textile mills, had been partially offset by an upward trend in instruments, aircraft, missiles, space vehicles, and electrical machinery, all heavily supported by the nation's military and space programs in the 1950s and 1960s. But the post-Vietnam slump in all of these except for instruments, left the state's employment growth almost at a standstill until after the middle of the decade. Writing in *Fortune* in 1974 one experienced observer of the high tech scene commented:

The famous Boston–Cambridge complex has gone into a decline, partly because of the excessive dependence on federal contracts, which stopped coming, and partly because most of the technologies the Boston companies bet on failed to catch on [7].

The state's very modest endowment of natural resource and locational advantages, aggravated by dependence on imported oil, added up to a bleak outlook for its economic future. But during the next five years, 75,000 employees were added to its high technology work force, an increase of over 30 percent, and unemployment fell to well below the national average, where it has remained ever since.

High tech concentrations in the United States whose rapid expansion have attracted the most attention, like those in Massachusetts, are primarily engaged in the design, development and production of electronics-based goods and services, most significantly computer hardware and software, instruments, communications equipment, industrial apparatus and their parts and components, including the integrated circuits engraved on silicon chips whose revolutionary advances gave birth to the electronics boom. The vastly reduced cost and improved performance of integrated circuits and the invention of the microprocessor gave impetus to an explosion of opportunities for the commercial application of solid state electronics to information processing and communication, and to instruments and apparatus for measuring, sensing, testing and controlling an enormous variety of phenomena. Advances in computer software and hardware have continually extended these opportunities, opening up new markets and expanding old ones.

The term "high tech" is not, of course, confined to electronics-related activities. We have settled on its use here to describe establishments that are engaged in the design, development or production of new products or processes through the systematic application of scientific or technical knowledge, using largely state-of-the-art techniques. Some establishments in a great many different industries meet these criteria, but for practical purposes we define a high tech industry as one that includes a relatively large proportion of such establishments.

There is far from hearty agreement about which industries should be classed as such. The most common indicators are a relatively high proportion of scientists and engineers among the work force and a relatively large expenditure on research and development. At the present time the most rapidly growing high tech industries are tied in one way or another to advances in solid state circuitry and computer hardware and software.

On the basis of the three-digit Standard Industrial Classification (SIC) manufacturing industries that the Massachusetts Division of Employment Security (DES) classifies as high tech [22], the state had about 235,000 high tech employees at the end of the 1970s. If computer and data processing services are added, the total approached 250,000 by 1980, most of it concentrated within about 30 miles of Boston, not counting the overflow into southern New Hampshire.

By coincidence, Santa Clara County in California, better known as Silicon Valley, has about the same number of high tech employees, and the entire San Francisco Bay Area has about 30 percent more. Growth in such employment in the late 1970s was substantially higher in Santa Clara County than in Massachusetts. However, comparisons are hazardous because of inconsistencies in employment data and differences in the high tech proportions of different industries in the two areas.[1] No other region of similar size in the United States approaches the high tech concentration of either of the two areas. Massachusetts had, by 1979, a higher proportion of its manufacturing work force employed in such industries than any of the other leading industrial states (see table 1). With 3 percent of the nation's labor

Table 1
High tech employment as percent of manufacturing employment in top ten industrial states, 1979

State	Total manufacturing employment (in thousands)	High tech manufacturing (in thousands)	Percent of total manufacturing	Rank
Massachusetts	672.7	222.0	33.0	1
California	2,003.1	574.9	28.7	2
New York	1,500.0	375.0	25.0	3
New Jersey	792.2	182.2	23.0	4
Florida	442.8	98.3	22.2	5
Illinois	1,283.1	242.5	18.9	6
Pennsylvania	1,390.1	209.9	15.1	7
Texas	1,018.4	143.6	14.1	8
Ohio	1,383.8	161.9	11.7	9
Michigan	1,153.8	92.3	8.0	10

Source: [21, p. 7].

force, it has 6.5 percent of the country's employment in high tech industries. But these figures, based on three-digit SIC categories, do not do justice to its contribution to high technology. For one thing, three-digit industries generally include some four-digit industries that are not properly classed as high tech, and the proportion of employees in such industries is often greater outside of Massachusetts than inside. In Medical Instruments and Supplies (SIC 384), for example, sophisticated new products such as electronic equipment and membrane filters are produced in Massachusetts and California, while off-the-shelf items such as surgical scissors, first aid supplies and disposable thermometers are made in the Middle West [14].

Even more to the point, some high tech firms perform their research, development, testing, and evaluation in Massachusetts and ship off more routine manufacturing and assembly operations to states where labor and other costs are lower. Massachusetts' two leading minicomputer firms, Digital Equipment (DEC) and Data General, for example, employ more people outside of the state than inside [23], but the bulk of their product development is performed close to headquarters.

Table 2 shows employment in the 20 manufacturing industries in the state that the Massachusetts DES classifies as high tech, together with Computer and Data Processing. It also shows changes in employment between 1975 and 1979. During this time the total rose by over 30 percent while in computers it increased by 90 percent and in electronic components by 65 percent. High tech employment continued to grow in 1980 and 1981 at a reduced rate. The concentration of employment and of employment growth in electronic components and in computers is self-evident. Other important areas of growth were various instruments and electrical industrial apparatus.

Massachusetts' high tech development is largely indigenous, depending mainly on the growth of existing firms and the start-up of new ones by entrepreneurs with roots in the state, rather than on entrepreneurs, branches, or spin-offs from out of state. It claims a fair number of foreign branches, however [19]. Moreover, its emergence was virtually spontaneous, unabetted by efforts on the part of local interest groups or government to bring it off.[2] It contrasts in this respect with Silicon Valley, whose inception was carefully nurtured by Stanford University, under the leadership of Frederick Terman, beginning in the 1950s. Neither Harvard nor MIT in the Boston area

Table 2
Employment in three-digit high tech industries in Massachusetts, 1979

SIC	Industries	Employment		
		1979	Percent change 1975–1979	Absolute change 1975–1979
367	Electronic components and accessories	44,459	65	17,491
357	Office computing and accounting machines	39,611	90	18,729
366	Communications equipment	29,534	3	958
382	Measuring and controlling instruments	18,119	27	3,908
386	Photographic equipment and supplies	15,180	34	3,876
376	Guided missiles and space vehicles	12,096	11	1,233
364	Electric lighting and wiring equipment	8,993	14	1,144
385	Ophthalmic instruments and supplies	7,038	27	1,462
384	Surgical, medical, dental instruments, and supplies	6,471	54	2,266
383	Optical instruments and lenses	6,283	46	1,991
362	Electrical industrial apparatus	6,222	175	3,965
361	Electrical distribution and transmission equipment	5,813	(54)	(6,892)
369	Miscellaneous electrical machinery, equipment, and supplies	5,350	75	2,200
348	Ordnance and accessories	5,032	22	923
381	Engineering, laboratory and scientific instruments	3,306	21	578
365	Radio and TV receiving equipment	2,925	(5)	(144)
283	Drugs	2,693	(43)	811
387	Watches, clocks, and clockwork–operated devices	1,383	(13)	(206)
363	Household appliances	1,347	13	152
379	Miscellaneous transportation equipment	109	32	(51)
	Totals	221,964	31	54,394
737	Computer and data processing services[a]	11,477	130	6,412

Source: Massachusetts Division of Employment Security, *Employment & Wages, State Summary*, 1975 and 1979.
Note: Based on Massachusetts Department of Employment Security definition.
a. Not included in DES definition.

have involved themselves seriously as institutions in the local technical economy. Nevertheless, the graduates and staff of MIT have provided the single most important source of entrepreneurs to the region.

Hundreds of high tech firms populate the Boston area. Although accurate information on numbers of enterprises is not available, there were almost 900 establishments, including branch plants, in 1980 in the seven fastest growing high tech manufacturing industries in the state, not counting the 700 Computer and Data Processing Service establishments. Of the latter, about two-fifths represented computer programming and software companies, and another two-fifths data processing services.[3] The total number of high tech establishments grew by 50 percent between 1975 and 1980. Most computer firms were founded in the 1960s and 1970s. Dun and Bradstreet data for the electronic computer industry (SIC 3573) show that, of the 54 Massachusetts firms with more than 15 employees in 1979, all but six were founded after 1960 [15]. (The computer industry includes manufacturers of accessories and peripherals as well as central processors.) The state's most successful computer firm, DEC, was founded in the 1950s, as was another market leader, Wang Laboratories.

Massachusetts is also the home of a number of large, pre-war electronic firms, such as the Raytheon Corporation, and the location of branch plants of others such as General Electric and GTE Sylvania. Most have specialized in military and space contracts and employment in these areas was not at the forefront of the state's high tech boom in the late 1970s. Employment in Guided Missiles and Space Vehicles (SIC 376) rose only 7 percent between 1975 and 1980. Some pre-war firms are among the leaders in the new technologies that were on the upswing in the late 1970s, but newer firms were critical to the pattern of development that occurred in Massachusetts.

Four additional characteristics of the high tech industries that have flourished in the state are worthy of note.

First, Massachusetts' economy reflects the notable degree of regional specialization that is evidenced within the electronics industry as a whole. Virtually no advanced integrated circuits are manufactured for the commercial market in Massachusetts, and while the state contains 13 of the nation's top 100 firms in the data processing industry, they are represented almost entirely by one branch, the minicomputer, together with the closely related word processor [1]. Minicomputers stand in between the larger mainframe and the small business and personal computers in terms of capacity, performance, and price, but these distinctions are becoming increasingly blurred with advances in the capabilities of small computers. Minicomputers' first applications were for industrial control and laboratory instrumentation, but by 1978, about half were in use for commercial processing and automation [18]. Increasingly, they are used for data processing and communications.

The market for minicomputers was created when DEC introduced its PDP-8 in 1967. It was the first computer to sell for under $20,000 [5]. The firm now claims 40 percent of the minicomputer market and is second to IBM in total computer sales. With six of the top nine money-makers among minicomputer manufacturers (DEC, Data General, Wang, Honeywell, Prime, Nixdorf) and a number of smaller firms, Massachusetts is the heart of the industry that has experienced the greatest absolute growth in sales of any computer sector in the late 1970s. In 1980, minis accounted for 34 percent of the nation's $26 billion computer industry, and over 70 percent of their value came from Massachusetts firms [1].

Second, while some Massachusetts enterprises are now entering the personal computer market, historically the state has turned out electronic equipment aimed almost entirely at the producer capital market. Hand calculators and electronic games, for examples, are noteworthy by their absence.

Third, the final products produced in the state have tended to be for relatively specialized uses. Minicomputer manufacturers historically relied heavily on Original Equipment Manufacturers (OEMs) to market their products to final users. OEMs package the computers of other firms together with peripherals and their own software to suit the needs of individual clients. The optical, medical and other instruments produced in the state tend, even more than computers, to be aimed at small and specialized markets rather than general purpose, off-the-shelf distribution [16].

Finally, the rapid growth of Massachusetts' high tech industries toward the end of the 1970s was driven by an explosion of new products rather than new processes for manufacturing them. The impetus behind the development of new products was mainly new technology rather than new demand. Although products are, naturally, designed to meet a demand, these were stimulated not by a change in demand but by technological opportunities that were becoming available to the civilian market.

The Roots of Massachusetts' High Tech Boom

Now, let us consider the factors that underlay the revitalization of Massachusetts' high tech economy. The stage was set by a nationwide boom in the commercial market for electronic computers and related industrial equipment and instruments. The drastic reductions in size and cost of computers which had occurred in the late 1960s and early 1970s, together with advances in software design, generated an explosion of opportunities for civilian applications of technologies that had formerly been accessible mainly to the federal government. Semiconductor sales to government fell from 50 percent of the total in 1960 to only 15 percent in 1975 [28]. Recovery from what was at the time the nation's worst postwar recession also helped to spur demand. Employment in high tech industries listed in table 2 grew 25 percent nationwide between 1975 and 1979, compared with 32 percent in Massachusetts.

Table 3 presents a picture of the state's relative share of the nation's employment in the fastest growing high tech industries in Massachusetts in 1975 and again in 1979. Those shares should be compared with the state's less than 3 percent of U.S. population and employment. The fourth column shows the share of the state's employment growth in an industry that was "explained" by U.S. growth. Office Computing and Accounting Machines substantially outpaced national growth while Measuring and Controlling Instruments fell far behind.

The main question we now focus on is, What were the conditions that made it possible for Massachusetts to capture a disproportionate share of the overall increase in the nation's high tech activity? To find an answer, we need to consider (1) the particular resource and other locational factors that such industries depend on and the state's ability to supply them, (2) the way in which spatial concentration, or agglomeration, of high tech firms enhances the productivity of those resources, (3) the factors that led relatively new enterprises to capture

Table 3

Massachusetts employment and change relative to United States, 1975 and 1979 for selected high tech industries

SIC	Industries	Massachusetts employment as percentage of U.S. employment		Percent change U.S. employment/percent change Massachusetts employment	Absolute increase Massachusetts employment (thousands)
		1975	1979	1975–1979	1975–1979
367	Electronic components and accessories	8.0	8.4	0.85	17.5
357	Office computing and accounting machines	7.2	10.0	0.43	18.7
382	Measuring and controlling instruments	8.3	7.7	1.44	3.9
386	Photographic equipment and supplies	9.3	11.4	0.32	3.9
376	Guided missiles and space vehicles	10.3	11.9	0.91	1.2
737	Computer and data processing services	3.5	4.2	0.68	6.4
385	Ophthalmic goods	15.4	15.3	1.00	1.5
384	Medical instruments and supplies	3.8	4.6	0.54	2.3
383	Optical instruments and lenses	19.3	19.6	0.98	2.0
362	Electrical industrial apparatus	1.1	2.5	0.11	4.0
369	Miscellaneous electrical mechanical equipment and supplies	2.4	3.0	0.53	2.2

Source: Computed from data in Massachusetts Division of Employment Security, *Employment & Earnings, State Summary*, and U.S. Bureau of Labor Statistics, *Employment & Earnings, United States*.

such a large share of the high tech market, together with the circumstances that made Massachusetts such a fertile spawning ground for such firms.

Physical Resources

The current wave of electronics-based high tech industries is unfettered by the constraints that have traditionally explained industrial location: the need to locate close to a natural resource or to where shipping costs to suppliers and markets are minimized. The natural resources employed are mobile and the very high value-to-weight ratio of products makes transport considerations irrelevant, access to good air freight service being the one transportation requirement. *Speed* of transportation and close communication among suppliers, customers, and competitors provide significant advantages to firms in these rapidly evolving industries, however. Nevertheless, access to a number of "man-made" resources provides important economic advantages to high tech establishments, most importantly a skilled labor force, a technological infrastructure and a venture capital market.

Labor Supply

Labor is, in theory, mobile but its mobility cannot be achieved without a cost to the employer, and this cost is much higher in some locations than in others. The most critical manpower need in high technology industries is for scientists, engineers and other technical personnel. In addition, high tech firms require other skills, ranging from low paid operatives to more experienced and flexible production line workers and skilled craftsmen. Requirements vary from one product to another. Manufacturers of semiconductors in Silicon Valley require a demanding combination of highly trained engineers and low skilled production line employees in their fabricating plants, for example [28]. Table 4 indicates the relatively high proportion of professional and technical personnel employed in Massachusetts in those industries in which such employees constitute 20 percent or more of all workers. Note that in Office Computing and Accounting Machinery the percentage of 35.6 is more than three times the average for manufacturing as a whole. In electronic components, however, a diverse industry in the state, the percentage is only slightly greater than the percentage for all industries combined, though twice the

Table 4

Professional and technical employees in industries in which they constitute 20 percent of workers, Massachusetts, 1976

SIC	Industry title	Employment[a]		Percent professional or technical
		All	Professional or technical	
	All industries	2,299,200	428,000	18.6
	All manufacturing	595,200	64,300	10.8
	Selected durable goods industries			
194	Sighting and fire control equipment	3,500	1,900	55.2
383	Optical instruments and lenses	4,700	1,800	37.8
357	Office, computing and accounting machinery	23,100	8,200	35.6
343	Plumbing and heating products (except electrical)	1,200	400	31.9
381	Engineering and scientific instruments	1,900	600	30.1
382	Instruments for measuring and controlling	9,600	2,800	28.9
192	Ammunition (except small arms)	11,500	3,300	28.6
361	Electrical distribution and transmission equipment	19,300	5,000	26.0
386	Photographic equipment and supplies	12,100	3,100	26.0
366	Communications equipment	22,000	5,200	23.4
367	Electronic components and accessories	30,300	6,600	21.8
	Selected nonmanufacturing industries			
89	Miscellaneous services[b]	32,600	19,500	59.7
82	Educational services	220,500	128,600	58.3
80	Medical and other health services	203,200	90,500	44.5
81	Legal services	10,500	3,600	34.6
86	Nonprofit membership organizations	48,100	16,800	34.2
84	Museums and art galleries	2,200	500	23.8
91	Federal government	57,800	12,900	22.3

Source: Massachusetts Division of Employment Security. *Variety and Distribution of Occupations in Massachusetts, 1976*, March 1980, p. 3.
a. 1976 Wage and Salary Employment (excludes self-employed).
b. Engineering and architectural services; nonprofit educational and research agencies; accounting and bookkeeping services; other N.E.C.

average for manufacturing. Firms will generally locate at the source of professional talent or where they can attract it from outside easily. Best of all for such firms is to set up shopless where the spectrum of different skill requirements can be met without wages and salaries being bid up to noncompetitive levels.

Ten of the state's academic institutions supply most of the scientists and engineers to the local labor market. A survey by the Massachusetts High Technology Council, whose member firms make up about 50 percent of high tech employment in the state, showed that about 80 percent of the college graduates that they hired between 1978 and 1980 held degrees from Massachusetts institutions [24]. In 1981 almost a thousand Bachelor's degrees in electrical or computer engineering were awarded in the state (5.5 percent of the nation's total), 330 Masters' degrees, and 57 Doctorates, not including degrees in related disciplines awarded at Harvard, where they are not classified as engineering degrees [37]. In 1975 over 9 percent of the nation's Ph.D.s in mathematics, computer sciences, and electrical engineering combined were awarded by Massachusetts institutions [33]. MIT supplied most of the state's Ph.D.s and about half of the Master's in electrical and computer engineering. Far more important than numbers is the quality of MIT's degrees. In two recent surveys MIT's electrical engineering and computer science departments were ranked number one in the nation [8,16]. Northeastern University in Boston, which is said to have the largest engineering enrollment in the country and supports extensive evening and work study programs, is second to MIT in the number of electrical and computer engineering degrees granted in the state.

Massachusetts' own institutions are especially important to its economy in view of evidence that New England attracts few engineers and scientists from out of state while doing a good job of holding onto its own. A study conducted for The Center for Policy Alternatives in 1979 [33] suggested that, in 1976, as many as 92 percent of electrical engineers who had received their last schooling in New England may have remained there.[4] The Boston area's unique concentration of academic institutions, together with outstanding cultural amenities, creates an environment that no doubt helps to entice degree holders to remain. The relatively large supply of engineers and various types of computer analysts in the Boston area is reflected in the fact that salaries are not above those paid in other metropolitan areas and are lower than in some centers of high tech development [30,34].

In addition to scientists and engineers, Massachusetts' economy provides a greater than average proportion of technicians, skilled and semiskilled machinists, metal workers, and related craftsmen, and a lower than average proportion of operatives, insofar as one can judge from the numbers actually employed in such classes [21]. A large pool of unskilled workers who will accept low wages is not available in the state, reflecting in part the population's relatively small proportion of minorities. Minorities make up only 6.7 percent of the state's labor force, compared with more than 11 percent in the nation as a whole. By contrast, the labor demand generated by the specialized needs of the semiconductor industry in Santa Clara County was able to attract a "massive influx" of unskilled, predominantly minority workers, primarily Mexican-American and Filipino-American, who had been displaced from California and other Southwest agricultural work [28]. In 1970, 17.5 percent of the population in Santa Clara county was made up of Spanish-Americans, and 35 percent of production workers were reported to be minority women [28, table 13b, pp. 77c, 77d].

Wage rates in Massachusetts tend to be slightly below national averages for workers in corresponding job classifications [6], but there is no evidence that this is an important factor in accounting for the location of high tech industries in the state. On the other hand, a stable supply of experienced workers is, according to the manager of one major instruments company, the main reason that its operations are located in the state.

Technological Infrastructure

Massachusetts inherited a technological infrastructure of special importance to new and growing electronics firms. The state has historically supported a large machinery industry, begun in the nineteenth century to serve textiles and other nondurable mills. During and after World War II, its emphasis shifted to supplying defense and space contractors, increasingly linked to the electronics industry. As the electronics industry grew, the infrastructure expanded to meet its needs. The 65 percent rate of growth in employment by suppliers of electronic components and accessories in the late 1970s was second only to that of the computer industry and greater in absolute terms.

The infrastructure includes a network of job shoppers that supply made-to-order circuit boards, precision machinery, metal parts, and subassemblies, as well as electronic components, all particularly critical to new start-ups that are developing prototypes and to manufacturers of customized equipment for small markets. In addition, dozens, if not hundreds, of consulting firms, specializing in hardware and software populate the region to serve new firms and old. Faculty at the area's universities augment the supply. According to a member of MIT's electrical engineering faculty, the highest level of technology in components and parts is available in the Boston area. Firms can get what they want quickly and supervise its production. At the same time, the very best in software expertise can be had. The only shortcoming is a lack of proximity to the leading semiconductor manufacturers.

While parts and subassemblies can, in principle, be ordered from out of state, in the design stage close contact with suppliers is more than a convenience. Freeman, noting the shorter lead time in development of American electronics products compared with British, suggested that one reason is that components and subassemblies of all types are much more quickly available in the United States [13]. This, he says, "applies to standard 'off-the-shelf' components, which often have long delivery delays in Europe, and to 'specials' made for a particular customer. Some European firms fly in components from the United States rather than wait, but if they intend to use European components at the production stage, this creates serious design problems" [13, pp. 67–68].

Venture Capital

Among the top 100 venture capital investors in the United States in 1981, the value of total investments by Boston firms stood fourth in the nation, after New York, San Francisco, and Chicago [43, table, p. 82]. Boston's total was slightly more than a third that of New York and a little more than half that of the Bay Area. Its relatively high rank is probably more a consequence than a cause of the state's high tech boom. Venture capital investors are drawn to locations where promising entrepreneurs proliferate. Nevertheless, some students of the subject argue that Boston investors have historically been more venturesome than those in most other cities, often tracing their attitude toward risk back to the financiers of the eighteenth-century whaling fleets. But another view is that Boston investors in this century were conservative and reluctant to risk capital in new ventures until the enterprising Boston company, American Research and Development, came along. It took it upon itself to support new innovative companies in the 1950s and to help guide them through the perilous early stages of development. ARD gave DEC its start and, itself, became the first publicly owned venture capital company in the country. In any case, it appears that in the postwar era, new firms were in a better position to find venture capital in Boston than in many other parts of the country.

Other Resources

The state provides excellent building space at relatively low cost, good surface and air transportation, and attractive residential neighborhoods with easy access to work sites. Abandoned mills have served as inexpensive quarters for young firms' labor-intensive operations. Frequent and direct air transport service to major cities is critical to an industry in which speed of delivery often makes the difference between winning and losing a sale and manufacturers guarantee overnight delivery of replacement parts. All of these requirements can be met in some other locations as well, but not necessarily in combination with the additional resources that have helped to spur development in the state.

Agglomeration Externalities

For firms in some industries or at some stages of development there are important advantages in locating near to complementary and competitive enterprises as well as to customers. These advantages result from "external economies of scale." Growth in size and number of firms in the same and related industries within a given geographical area leads to economies in production or marketing for all such firms. So long as the externalities of agglomeration are, on balance, positive in an industry, we expect a tendency for it to grow faster in a region the greater the degree of agglomeration there, other things being equal. This may help to explain the fact that Massachusetts' high tech industries outpaced the national growth rate and also the tendency for sectors of the industry to be spatially concentrated in a few locations in the United States.

Agglomeration externalities are widely acknowledged in the literature on regional location and urbanization, but usually in the context of the generalized benefits enjoyed by firms located in close proximity to a wide range of urban services. Vernon [42], however, recognized the specialized advantages of agglomeration for certain industries in New York City that survive by continually innovating, such as publishing, the arts, and garment manufacturers with frequent style changes. Hollywood's concentration of television and motion picture producers is another case in point. New industries, undergoing rapid technological development, are in a similar position to benefit from agglomeration externalities specific to their industries. The large amount of regional specialization in many high tech sectors suggests that, for them, such advantages are significant. Sixty-seven percent of the computer industry in the United States is located in five states. A high proportion of the nation's merchant semiconductor industry, as we saw, is headquartered in Silicon Valley, while the producers of over two-thirds of all minicomputers are centered in Massachusetts. These concentrations cannot be attributed to natural resource or transportation cost advantages.

One thing that agglomeration has done for Massachusetts is to enhance the resource advantages for high tech firms that were described in the preceding section, by expanding the labor market, the technological infrastructure, and the venture capital market. Choices for job hunters and horizontal and vertical job mobility are expanded by agglomeration, and opportunities for associating with colleagues who share similar interests are enhanced. All help to attract and hold skilled professionals within a regional labor market. For an employer, expansion of the labor market is particularly important in computers and semiconductors where job turnover is very high and technical skills in short supply. New and expanding firms hire their "know-how" by bidding experienced employees away from competing firms. Finding and attracting such employees is greatly facilitated for employers who are surrounded by hundreds of related enterprises.

The agglomeration of innovative enterprises and the tendency of new ones to spin off from them has drawn venture capital to the Boston and San Francisco areas as we saw earlier. Expansion of the venture capital market in a region in turn makes it even more attractive to new ventures. Capital is, of course, mobile, but, all else being equal, venture capital firms prefer to put their money into enterprises whose proximity makes it easy to exercise oversight and guidance during the early stages of development.

Massachusetts inherited a strong technological infrastructure, but the agglomeration of electronics firms encouraged its further growth and diversity. Producers of electronics products are caught up in a network of mutual interdependencies, linking manufacturers of electronic components, parts and subassemblies, makers of computers and their peripherals along with their distributors, designers of software, manufacturers of industrial equipment and instruments that incorporate microprocessor and other computer technologies, makers of equipment for testing their performance, and so forth. There are obvious advantages for such mutually dependent firms in locating close to each other.

Beyond enhancing Massachusetts' natural advantages, agglomeration permits its entrepreneurs to be at the center of action and sources of information. Knowledge of current developments in technology, products, and markets is critical to firms in a rapidly evolving industry. Keeping tabs on what the competition is up to and being quick to identify and take advantage of new market niches are essential to success when less than a year may elapse before one new product is replaced by another.

One by-product of geographical concentration of electronics firms seems generally agreed to be the most important one in producing new economic growth in Massachusetts. That is its stimulus to hard work, new ideas, and entrepreneurial activity. The "pressure cooker" atmosphere induced by close proximity to competitors is an inducement to turn out new products and get them to the market quickly. The example of colleagues "making it" in their own backyard seems to prod young engineers and scientists to develop new products and create their own enterprises with which to launch them. Speaking of former colleagues who had succeeded in founding a major new enterprise, a former vice-president of Data General, who left to start his own computer firm, had this to say: "These guys were just like you and me. There was nothing unique or special about them. So I figured if they can do it, why can't I?" [36, p. 20].

The external benefits of agglomeration described here are especially advantageous to new or small firms, sometimes allowing them to benefit from economies of scale or of vertical integration that only large enterprises could otherwise enjoy. As the size of a spatial cluster grows, however, negative externalities from congestion may begin to overtake the positive ones. There is evidence that high land and housing costs in Santa Clara County has caused some establishments to relocate, but to date, Massachusetts has not suffered from such impacts.

The Role of New Firms and Their Sources

The nationwide high tech boom was, as we saw, driven mainly by technological opportunities opened up by advances in semiconductor and computer technologies that led to smaller and cheaper computers with higher performance and to an explosion of possibilities for new applications. With minor exceptions, advances in these fields were led by firms that had been founded after the invention of the transistor at Bell Laboratories and the development of the computer in the 1940s. New firms such as Fairchild and Intel in California were at the forefront of advances in semiconductor technology that followed, along with Texas Instruments, a small company that transferred into electronics from research in petroleum exploration equipment. In minicomputers, DEC, Data General, Wang, Prime, and Computervision in Massachusetts, and Hewlett Packard in Palo Alto, are all children of the postwar electronics revolution. Almost 80 percent of all minicomputer sales in 1980 and 1981 were accounted for by postwar firms.[5]

In Massachusetts, new firms have also made their mark in instruments (e.g., Teradyne, Analog Devices) and in software and data processing services. Pre-war firms, such as GenRad and the Foxboro Company have also been successful in manufacturing instruments and industrial apparatus. But, as we saw earlier, virtually all of the computer firms in the state were founded in the 1950s or later, and the pattern, as reflected in Dun and Bradstreet data, is similar for the four other major computer manufacturing states [15]. The same can be said for the one instrument industry for which comparable data have been published, medical instruments [14].

If we accept the fact that a succession of postwar firms played the central role in the high tech boom of the late 1970s, then a comparative advantage in spawning new firms during the postwar era is a third factor in explaining why a region's high tech growth would outpace its competitors.

Massachusetts' advantage in this respect springs from two sources: it is rich in the origins of new entrepreneurs, and entrepreneurs tend to set up shop near to their origins. Entrepreneurs in the electronics fields come mainly from the staffs of universities and their research labs and from other high tech firms. MIT and Harvard have historically been leaders in the development of computer hardware and software. Beginning in the 1930s and during and shortly after World War II, each sponsored laboratories that performed pathbreaking research in these fields as well as in radar, instrumentation and other electronics-based technologies.

Jay Forrester, at MIT's Digital Computer Laboratory, developed one of the first high speed digital computers, the landmark Whirlwind, and invented the magnetic core memory.[6] At Harvard, Howard Aiken, with support from IBM, developed the Automatic Sequence Controlled Computer in the early 1940s. MIT's Draper Instrumentation Laboratory, founded during World War II to deal with problems of guidance and inertial navigation instrumentation, continued into the postwar era to sponsor research related to ballistic missile and space craft guidance and navigation. MIT's Lincoln Laboratory was founded shortly after the war to perform research for the Air Force in radar, computer technology, and space communications, while the Radiation Lab, founded during the war, became a leader in the development and application of radar. It was later replaced by the Research Lab for Electronics. At Harvard, the Cruft Laboratory, established during the war, was the first computer laboratory in the nation. Most of the laboratories still exist, and others have been added, such as MIT's Artificial Intelligence Laboratory, a pioneer in its discipline. Most received government financing, but some have been privately supported.

Research laboratories in Massachusetts have been an extraordinarily rich source of new entrepreneurs in the state. Roberts [25,26] located more than 175 new Massachusetts firms that had been founded by former full-time employees of four of MIT's research facilities and three engineering departments during the 1960s alone, and he believes that by no means all were located. Eighty percent of them had survived after five years. Earlier, as we saw, Kenneth Olson founded DEC and later introduced the first minicomputer, designed after one whose development he had supervised at MIT's Lincoln Laboratory. An Wang established his firm in 1951, after making an important contribution to the development of computer memory at Harvard's Computation Laboratory. Many others have succeeded in commercializing products that they themselves helped to develop at one such laboratory.

The ready market provided by military and space procurement contracts was a boon to new firms in the 1950s and 1960s. This fact raises the question of whether MIT's unusual success in "parenting" new firms at this time was tied in part to its willingness to accept military contracts at a time when many other academic institutions were turning them down.

The second main source of founders of new firms is other high tech firms. In the study referred to above, Roberts found 39 firms that had spun off from one large employer alone in Massachusetts [25]. Engineers and scientists repeatedly leave their employers to commercialize and market new products whose concepts they helped to develop in the laboratory of a former employer. It is fairly common for a single entrepreneur to have started several firms, selling out his share in a company once the product is launched to try his luck with another new product and a new enterprise. Thus, many spin-offs have produced several generations of new firms.[7]

It would require a major research effort to systematically document all of the spin-offs in Massachusetts alone, but even a cursory reading of the trade journals confirms the strong lineal descent described above (see, for example, [44]). Indeed, it is more of a challenge to find new enterprises whose founders did not come from an academic laboratory or another high tech firm than the other way around.

Among the most successful firms in Roberts' sample he found a high degree of technology transfer from MIT laboratories. A more recent set of interviews by the Center for Policy Alternatives at MIT, which covered officers of 22 randomly selected computer firms founded in Massachusetts between 1965 and 1975, discovered that half of their products were the result of direct technology transfer from previous employers and another quarter indirect transfer [41].

It is evident that a major force in the expansion of a region's high tech economy has been the three-tiered tendency for lots of new growth to be generated by new firms, for new firms to be spawned by existing firms, and for the new founders to choose to locate near the firms from which they spin off. Like agglomeration externalities, the tendency gives an advantage to a region with a head start: expansion builds on itself. The region benefits not only from expansion of its existing firms, but by capturing more than its share of the nation's growth due to new firm formation as well. In markets where opportunities for new firms are great, these advantages are significant.

It should not be overlooked that the spectacular success of a single firm can have a profound influence on a region's economic development. DEC is directly responsible for 10 percent of high tech employment in the state and indirectly for a great deal more, not only by virtue of its spin-offs but through suppliers of hardware and software to its customers. Fairchild in Palo Alto, Texas Instruments in Dallas, Control Data in Minneapolis, Motorola in Phoenix, are other firms whose successes have made an important difference to their local economies.

Although there are well over a hundred computer manufacturing establishments in Massachusetts, at least 80 percent of their employment is in establishments that have more than 500 workers and over two-thirds are in establishments with more than 1,000.[8] The number employed in firms with more than a given number of employees is even larger than it is for establishments of a given size. Thus, the most conspicuous advantage of a state's having many small computer firms appears to be the increased chance that some small firm in the state will grow to be a DEC or a Wang. The transition from being a small to a large firm is strewn with obstacles. The shift from an entrepreneurial style that generates new products to one that will usher a growing firm through the organizational and financial challenges facing a large enterprise often proves too much for the managers of creative new companies. Also, a high percentage of successful new firms are bought out by large companies early in their careers. Large firms account for most of the employment in the state among manufacturers of instruments for measuring and controlling as well, but in electronic components, optical and medical instruments, and in software, all or most employees work for small firms.

It is evident that the importance of new enterprises in spearheading innovations in electronics during the past two and a half decades has influenced not only the pace and direction of innovation but the locational pattern of the industry as well. The fact that most new enterprises are founded by ex-employees of other firms or of research labs in the same location and the strong advantages for new firms of agglomeration externalities, has created pressures toward geographical concentration of innovative new enterprises. It has also meant that a region with a head start enjoys an advantage over late developers in capturing new growth. New or small enterprises have not always been at the forefront of innovative activity. In the early days of electronics and computers, for example, the enormous amounts of capital and numerous patents that needed to be controlled barred firms lacking substantial financial backing from entering the competition [13]. Three characteristics of the producer durable electronics that characterized the Massachusetts high tech economy seem to have permitted the success of new enterprise.

First, the opportunities for innovation opened up by fundamental advances in technology were, and remain, far too numerous to be exploited by a few firms. Hundreds of small market niches were created, often too narrow or specialized to entice large firms. Second, for the most part, leaders in markets for older electronic equipment hesitated for some time before making serious entries into the markets for smaller computers, leaving the doors open to newcomers. Finally, traditional entry barriers have been relatively weak. Most important, initial capital costs are relatively low and patents are not very effective.

There is abundant, if spotty, evidence that firms in the Massachusetts sectors of the industry have succeeded with small initial investments. DEC was founded with $70,000 in 1957 [23]. Data General began with $800,000 in the early 1970s [17]. One study of a sample of 15 Massachusetts high tech start-ups in 1975 found a median capital outlay of $15,000 and a range of $3,000 to $300,000, and another study of 23 spin-offs from large Massachusetts high tech firms showed a range from $3,000 to $600,000, with an average of $76,000 [35]. The recent interviews conducted at The Center for Policy Alternatives, of 22 computer firms founded in the state between 1965 and 1975, discovered an average first year equity of $50,000 [4].

Patents have not generally provided very effective barriers to entry into the market for electronic computers and their components

[13,32,40]. Until recently, even systems software was not patentable.[9] A recent statistical analysis of R&D and patents covering a sample of over 2,500 U.S. manufacturing firms [4] found that firms in the computer industry (SIC 3570 and 3573) do not use patents extensively to protect the output of their research departments, in spite of the fact that that industry is the most R&D intensive one in the sample.[10]

Massachusetts and Silicon Valley Compared

While the focus of this study is on the high tech economy of Massachusetts, the striking similarities between that phenomenon and the one on the other side of the continent in Silicon Valley deserve some attention. The analogies between the two are, on the whole, more compelling than the contrasts, but it must be added that there is room for further study in this area.

Each began its takeoff after World War II with heavy support from U.S. military and space programs. In Massachusetts, the four two-digit industries that contain most of its high technology[11] grew almost enough during the quarter century before 1975 to offset the decline in the state's traditional mill industries which became increasingly severe during that period. The four expanding industry groups contain many sectors that were neither high technology nor government supported and some, such as Aircraft and Parts, which were supported by the military but are not regarded as high tech in Massachusetts. Many of those subsectors were well established in the state before the beginning of World War II. But comparisons of long term trends in three or four-digit SICs are not possible because of serious gaps in data at the state level and major reclassifications of SICs, especially in the newly emerging high tech industries, in the late 1960s, and early 1970s.

Out in the Bay Area, high tech replaced apricot and walnut orchards rather than textile mills, but there, too, it emerged soon after World War II and owed its early support almost entirely to military and space contracts [28].

By the end of the War Massachusetts contained the country's most distinguished combination of academic-based laboratories supporting research at the frontiers of electronic and computer technologies, and also some well established electrical and electronic companies such as Raytheon and General Electric, both sectors heavily supported by government contracts. But Santa Clara County, which later came to be known as Silicon Valley, had the important advantage at that time of proximity to the emerging aircraft and space industry which was to become the major customer for semiconductors and, indeed, the only customer for integrated circuits for many years.[12] This proximity attracted well established electrical and electronics firms into the county in the 1940s and 1950s and a number of larger national firms established research labs there, e.g., IBM and Lockheed [28]. Thus, in the early postwar period the two regions were on the way to becoming the country's leading centers of the new electronics-based technologies.

Academic centers of excellence are at the heart of both local economies. If the Harvard–MIT axis has its equal anywhere, it is in the San Francisco Bay area, which claims the University of California at Berkeley as well as Stanford. The analogy is even more complete when electrical engineering (including computer science) departments are compared since MIT, Stanford, and Berkeley are generally recognized today to have the nation's leading departments in that field.[13] Both areas have large engineering enrollments in other colleges, but these must be regarded more as consequences than as causes of regional high tech growth. Some say that another common bond between Stanford and MIT is the spirit of entrepreneurship that motivates their graduates and faculty. Although there is lots of anecdotal evidence on this score, it is difficult to assess.

At this point analogies between the two universities give way to contrasts. While MIT's electrical engineering department held a long established reputation at the end of World War II, Stanford's was transformed in the postwar era when Frederick Terman, a professor of electrical engineering at Stanford, returned from administering a wartime project at Harvard, with the aim of raising the West Coast department to a level of eminence and creating a community of technical scholars within the region [11;27;28;39]. He became dean of engineering and later vice-president of the university. His success in attracting government and business financing for this purpose is now legendary. At the same time, it was his idea to develop a research park on the Stanford campus in the hopes of attracting science-based firms whose employees would interact with the university. It opened in

1954, and one of its first tenants was William Shockley's semiconductor firm, which was also the first semiconductor enterprise in the region. Its founder brought with him several experts from Bell Laboratories, where he was one of three scientists credited with invention of the transistor. The firm's most important impact on the region began when eight of these experts left to found Fairchild Semiconductor, headed by Robert Noyce. That firm now counts over 80 enterprises among its offspring or their offspring in the region [31].

Terman assisted many new companies in getting started, among them Varian Associates and Hewlett-Packard, and fostered industry-university cooperation. Stanford's educational arm has been extended into the local high tech community through live, interactive television courses, piped into company quarters, which permit employees to earn degrees without leaving the plant. No dissertation or residency is required for the Master's degree. Currently about 350 students at 50 companies are enrolled in what is called Stanford's Honors Co-op Program [39]. Employers pay double the normal tuition for their employees.

By contrast, the administration of neither MIT nor Harvard has deliberately striven to promote local growth. The notable exception is MIT's Enterprise Forum, a highly regarded monthly gathering at which fledgling entrepreneurs have a chance to present their problems to a panel of experts in a public setting. Neither Massachusetts institution offers continuing education or degree programs in science and technology for nonresidents, and all advanced degrees at MIT require dissertations.

In spite of Stanford's deliberate and successful effort to create a technology-based economy in its backyard, it is difficult to judge the extent to which it was actually responsible for the growth that occurred there. The area's amenities, its underutilized building space in the beginning, and its proximity to UC Berkeley and to the aerospace industry might well have been sufficient to get the ball rolling on their own. In Massachusetts, however, the importance of the university connection is indisputable. It is almost impossible to imagine that the defense- and space-related growth in the postwar period would have occurred on anything like the scale that it did without the stimulus of the academic research labs supported by MIT and Harvard and the outstanding scientific and engineering talent they turned out. These same laboratories played critical roles in spawning the new firms that later were responsible for the high tech revival of the late 1970s. Unlike California, which attracts many engineers and scientists from out of state,[14] Massachusetts depends very heavily on graduates of its own degree programs to provide the technical talent to high tech firms and the entrepreneurship to get them started.

The most apparent difference between the two high tech centers is in what they produce. Silicon Valley has been, since its beginning in the early 1950s, the heart of technological development in the world's semiconductor industry. It can claim a greater share of the advances that have led up to today's silicon chip, following Bell Laboratory's invention of the transistor, than any other site. It should be mentioned, however, that Texas Instruments and Motorola are located elsewhere. Research, development, design, and fabrication of integrated circuits and microprocessors are an important part of the county's high tech industry, while assembly operations generally occur out of state. Computer and instrument firms also crowd the area, probably due in part to the advantages for them of proximity to the center of semiconductor design and manufacture. Such firms often integrate backward, while chip makers integrate forward. They account for more employment in the county than do semiconductor manufacturers [2]. Silicon Valley is, therefore, also the home of some of the nation's leading makers of computers, especially microcomputers, for example, Tandem, Apple, and Hewlett-Packard, which also makes minicomputers.

Massachusetts, on the other hand, produces no advanced integrated circuits to speak of for the merchant market, and its computer industry is, as we saw, heavily concentrated among minicomputers and their close relatives. But both regions contain also a large and diverse mix of enterprises producing instruments, specialized computers, and their peripheral equipment and both claim very large software industries. Each of them is populated by hundreds of small, young firms, one or more of which could grow up to be another DEC or Intel.

The reasons for the contrasting emphasis on semiconductors in Santa Clara County and minicomputers and related equipment along 128 have their roots in early postwar history. When Shockley left Bell Laboratories with a handful of engineers to set up a firm in Stanford dedicated to the further development of the transistor, he laid the cornerstone for the phenomenon which changed the face of the region.

It is of interest that Massachusetts was at one time the leading center of semiconductor manufacturing. Raytheon was the major producer for the open market in the early 1950s, and a new firm, Transitron, founded by a Bell Labs engineer, was second only to Texas Instruments in the late 1950s [5]. But neither Massachusetts firm's market survived the revolution in production techniques of the late 1950s or development of the integrated circuit. Failure to concentrate sufficiently on production processes may have been at the root of their failure, but one can at best speculate as to the difference that their continued success would have made to the economy of the region.

Had Shockley decided to settle along Route 128, or in some third location, the explosive growth of the semiconductor industry might not have taken place in Santa Clara County. But his choice of Palo Alto was not an accident. He holds a degree from Stanford and was looking for a site to which he could attract the nation's top engineers. William Hewlett and David Packard, founders of the earliest and one of the most successful manufacturers of instruments and later computers in that region, also received their undergraduate engineering degrees from Stanford.

In Massachusetts, the seeds of the minicomputer boom were planted by Kenneth Olson, the first and most successful manufacturer of such equipment in the world. But neither was his locating near Route 128 an historical accident. He had managed the project at MIT's Lincoln Laboratory that developed the TX-O, the first high speed, transistorized computer and the model for DEC's PDP-1, after circuits were modified to take account of technological advances. It was followed several years later by the classic PDP-8. The circuit designer from Lincoln Lab was also part of DEC's first team. As we saw, research laboratories at MIT and Harvard were in on the ground floor of the computer revolution. An Wang's founding of what was to become another major minicomputer firm grew out of work at Harvard's Computer Laboratory.

The agglomeration advantages that were noted in Massachusetts are even more evident out West. In semiconductors, dependence on an infrastructure of suppliers is if anything greater, interrelationships between sectors of the high tech industry even stronger and the rate of change of technology still faster, placing even greater emphasis on the need to be in close touch with the generators of new technological developments.[15]

The explosive growth in semiconductor design and technology in Silicon Valley thus reinforces evidence from Massachusetts of the power of agglomeration externalities and of the centripetal force of spin-offs in moulding the spatial concentration of firms in the new electronics industries.

The processes by which minicomputers, on the one hand, and silicon chips, on the other, are produced are widely different. Computers are assembled from modular components (much like consumer audio high fidelity equipment) which, in turn, can be manufactured in large part from standardized components. Chip fabrication, by contrast, involves three stages, two of which are extremely complicated and sensitive processes requiring advanced techniques. There is no reason that one industrial process could not have been as easily performed in either the East Coast or the West Coast location, however, except possibly for the fact that Massachusetts does not have a very large pool of low wage labor to draw upon for work in the semiconductor wafer fabrication plants. Silicon Valley was able to attract immigrant workers from the excess supply in the Southwest [28].

The most stunning parallel between the two regions is in the youthfulness of the dominant enterprises. Virtually all are children of the transistor-computer generation rather than headquarters or branches of pre-war giants in the electronics or office machines industries. With few exceptions, the leaders in the new wave of high technology in both places started up after World War II. We attribute the parallel in California to most of the same factors that explain the importance of new enterprises in Massachusetts' high tech economy: the presence of many small market niches,[16] low barriers to entry, failure of the industrial giants to move quickly into new markets, and agglomeration externalities. Opportunities for exploiting economies of scale appeared earlier in the semiconductor industry than in minicomputers and in some other electronics industries, raising barriers to entry. But more recently the increasing importance of customized chips shows signs of erasing scale advantages and appears to be reopening opportunities for smaller—though not very small—enterprises.

In sum, then, though developments in the two regions display some quantitative and qualitative differences, the overall picture has been remarkably similar and West Coast experience supports our conclusions regarding the forces that have tended to generate spatial concentration of electronics-based high tech industries.

Summation

The Boston area's two great universities, MIT and to a lesser extent Harvard, seem to have provided the most critical stimulus to high tech development there. Their outstanding scientific and engineering laboratories, founded around the time of World War II, came to be singular sources of new ideas, technical manpower and, perhaps most important, entrepreneurs who founded the new firms that became the backbone of the state's recent high tech boom. A large and distinguished academic community also has contributed to a cultural environment that makes the Boston area an attractive place for new firms to be established.

Together with its academic institutions and laboratories, Massachusetts' inheritance from pre-war decades of a few well established electronics firms and a large technological infrastructure positioned it early on to exploit the worldwide ground swell in markets for computers and other electronic products. The head start was particularly important because of two propensities that characterize the industry. First is the explosive tendency for successful new enterprises to spin off from other newly established firms. Second is the importance of agglomeration externalities in stimulating and supporting growth of new firms. Both helped to concentrate expansion in the industry close to its origins. Finally, it should not go unnoticed that in Massachusetts, as well as in Silicon Valley, the early successes of a few individual entrepreneurs powerfully influenced the direction and magnitude of regional development.

None of these factors would have exerted the same pressures toward concentration of the new industries in the region were it not for the fact that those industries were especially hospitable to new enterprises.

The most important of our findings for planners and policymakers who seek to duplicate the 128 experience in other regions would seem to be four. First, Massachusetts' electronics boom occurred basically without the benefit of concerted efforts to make it happen by academic institutions, government bodies or other interest groups. This does not prove that such efforts are necessarily futile, but that they are far from crucial in some cases at least.

Second, the academic institutions that provided much of the momentum are steeped in a tradition of research at the frontiers of developments in electronics, computer science, and instrumentation and compete with a handful of other universities for top ranking in graduate programs in these fields. It remains to be seen whether institutions of lesser rank can provide the same stimulus to innovation.

Third, Massachusetts' new industrial growth was propelled by firms that had gotten their start there after the onset of the electronics revolution, rather than by the expanding and branching into the state of large, established companies. The new firms were especially prolific when it came to spinning off other new firms.

Finally, agglomeration externalities that accrue to firms from close proximity to others engaged in closely related activities in these rapidly evolving industries argue in favor of attempts to achieve a degree of specialization among high tech industries in a given region rather than diversity.

Notes

Based on Nancy S. Dorfman, *Massachusetts' High Technology Boom in Perspective: An Investigation of Its Dimensions, Causes and of the Role of New Firms*, CPA 82-2. The study was funded in part by a grant from the IBM Foundation and by the Japan Steel Professorship at MIT. This paper was originally published in *Research Policy* 12 (1983), 299–316. © 1983, Elsevier Science Publishers B.V. (North-Holland).

1. Data are based on the three-digit SICs that the California Department of Employment Security defines as high technology in [2], using *County Business Patterns* instead of state Division of Employment Security data, which is used elsewhere in this study. In Massachusetts CBP data show high tech employment increasing about 30 percent compared with about 70 percent in Santa Clara County. But Computers and other Office Machines (SIC 357) employment in Massachusetts as reported by CBP is significantly lower in 1979 than that reported by DES and other sources. It has not been possible to resolve this discrep-

ancy but the weight of evidence indicates that CBP understates such employment in Massachusetts.

2. A Boston venture capital firm, American Research and Development, however, is credited with having given a big push to the development of the local high tech economy in the 1950s.

3. Data on employment in Computer Programming and Software Services (SIC 7372) is drawn from U.S. Department of Commerce, *County Business Patterns* (CBP), which is reported by four-digit SIC categories in contrast to the three-digit State Employment Security data on which most of the present analysis is based. Because CBP appears to understate total employment in a number of high tech industries, we have not relied on their data for most purposes.

4. Based on a special cross tabulation of the National Science Foundation's Survey of Scientists and Engineers in 1976. The data are subject to a number of possible biases. Most important, respondents were asked where they received their most recent education rather than degree, so that the site of continuing education might have been reported rather than the location of the degree-granting institution. Also there may have been a greater tendency for degree holders who have remained in the region to respond.

5. Computed from table IV of [30]. Honeywell, one of the few pre-war firms, with the largest minicomputer sales of any older generation firm, bought out a small computer firm in Massachusetts in order to establish a base in the field to tie into its industrial process control activities. Hewlett-Packard, which was established in 1939 when the two founders began to manufacture instruments in a Palo Alto garage, we count as a member of the postwar generation of electronics firms.

6. Forrester later headed MIT's Lincoln Laboratory where Kenneth Olson supervised development of the TX-O computer on which he later modeled the first commercial minicomputer.

7. Henry E. Kloss, who successively founded Acoustic Research, KLH, Advent, and Kloss Video is one of the better-known examples.

8. Estimated from U.S. Department of Commerce, *County Business Patterns, 1979, Massachusetts,* table 1C.

9. In a recent Supreme Court decision, however, it was held that software incorporated in hardware is patentable (Diamond *v.* Diehr and Lutton, 49 L.W. 4194, March 1981).

10. Company data in the survey were taken from Standard and Poor's Compustat tapes.

11. SIC 35 Machinery except industrial, SIC 36 Electrical equipment and supplies, SIC 37 Transportation equipment, and SIC 38 Instruments.

12. In 1962 defense accounted for 100 percent of integrated circuit production, according to [38, table 4-8, p. 91].

13. MIT ranked number one, and Stanford and UC Berkeley each a close second among electrical engineering departments in the nation in the surveys of faculty rankings of their peers in graduate programs, reported in references [8;16]. Stan-

ford was ranked first and MIT second in computer science in [8], and the three universities along with Harvard led the field in terms of overall quality.

14. This observation is based on a conversation with a former "head hunter" employed by a Silicon Valley firm and on numerous examples that have appeared in the trade press.

15. The semiconductor industry has attracted many small companies that manufacture diffusion furnaces, ion implantation machines, epitaxial growth systems, and mask-making systems, all part of a necessary support structure.

16. The government's policy of second sourcing helped to support small semiconductor firms.

References

[1] Pamela Archibald, The Foremost Companies in the Data Processing Industry, *Datamation*, June (1982).

[2] Association of Bay Area Governments, *Silicon Valley and Beyond, High Technology Growth in the San Francisco Bay Area* (Berkeley, December 1981).

[3] W. L. Baldwin, *The Impact of Defense Procurement on Competition in Commercial Markets: Case Studies of the Electronics and Helicopter Industries* (Federal Trade Commission, December 1980).

[4] J. Bound, C. Cummins, Z. Grilliches, B. H. Hall and A. Jaffe, Who Does R&D and Who Patents? National Bureau of Economic Research, Inc., Conference on Patents and Productivity, Cambridge. October 2–4, 1981.

[5] Ernest Braun and Stuart MacDonald, *Revolution in Miniature, the History and Impact of Semiconductor Electronics* (Cambridge University Press, 1978).

[6] Lynn E. Browne, How Different Are Regional Wages? *New England Economic Review*, January/February (1978), 33–43.

[7] Gene Bylinsky, *The Innovative Millionaires* (Charles Scribner, New York, 1976).

[8] Conference Board of Associated Research Councils, *An Assessment of Research Doctoral Programs in the United States* (National Academy Press, Washington, DC, 1983) reported in the *New York Times,* January 17 (1983), 1, B7.

[9] DP Industry Profile, *Datamation*, May 25 (1979), 10.

[10] Nancy S. Dorfman, *Massachusetts' High Technology Boom in Perspective: An Investigation of Its Dimensions, Causes and of the Role of New Firms,* CPA 82-2 (Center for Policy Alternatives, MIT, April, 1982).

[11] Datamation Top 100, *Datamation*, June (1982).

[12] *Electronics*, April 17 (1980), 349.

[13] Christopher Freeman, Research and Development in Electronic Capital Goods, *National Institute Economic Review* 33 (1965), 40–97.

[14] John S. Hekman, Can New England Hold onto Its High Technology Industry? *New England Economic Review*, March/April (1980), 35–42.

[15] John S. Hekman, The Future of High Technology in New England: A Case Study of Computers, *New England Economic Review*, January/February (1980), 4–17.

[16] How Engineering Faculties Rate Each Other, *Science*, December 3 (1982), 980.

[17] Tracy Kidder, *The Soul of a New Machine* (Little, Brown, Boston, 1981).

[18] Sarah Kuhn, *Computer Manufacturing in New England: Structure, Location and Labor in a Growing Industry* (Harvard-MIT Joint Center for Urban Studies, March 1981).

[19] Jane S. Little, Foreign Direct Investment in the United States: Recent Locational Choices of Foreign Manufacturers, *New England Economic Review*, November/December (1980).

[20] Robert T. Lund, Marvin A. Sirbu, Jr. and James M. Utterback, *Microprocessor Applications*, CPA 79-3 (Center for Policy Alternatives, MIT, May 15, 1979).

[21] Massachusetts Department of Employment Security, *Variety and Distribution of Occupations in Massachusetts, 1976* (March 1980).

[22] Massachusetts Division of Employment Security, *High Technology Employment in Massachusetts and Selected States* (April 1981).

[23] Massachusetts Division of Employment Security, *Employment in Massachusetts' Minicomputer Industry* (Fall 1979).

[24] Massachusetts High Technology Council Inc., *Results of Survey on Human Resource Needs* (1981).

[25] Edward B. Roberts and H. A. Wainer, New Enterprises Along Route 128, *Science Journal*, December (1968), 2, 79–83.

[26] Edward B. Roberts, A Basic Study of Innovations, *Research Management*, July (1968).

[27] Ronald Rosenberg, The Learning Center at Top End of Silicon Valley, *The Boston Globe*, November 6 (1982), 1.

[28] Analee Saxenian, *Silicon Chips and Spatial Structure: The Industrial Base of Urbanization in Santa Clara County, California*, Working Paper 345 (Institute of Urban and Regional Development, University of California, Berkeley, March 1981).

[29] David Schwartzman, *Innovation in the Pharmaceutical Industry* (Johns Hopkins Press, Baltimore, 1976).

[30] Scientific Manpower Commission, *Salaries of Scientists, Engineers and Technicians* (Washington, DC, November 1979).

[31] Semiconductor Equipment and Materials Institute, Inc., *Silicon Valley Genealogy* (Mountain View, California, 1983).

[32] Daniel Shimshoni, Aspects of Scientific Entrepreneurship, Ph.D. thesis, Harvard University, May 1966.

[33] Marvin A. Sirbu, Jr., Karen DeVol and Eustaquio Heis, *High Technology Manpower in Massachusetts,* CPA 79-5 (Center for Policy Alternatives, MIT, August 1979).

[34] Source Edp, *1981 Local Metropolitan Computer Salary Survey* (Boston, 1983).

[35] Christopher L. Taylor, New Enterprises Descended from a Technically Based Company, Master's thesis, Sloan School of Management, MIT, June 1981.

[36] *The Boston Business Journal,* March 7 (1983), 20.

[37] *The Boston Globe,* February 9 (1982), 45.

[38] John E. Tilton, *International Diffusion of Technology: The Case of Semiconductors* (The Brookings Institution, Washington, DC, 1971).

[39] Elizabeth Unseem, *Education and High Technology Industry: The Case of Silicon Valley, Summary of Research Findings* (Department of Sociology, University of Massachusetts, Boston, August 1981).

[40] James M. Utterback and Albert E. Murray, *The Influence of Defense Procurement and Sponsorship of Research and Development on the Development of the Civilian Electronics Industry* (Center for Policy Alternatives, MIT, June 30, 1977).

[41] James M. Utterback and Goran Reitberger, *Technology and Industrial Innovation in Sweden, A Study of New Technology-Based Firms,* CPA 83-06 (Center for Policy Alternatives, MIT, May 13, 1982).

[42] Raymond Vernon, *Metropolis 1985* (Doubleday, Garden City, NY, 1963).

[43] *Venture,* June (1982), 82.

[44] The Splintering of the Solid State Electronics Industry, *Innovation* 8 (1969), 2.

Lowell: A High Tech Success Story

Patricia M. Flynn
Federal Reserve Bank of Boston
September 1984

Lowell—a mill town between Boston and the New Hampshire border—has often been touted as a model of high tech revitalization. Once a thriving center of cotton textile manufacturing, the city fell on especially hard times from 1929 through the 1950s as the textile industry fled South, leaving the economy stagnant and unemployment high.

Then, in the 1960s, things began to change due to the efforts of a few aggressive individuals, a considerable sum of money, the coming boom in the high technology sector, and some extraordinary luck. The city was able to wrangle nearly $44 million in state aid and another $54 million in federal and local funds to clean up the area, for example. Native son Paul Tsongas, then a member of Congress, helped get part of the city declared a national park, making it the first national park created east of the Mississippi in the twentieth century.

Perhaps the most significant development was the decision in 1976 by Wang Laboratories, a small computer company at the time, to move its headquarters to Lowell. Although local officials had wanted a larger company to occupy the parcel that Wang subsequently purchased, they soon learned to live with it. Wang immediately went through a period of explosive growth and soon became the single largest employer in the area. Later more computer companies and other high tech firms moved in as well. Without a doubt, Lowell benefited mightily from its proximity to Boston and the high technology infrastructure of eastern Massachusetts.

In this 1984 paper, Flynn, an associate professor at Bentley College then on leave as a visiting scholar at the Federal Reserve Bank of Boston, outlines the dimensions of the dramatic turnaround in Lowell. More impor-

tant, she provides some insights on the unique nature of Lowell's boom, and on the dangers of seeking to replicate the "Lowell model" in other regions.

High technology has been heralded as a panacea for most, if not all, of America's economic ills. It is not surprising, therefore, that high technology has not lived up to all of our expectations. Yet while debate continues over both the quantity and quality of jobs in high technology industries, states throughout the country are actively seeking to attract these employers. Case studies of the impact of high technology employment in particular localities can provide a better understanding of the strengths and weaknesses of this sector and can offer guidance in developing local and regional economic development strategies.

This article is about a high technology "success" story: Lowell, Massachusetts. Lowell today is viewed as a "model of reindustrialization" for older cities throughout the United States that have lost jobs in their traditional manufacturing industries. Section 1 describes the transformation of the Lowell Labor Market Area, located 25 miles northwest of Boston, from a stagnating, depressed economy into a thriving center for high technology employment. (See the map.) The Lowell area, which includes the towns of Billerica, Chelmsford,

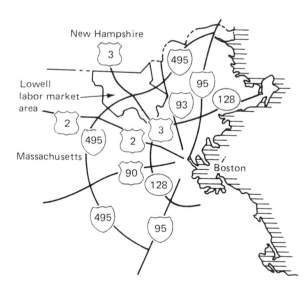

Lowell labor market

Dracut, Dunstable, Tewksbury, Tyngsborough, and Westford in addition to the city of Lowell, had a population of 227,000 in 1980. The long-term prospects of economic growth and development in the Lowell area are addressed in section 2. The article concludes with a section on the feasibility of extending the Lowell model to cities and towns suffering economic decline today.

1. The Revitalization of the Lowell Economy

A Brief History

An infusion of textile mills in the nineteenth century transformed Lowell from a sparsely populated rural area into the state's second largest city and the heart of the U.S. textile industry. During the period 1826 to 1850 the population of Lowell expanded from 2,500 to over 33,000; by 1920 the population had more than trebled to over 112,000.

The impetus behind this growth came from manufacturing—specifically textiles. Employment data for the textile industry in Lowell in the nineteenth century are not available; however, production statistics for the period 1835 to 1888 indicate a substantial growth of jobs. For instance, the number of textile mills in Lowell rose from 22 to 175, and the output of cotton cloth rose from approximately 750,000 to almost 5,000,000 yards per week. By the early 1920s, employment in the textile industry accounted for over 40 percent of all manufacturing employment in Lowell.[1]

Lowell's dramatic growth came to an abrupt halt in the late 1920s. Manufacturing employment in the city fell almost 50 percent between 1924 and 1932. This decline partially reflected the Great Depression experienced throughout the country. In addition, however, much of New England's textile industry shifted to the South during this period. Hence, when the national economy recovered from the Depression, Lowell did not. Instead, the area experienced economic stagnation for the next three decades.

In the 1960s the Lowell economy witnessed a revival that spilled over into the entire labor market area. Population and employment expanded faster than that of the state and the nation throughout the 1960s and the 1970s. Local employment growth was particularly

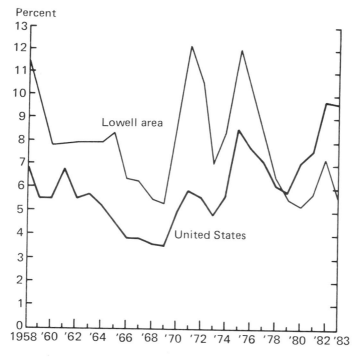

Chart 1: Unemployment rates in the Lowell area and the United States, 1958–1983. Prior to 1973 the unemployment rates are for the Lowell standard metropolitan statistical area. Thereafter they refer to the Lowell market area. These two areas are virtually identical. (Source: Massachusetts Division of Employment Security, and the U.S. Department of Labor, *Employment and Earnings, Bureau of Labor Statistics Centennial, 1884–1984.*)

rapid after the nationwide recession in the mid-1970s—growing over 6 percent a year on average from 1976 to 1982, a rate more than double that of both Massachusetts and the country overall.

This relatively fast employment growth significantly reduced the local unemployment rate compared to the nation's. (See chart 1.) The historically large gap between Lowell's unemployment rate and the national rate began to narrow in the late 1960s and closed considerably after the recession in the mid 1970s. Since 1979 the Lowell area's unemployment rate has been below that of the United States. In March 1984, the local area's unemployment rate fell to a postwar low of 4.3 percent. Comparable rates for Massachusetts and the nation were 5.8 percent and 8.1 percent, respectively.

Employment by Industry

Although the Lowell area maintained its tradition of being more oriented to manufacturing than either Massachusetts or the nation, the manufacturing base in the local economy declined in both absolute and relative terms during the 1960s and early 1970s. In the early 1970s, however, employment patterns within Lowell's manufacturing sector became mixed. While significant employment losses continued in the nondurable goods manufacturing sector, several durable goods manufacturing industries experienced rapid growth. The electrical and electronic equipment industry, for example, grew at a rate of over 9 percent a year between 1970 and 1976, a rate more than three times that of total employment in the Lowell area. The nonelectrical machinery industry also experienced above average growth.

In the late 1970s, expansion of the durable goods industries overwhelmed growth in the services sector, reversing the shift away from manufacturing in the local economy. In contrast, the manufacturing employment base in both Massachusetts and the nation continued to decline. (See chart 2.) Lowell's nonelectrical machinery industry, which includes the computer industry, led the local employment boom, expanding an average of 43 percent a year from 1976 to 1982. The instruments industry grew by 24 percent a year during that

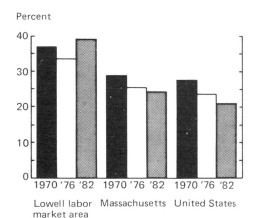

Percent

Lowell labor market area   Massachusetts   United States

Chart 2: Manufacturing employment as a percent of total nonagricultural employment. (Source: U.S. Department of Labor, Bureau of Labor Statistics, *Employment and Earnings, States and Areas, 1939–1982,* vol. 1; and *Employment and Earnings, July 1983.*)

period. In addition, employment in the transportation equipment industry, which is dominated locally by the guided missiles and space vehicles industry, expanded by 15 percent a year. Comparable rates of employment growth at the state and national levels were less than 7 percent for the nonelectrical machinery industry and below 6 percent in the instruments industry, while there were actual declines in the transportation equipment industry. (See appendix table 1.)

By 1982, 39 percent of all nonagricultural employment in the Lowell area was in manufacturing compared to 24 percent in Massachusetts and 21 percent in the nation. (See appendix table 2.) More than one in every four of Lowell's workers were employed in the durable goods manufacturing sector alone.

High Technology Employment

The bulk of the fast growing manufacturing industries in the Lowell area are associated with high technology employment. The term "high technology" generally refers to industries that operate at the "cutting edge" of new technologies. These industries are usually identified by their relatively high proportions of research and development (R&D) expenditures and of professional and technical workers. Based on the Massachusetts Division of Employment Security definition, high technology manufacturing employment accounted for 24 percent of all employment in the Lowell area in 1982.[2] By comparison, such employment accounted for less than 10 percent of total employment in Massachusetts and less than 4 percent of all employment in the United States in 1982.

Three industries—office, accounting, and computing machines; guided missiles and space vehicles; and electronic components and accessories—were responsible for over 90 percent of the local high technology growth from 1976 to 1982. In fact, the office, accounting and computing machines industry accounted for over 70 percent of the growth in high technology manufacturing employment in the Lowell area and 45 percent of total job growth.

Employment by Occupation

The occupational composition of the traditional manufacturing industries in the Lowell area differs significantly from that of the high technology industries entering the area. Statewide data indicate that the high technology industries, vital to the Lowell economy, have a much higher percentage of their employment in professional and technical occupations. (These occupational data are not available specifically for the Lowell area.) In addition, the high technology industries employ a relatively large percentage of skilled production workers. A substantially lower percentage of the work force in these newer industries is in low-skilled and unskilled jobs.

More specifically, a comparison of the occupational composition of four traditional industries in which the Lowell area has lost the greatest number of jobs in recent years (apparel, leather, textiles, and food) with that of the four high technology industries in which job growth has been the largest (office, accounting and computing machines, guided missiles and space vehicles, electrical and electronic equipment, and instruments) indicates:

• Professional workers accounted for less than 2 percent of the employment in the four traditional industries, but comprised between 9 percent and 26 percent of the workers in the four high technology industries. (See table 1.)

• Engineers made up 1 percent or less of the work force in the traditional industries, in contrast to 8 percent to 20 percent of the workers in the high technology industries.

• Skilled technician workers were less than 2 percent of the total in the traditional industries, while the range in the high technology industries was from 6 percent to 11 percent.

• Low-skilled and unskilled operatives and laborers held one-half to three-quarters of the jobs in the apparel, leather, and textile industries, compared to approximately one-fifth to just over one-third of the jobs in the newer industries.

However, while professional and technical occupations account for a greater share of jobs in the newer industries than in the traditional industries, blue-collar and clerical jobs continue to account for the majority of workers in these high technology industries. In fact, unskilled assembler (which does not include the higher paid electrical and electronic assembler) was the largest occupation in the office, accounting and computing machines, electrical and electronic equipment, and instruments industries in Massachusetts in 1980; assembler was the second largest occupation, following engineer, in the guided missiles and space vehicles industry.

Table 1
Occupational distribution of selected traditional and high technology manufacturing industries in Massachusetts, 1980

Occupation	Traditional industries				High technology industries			
	Apparel	Leather	Food and kindred products	Textiles	Office, accounting and computing machines	Guided missiles and space vehicles	Electrical and electronic equipment	Instruments
Managerial and professional specialty	5.7%	8.6%	11.9%	9.6%	31.4%	30.6%	20.9%	21.2%
Executive, administrative, and managerial	4.7	7.1	10.4	7.7	14.8	4.9	9.6	11.6
Professional specialty	1.0	1.5	1.5	1.9	16.6	25.7	11.3	9.6
Engineers	0.2	0.5	0.4	1.0	10.8	19.4	8.3	8.0
Technicians, sales, and administrative support	11.8	16.4	19.3	18.3	36.3	26.0	22.4	27.9
Technicians	1.0	0.5	1.0	1.7	11.1	8.6	6.6	9.8
Sales	1.5	2.5	4.4	1.5	1.9	0.0	1.9	2.2
Administrative support (including clerical)	9.3	13.4	13.9	15.1	23.3	17.4	13.9	15.9
Service	1.2	2.0	3.4	1.6	2.2	2.2	1.8	2.0
Farming, forestry, and fishing	0.0	0.0	0.0	0.0	0.0	0.0	0.0	0.0
Precision production, craft and repair	9.3	10.6	20.7	16.3	11.1	13.7	18.6	18.6
Mechanics, repairers, and construction trades	1.3	1.7	4.7	8.0	3.9	4.9	4.0	5.4
Precision production	8.0	8.9	16.0	8.3	7.2	8.8	14.5	13.2
Operators, fabricators, and laborers	72.0	62.5	44.7	54.1	19.0	27.5	36.2	30.4
Total	100.0%	100.0%	100.0%	100.0%	100.0%	100.0%	100.0%	100.0%

Source: U.S. Department of Commerce, Bureau of the Census, 1980, Public Use Tapes, unpublished.
Note: Columns may not sum to 100.0% due to rounding.

Earnings and Wages

Many of the fast-growing high technology firms in the Lowell area pay well relative to the service-producing sectors and to the more traditional manufacturing industries in the area. Average annual earnings in the services and retail sectors, for instance, were almost 25 percent and 40 percent, respectively, below the average for all industries in the Lowell area in 1980. In contrast, in the durable goods manufacturing sector, which includes the high technology industries, average annual earnings were approximately one-third higher than the average for all local industries in 1980.

The better-paying high technology sector, however, showed substantial diversity with respect to earnings. In the nonelectrical machinery industry, average annual earnings were more than 40 percent above the average for all industries in 1980—more than double those in the apparel industry, more than 75 percent above those in the leather industry, and more than 30 percent above those in textiles.[3] However, in the electrical and electronic equipment industry, average annual earnings were 6 percent below the average for all industries, and 13 percent below the average in textiles.

Data on wages paid to production workers further illustrate the pay diversity within the high technology sector. In 1979 average hourly wages of production workers in the Lowell area were $4.71 an hour in the nonelectrical machinery industry and $6.17 an hour in the transportation equipment industry. These wages compared favorably with those paid in textiles ($4.55 an hour) and in apparel ($4.28 an hour).[4] In contrast, average wages of production workers in the electrical and electronic equipment industry were $3.83 an hour—considerably below those paid in the declining, traditional industries.

While most of the newer industries in the Lowell area pay their production workers wages that on average exceed those paid by local traditional industries, Lowell's production workers remain a considerable bargain. In 1982, for instance, average hourly wages of manufacturing production workers in the Lowell area were 9 percent below the state average and 19 percent below the national average.[5] In fact, in recent years local production wages have fallen relative to Massachusetts and the United States. The increasing differential results from the fact that in both the nation and the Lowell area the job expansion has occurred primarily in those manufacturing industries in which Lowell's production wages are low relative to national averages. Jobs have declined in those industries where local employers were paying rates above the national average. For example, in March 1979, the last month for which such data are available, production workers in the Lowell area were earning less than two-thirds the national average for production workers in the nonelectrical machinery and the electrical and electronic equipment industries. In contrast, local textile and apparel manufacturers were paying wages above the national average for these industries.

In sum, while high technology raised earnings and wages in the Lowell area relative to its traditional manufacturing and services sectors, relative to the state and the nation, production wages remain low and this wage gap has widened in recent years.

2. The Future of Lowell

How long Lowell's success will continue is subject to debate. Dynamic employment growth in the area has absorbed most of the earlier labor surpluses. With unemployment around 4 percent, finding workers at all skill levels has become exceedingly difficult. In the 1960s and 1970s employers were able to entice local residents, particularly women, who were not already in the labor market to come to work. Now labor force participation rates of both men and women in the Lowell area are considerably above the national averages.

Workers may, of course, migrate to the local area in search of jobs. Unemployment in the New England region, however, is also quite low. Moreover, the relatively large baby boom generation has already been absorbed into the labor market. As the supply of youth entering the world of work declines, critical labor shortages are predicted for the New England area. The most recent source of new workers in the Lowell area are low-skilled and unskilled immigrants and refugees. Cambodians, Laotians, and Vietnamese for example, are being hired in both the traditional and high technology sectors. The International Institute of Lowell helps these workers apply for jobs and in some cases provides staff for English courses that are offered at the factory during work hours. Higher wages will probably be needed to attract more skilled workers to the area.

The dominance of high technology employment in the area also raises questions about long-term economic development in the Lowell area. The term "high technology" encompasses a wide range of industries. However, as noted above, one industry stands out in the recent history of Lowell: office, accounting, and computing machines. In spite of its growing base, this industry's growth rate has increasingly overshadowed that of other high technology industries as well as industries in other sectors. By 1982, the office, accounting and computing machines industry accounted for 40 percent of all manufacturing employment in the Lowell area.

While numerous examples exist, Lowell need only look to its own past to see the vulnerability of an area when one industry becomes dominant. As industries mature, a shift to standardized production processes and greater reliance upon less-skilled labor set the stage for firms to relocate production jobs to lower cost areas and countries. Industrial life cycles thereby threaten the income and employment security of a "dependent" community. The textile industry experienced a life cycle in which manufacturing jobs shifted from New England to the South and subsequently to the Far East and Latin America. Lowell's economic base was devastated by this relocation of jobs. Production sites of electronics products including watches, radios, and semiconductors have spread from the United States to countries such as Scotland and Ireland and from there to Hong Kong, Singapore, and Taiwan. More recently, production of semiconductors has shifted to Malaysia, Thailand, Indonesia, Sri Lanka, and the Philippines. In the computer industry as well, manufacturing jobs are now spreading out from the primary R&D centers.[6]

The vulnerability of a particular community or region to the destabilizing effects of production life cycles depends on the area's industrial mix and the stages of development of those industries. Common sense suggests a policy of industrial diversity. The success of a booming, dominant industry, however, can "crowd out" alternative employment and can actually accelerate the departure of traditional manufacturing from an area. In the Lowell area, labor shortages, particularly in the blue-collar and clerical fields, attributable to the growth of high technology firms, are spilling over into other sectors less able to compete for workers in terms of both wages and image. At the same time, replacement needs of employers in the more traditional industries are becoming increasingly difficult to meet, as training programs in these fields take a back seat to skill training for the fast growing, newer industries.[7] The combination of product life cycles and the potential "crowding out" effects of a successful industry, thus, suggest a need to cultivate a diversity of firms and industries in an area even during prosperous times if economic growth and development are to continue in the long run.

A local or regional economic development strategy can focus on high technology without becoming dominated by one industry. Industries, or components thereof, pass through high technology phases—characterized by rapid technological change, a relatively high degree of R&D expenditures, and a dependence on highly skilled workers. While the textile industry is often referred to as mature or traditional today, it represented high technology a hundred years ago. Similarly, industries considered high technology today, such as computers, information processing, robotics or powdered metals, may or may not be the high technology of tomorrow. Conditions that nurture technological change and innovation will encourage new firms and industries committed to R&D to enter the area.[8] These firms will also bring new production jobs.

3. Extending the Lowell Model

Lowell's high technology success story has been viewed nationwide as a "model of reindustrialization" for older cities and regions, such as Detroit and Pittsburgh, that are losing jobs in traditional manufacturing industries.[9] The likelihood and ability of other areas to replicate the "Lowell model" of local economic development will, however, vary considerably depending on the characteristics of the area in question.

A detailed analysis of Lowell's transition, including such factors as the ability to tap federal funding sources for local development projects, access to venture capital, and community attitudes toward business, is beyond the scope of this article. Focusing specifically on high technology employment, however, one finds that the Lowell area clearly offered the ingredients most sought by these firms. Interviews with local employers confirm the results of a recent congressional survey of high technology firms nationwide that found the availability of skilled labor and relatively low labor costs the two most important factors influencing location decisions.[10]

The Lowell area is located close to Boston, with its excellent reputation for academic institutions. Lowell is also close to Route 128, which by 1975 was densely populated with high technology firms. Thus, the Lowell area provided ready access to a large supply of both new and experienced professional and technical talent. For example, after having started business in a small office above a garage in Boston, Dr. An Wang (founder and chief executive officer of Wang Laboratories Inc.) chose the city of Lowell as the site for his company's worldwide headquarters. The Lowell area also benefited from entrepreneurial spillovers of high technology firms. Apollo Computer and Automatix, Inc., a robotics firm, were spin-off firms started by former employees of high technology firms located along Route 128.

In addition, the Lowell area provided a good source of relatively low-cost, low-skilled labor. As noted above, unemployment rates in the local economy had been well above the national norms for several decades. Average wages of production workers in the Lowell area were considerably below those in the state and in the United States. Furthermore, given the particular mix of alternative employment opportunities in the area, high technology firms could pay employees significantly less than the national averages for production workers in these industries, yet compare favorably to local wages in the traditional manufacturing industries—textiles, apparel, and leather. Modern facilities, good promotion prospects, and fringe benefits packages that often include dental insurance, stock options, and pension plans, also gave the fast-growing, high technology companies an edge in both recruitment and retention of local workers.

Many of the areas seeking to "reindustrialize" their economies today do not share Lowell's labor market characteristics. The Detroit and Pittsburgh areas, for example, have proportionately fewer engineering and technical workers available than the Route 128 area in Massachusetts, the Silicon Valley in California, or Research Park Triangle in North Carolina. Lack of a high technology employment base cuts off the source of entrepreneurial spin-off firms as well.

Detroit and Pittsburgh do have a relatively large supply of production workers, many of whom have lost jobs in the declining

Table 2
Average hourly wages of production workers, 1982

Industry	Pittsburgh SMSA	Detroit SMSA	Massa- chusetts[a]	United States
Manufacturing, total	$10.66	$11.85	$7.58	$ 8.50
Durable goods	11.13	12.12	8.04	9.06
Primary metals	12.73	13.37	7.94	11.33
Fabricated metals	10.68	10.76	8.09	8.78
Nonelectrical machinery	10.52	12.49	8.35	9.29
Electrical and electronic equipment	9.54	8.19	7.36	8.21
Transportation equipment	NA	12.64	9.54	11.12
Nondurable goods	8.74	10.57	6.94	7.73
Textile mill products	NA	12.00	6.35	5.83
Apparel and other textile products	5.08		5.63	5.20
Paper and allied products	8.08	9.61	7.75	9.32
Printing and publishing	9.02	11.54	8.13	8.75
Chemicals and allied products	9.83	10.63	9.11	9.96

Source: *Employment and Earnings, States and Regions, 1939–82; Supplement to Employment and Earnings,* July 1983.
Note: NA = not available.
a. Production wages by industrial category in the Lowell area are not available after 1979.

automobile and steel industries. Average unemployment in 1982 was 16 percent in the Detroit area and 12 percent in the Pittsburgh area. In contrast to the Lowell area, however, relative wages of production workers in these two communities are significantly above national averages. In 1982, average hourly earnings of production workers in manufacturing were almost 40 percent above the national average in the Detroit area, and 25 percent above the national average in the Pittsburgh area. In some of the high technology industries, production wages in these labor markets are more competitive. However, by and large, they remain high, particularly compared to wages in Massachusetts. (See table 2.)

Aside from the question of national competitiveness, there is the issue of acceptance within the local communities of jobs in growing, newer industries. In contrast to the Lowell area, relative wages in the declining, traditional industries in many of the country's depressed areas far surpass those paid locally in high technology industries. The auto industry in Detroit and the steel industry in Pittsburgh are still among the highest paid sectors in these local economies. Thus, job changes between industries, even within the same occupation, could mean significant cuts in pay. In 1980 full-time assemblers, noted earlier as the largest occupational group in high technology industries in Massachusetts, were earning on average over 60 percent more in Detroit ($17,145) than assemblers in Massachusetts ($10,576); average annual earnings of assemblers in Pittsburgh ($14,090) exceeded those in Massachusetts by one-third.[11]

Furthermore, today's high technology industries offer fewer opportunities for workers to upgrade their occupations in Detroit and Pittsburgh than in Lowell. Statewide data indicate that a higher proportion of the workforce in the traditional industries in Michigan and Pennsylvania are in skilled production jobs than in Massachusetts.[12] For example, over 20 percent of the workers in Michigan's auto industry and in Pennsylvania's steel industry are in skilled craft and repair occupations. This is more than double the percentage of skilled production workers in the apparel and leather industries in Massachusetts. Almost three-quarters of all workers in Massachusetts' apparel industry are in unskilled operative and laborer jobs, compared to approximately one-half of those in the auto and steel industries in Michigan and Pennsylvania, respectively.

Moreover, the occupational mix of jobs in the newer industries differs by state, with Massachusetts' high technology work force more concentrated in higher skilled jobs. In the electrical and electronic equipment industry, for example, 18 percent of Massachusetts' workers are in professional and technical occupations, relative to 12 percent in Michigan and 14 percent in Pennsylvania. Skilled craft and repair workers also account for a higher share of the production jobs in this industry in Massachusetts than in Michigan or Pennsylvania.

Lastly, in addition to higher wages and the problem of local acceptance, the relatively high proportion of worker unionization in Pittsburgh and Detroit may deter high technology employers from entering these areas. This point may, however, be overemphasized by high technology employers, who have to date remained relatively free of unions. It is not clear whether former auto and steel workers would insist on union membership as a source of economic improvement and security in emerging industries given that their membership while in the smokestack industries did not provide them with job security.

The Lowell story shows that economically depressed areas can reverse the tides of decline and prosper once again. Today's high technology industries may or may not be the answer to economic renewal in Pittsburgh and Detroit—these industries do not have enough jobs to turn around all of the depressed areas in the country.[13] The lesson here is not that all areas can count on high technology industries to "work" for them. The lesson is that what "succeeds" in a city or region is a function of relative advantages, locally and nationally. To thrive locally, new industries should offer a better alternative to employment opportunities in the area—both current and of the recent past. For employers in growing industries to be attracted to these regions, the area must offer a location package preferable to those available in other parts of the country.

Appendix table 1
Change in employment by industry for the Lowell labor market area, Massachusetts and the United States, 1976–1982

Industry	Average annual percent change		
	Lowell labor market area	Massa-chusetts	United States
Construction	+0.3%	+2.8%	+1.6%
Manufacturing	+8.1	+1.2	−0.1
Nondurable goods	−3.3	−1.5	−0.4
Food and kindred products	−3.8	−2.7	−0.6
Textile mill products	−4.0	−4.1	−3.1
Apparel and other textile products	−4.9	−2.3	−2.0
Paper and allied products	+0.8	−1.6	−0.9
Printing and publishing	−1.8	+1.8	+2.6
Chemicals and allied products	−1.6	−0.8	+0.6
Leather	−8.4	−3.8	−2.6
Other nondurable goods	+0.1	−0.1	+1.0
Durable goods	+21.5	+3.1	+0.1
Lumber, wood, and furniture	−3.6	NA	−1.3
Primary metals	+1.0	−0.7	−3.4
Fabricated metals	+3.8	−1.0	−0.8
Nonelectrical machinery	+43.3	+6.9	+1.6
Electric and electronic equipment	+7.2	+5.5	+2.3
Transportation equipment	+14.7	−0.2	−0.5
Instruments	+23.6	+5.2	+4.1
Miscellaneous manufacturing	−0.4	−4.6	−1.5
Transportation, communication, and public utilities	+3.9	+0.9	+1.8
Wholesale and retail trade	+4.3	+1.6	+2.5
Finance, insurance, and real estate	+2.6	+3.7	+4.2
Services and mining	+6.8	+5.4	+5.3
Government	NA	−0.4	+1.0
Total nonagricultural employment	NA	+2.1	+2.1
Total private, nonagricultural employment	+6.2	+2.6	+2.4

Source: Massachusetts Division of Employment Security, ES-202 Data; *Employment and Earnings, States and Regions, 1939–82*; Vol. 1; *Employment and Earnings, 1939–78*, and *Supplement to Employment and Earnings*, July 1983.
Note: NA = not available.

Appendix table 2

Distribution of employment by industry for the Lowell labor market area, Massachusetts and the United States, 1982

Industry	Lowell labor market area	Massa- chusetts	United States
Construction	3.3%	3.0%	4.4%
Manufacturing	39.2	24.3	21.0
Nondurable goods	11.4	8.4	8.7
Food and kindred products	1.1	0.9	1.8
Textile mill products	2.9	0.8	0.8
Apparel and other textile products	0.9	1.4	1.3
Paper and allied products	1.0	1.0	0.7
Printing and publishing	2.6	1.7	1.4
Chemicals and allied products	0.5	0.7	1.2
Leather	0.8	0.7	0.2
Other nondurable goods	1.5	1.1	1.1
Durable goods	27.7	15.9	12.4
Lumber, wood, and furniture	0.3	0.4	1.2
Primary metals	0.7	0.6	1.0
Fabricated metals	0.9	1.8	1.6
Nonelectrical machinery	16.1	4.0	2.5
Electric and electronic equipment	4.0	4.3	2.2
Transportation equipment	3.5	1.2	1.9
Instruments	1.8	2.3	0.8
Miscellaneous manufacturing	0.5	1.4	1.1
Transportation, communication, and public utilities	3.9	4.5	5.7
Wholesale and retail trade	21.6	21.7	22.8
Finance, insurance, and real estate	2.8	6.4	6.0
Services and mining	16.1	26.0	22.6
Government	13.2	14.0	17.6
Total nonagricultural employment	100.0%	100.0%	100.0%

Source: Massachusetts Division of Employment Security, ES-202 Data; *Employment and Earnings, States and Regions, 1939–82*; Vol. 1; *Employment and Earnings, Supplement to Employment and Earnings,* July 1983.
Note: Columns may not sum to 100.0% due to rounding.

Notes

1. For more detail on Lowell's early history, see, for instance, Thomas Dublin, *Women at Work, The Transformation of Work and Community in Lowell, Massachusetts, 1826–1860* (New York: Columbia University Press, 1979); Arthur L. Eno, Jr., *Cotton Was King, A History of Lowell, Massachusetts* (New Hampshire: New Hampshire Publishing Company, 1976); George F. Kennegott, *The Record of A City: A Social Survey of Lowell, Massachusetts* (New York: MacMillan Publishing Co., Inc., 1912); H. C. Meserve, *Lowell: An Industrial Dream Come True* (Boston, MA: National Association of Cotton Manufacturers, 1923); Margaret Terrell Parker, *Lowell: A Study of Industrial Development* (New York: Kennikat Press, 1940).

2. The Massachusetts Division of Employment Security definition of high technology manufacturing employment includes the following 20 Standard Industrial Classification (SIC) three-digit level industries: Drugs (SIC 283), Ordnance and Accessories (SIC 348), Office and Computing Machinery (SIC 357); Electrical Distribution Equipment (SIC 361), Electrical Industrial Apparatus (SIC 362); Household Appliances (SIC 363); Electric Lighting and Wiring (SIC 364); Radio and TV Receiving Equipment (SIC 365); Communication Equipment (SIC 366); Electronic Components and Accessories (SIC 367); Miscellaneous Electrical Equipment and Supplies (SIC 369); Guided Missiles and Space Vehicles (SIC 376); Miscellaneous Transportation Equipment (SIC 379); Engineering and Scientific Instruments (SIC 381); Measuring and Controlling Instruments (SIC 382); Optical Instruments and Lenses (SIC 383); Medical Instruments and Supplies (SIC 384); Ophthalmic Goods (SIC 385); Photographic Equipment and Supplies (SIC 386); Watches, Clocks and Watchcases (SIC 387). See Helen B. Munzer and Eugene Doody, *High Technology Employment in Massachusetts and Selected States* (Boston, MA: Division of Employment Security, April 1981).

3. Further breakdowns for these data to the three-digit industry level are not available for the Lowell area.

4. Massachusetts Division of Employment Security, *Annual Planning Report, Fiscal Year 1980, Lowell, LMA*, p. 41.

5. U.S. Bureau of Labor Statistics, *Employment and Earnings, States and Regions, 1939–1982* and *Supplement to Employment and Earnings*, July 1983.

6. John S. Hekman, "The Product Cycle and New England Textiles," *Quarterly Journal of Economics* 94 (June 1980); John E. Tilton, *International Diffusion of Technology: The Case of Semiconductors* (Washington, D.C.: The Brookings Institution, 1971); Seev Hirsch, "The United States Electronics Industry in International Trade," in Louis T. Wells, Jr. (ed.), *The Product Life Cycle and International Trade* (Cambridge, MA: Harvard University Press, 1972); John S. Hekman, "The Future of High Technology Industry in New England: A Case Study of Computers," *New England Economic Review* (January/February 1980), pp. 5–17; Robert Premus, "Location of High Technology Firms and Regional Economic Development," Joint Economic Committee of Congress (Washington, D.C.: Government Printing Office, June 1982).

7. For a more detailed analysis of the effects of production cycles on skill requirements and an analysis of the responsiveness of educational institutions to labor market trends in the Lowell area, see Patricia M. Flynn, "Production Life Cycles and Their Implications for Education and Training," February 1984, final report to the National Institute of Education.

8. A detailed discussion of these conditions can be found in Office of Technology Assessment, Congress of the United States, *Technology, Innovation and Regional Development* (Washington, D.C.: U.S. Government Printing Office, 1984), and Roger Vaughan, *State Tax Policy and the Development of Small and New Businesses* (Washington, D.C.: Coalition of Northeastern Governors Policy Research Center, 1983).

9. See "High Technology Makes Lowell a Model of Reindustrialization," *New York Times*, August 10, 1982, p. 1; "Lowell: From Riches to Rags and Back Again," *Dun's Review*, July 1980. For a review of state initiatives to attract high technology employers, see Office of Technology Assessment, Congress of the United States, *Technology, Innovation and Regional Development, Census of the State Government Initiatives for High Technology Industrial Development, A Background Report* (Washington, D.C.: U.S. Government Printing Office, 1983).

10. Premus, "Location of High Technology Firms and Regional Economic Development."

11. U.S. Department of Commerce, Bureau of the Census, *Detailed Characteristics of the Population: Massachusetts; Michigan; Pennsylvania*; 1980.

12. Ibid.

13. See Lynn E. Browne, "Can High Technology Save the Great Lakes?" *New England Economic Review* (November/December 1983), pp. 19–33; Richard W. Riche, Daniel E. Hecker, and John U. Burgan, "High Technology Today and Tomorrow: A Small Slice of the Employment Pie," *Monthly Labor Review* (November 1983), pp. 50–58.

Economic Revitalization and Job Creation in America's Oldest Industrialized Region

Linda D. Frankel and James M. Howell
Bank of Boston
October 1985

By 1985 the transformation of Massachusetts' aging industrial base into a dynamic, new technologies-driven economy had garnered worldwide attention. Manufacturing jobs had stabilized, and unemployment had dipped below 4 percent, to the envy of many other regions around the world intent on revitalizing their own economies. Linda Frankel, executive director of the Boston-based Council for Economic Action, Inc., and the Bank of Boston's James Howell presented a paper documenting the state's transformation as the centerpiece of a European conference held in Paris entitled "The Job Machine."

What had been so remarkable was that job creation in New England had recently outstripped job growth in the rest of the United States by as much as 20 percent. Howell and Frankel attributed this phenomenon, first, to the presence of so many young high tech firms at the stage of development where employment growth was highest and, second, to the de facto relative manufacturing wage decrease in the region caused by the depressed state of manufacturing during the economic stagnation of the 1950s and 1960s in New England.

This paper also pointed out that low regional unemployment does not solve all of a region's problems. The effects of the Massachusetts Miracle varied dramatically around the state, for example, proving more beneficial to suburban areas and small towns than to cities in the region. Furthermore preliminary data were indicating many of the new manufacturing jobs created in the area's dynamic high tech industries appeared to be low-skill, entry-level positions with little opportunity for advancement.

There was no doubt that New England, and especially Massachusetts, was in better shape than it had been. But new economic development challenges lay ahead.

Introduction

The remarkable revitalization of New England's economy over the past decade—and especially that of Massachusetts—is now nearly legendary. Consider for a moment these summary statistics:

• In 1974 unemployment in New England averaged 12 percent; in 1985 the region posted unemployment rates in the 4.5 percent range; the current rate for Massachusetts—at 3.7 percent—is the lowest of any industrialized state of the United States.

• In 1974, of the 6.5 million people living in Massachusetts, 1.25 were on some form of welfare or public assistance; by 1985 much of this problem had been eliminated as economic growth absorbed these individuals into the labor market.

• Perhaps most pertinent to the deliberations of this meeting, in the period 1968 to 1975, New England lost 252,000 manufacturing jobs; in the period 1975 to 1980, New England created 225,000 new manufacturing jobs. In Massachusetts approximately 100,000 new manufacturing jobs were created—mostly as a direct result of the growth in the high tech industries. Sophisticated service sector job creation also played a role—especially in the Boston area—where 167,000 jobs were created in the 1975 to 1980 period.

The ability of the country's oldest industrialized region—New England—to create jobs on this scale has been truly significant. During the two most recent business cycle growth periods, job creation in New England has outpaced job growth in the United States by nearly 20 percent, and it is with this phenomenon of job growth that we are primarily concerned today.

Not surprisingly, the vigor of this revitalization process has captured the imagination of policymakers and journalists throughout the industrialized world. As the leading source of financing for the high technology firms that led the recovery, the Bank of Boston has played host to senior economic policy and development officials from a variety of cities, states, and even countries who have come to the Bank to gain a clearer understanding of the revitalization process. Specifically, our visitors have been searching for ways to transfer the high technology boom which so transformed New England to their own regions and to understand the economic factors that produced such a spectacular process of job creation.

In this paper we have attempted to synthesize many of these conversations. We have looked briefly at the region's history, outlined the overall parameters of the revitalization, and offered two explanations for its extraordinary job impact. Finally, we have noted two troublesome issues that appear to be emerging as the revitalization process itself matures.

As a final introductory note, we should add that while the broad focus of this analysis is on the six-state New England region, in many instances we will concentrate on the experience of Massachusetts. It was in Massachusetts that the recovery was most dramatic and some of its implications most clear. Before turning to a specific consideration of the recovery, let us review some basic facts about the New England region and its industrial history.

The New England Region: A Brief Geographical and Historical Overview

New England consists of the six most northeastern states of the United States. An area of relatively high population density and comparatively small size, the total land area is only 63 thousand square miles, a figure dominated by largely unpopulated areas in the northern states, particularly Maine. Total population for New England is 12.6 million. Total U.S. land area by comparison is 3.5 million square miles; total U.S. population 235 million. The region is highly urbanized, with 81 percent of the population living in eighteen key urban areas. Population patterns in the United States do mean, however, that the region has easy access to the Boston–New York–Washington Corridor, a market area of 61 million in population and $700 billion in personal income—roughly equal to the combined market of France and West Germany.

Despite a lack of natural resources, New England was the first area of the United States to industrialize—this process started as early as the 1820s. The region's proximity to Europe facilitated trade and provided a continuing supply of low-cost labor. Further, its population density supported the growth of commerce and financial institutions. Indeed, prior to 1850, New England and the neighboring mid-Atlantic states accounted for over 75 percent of the manufacturing employment in the country, and per capita income in New England substantially exceeded the national average.

Yet as Robert Eisenmenger has noted in his classic study, *The Dynamics of Growth in New England's Economy—1869–1963,* economic development has not been an easy process. As early as the post-Civil War period, New England began to lose many of its original locational advantages:

Its seaports surrendered trade to ports with better rail connections. The fertile agricultural lands of the West were developed. The nation's extensive iron-ore deposits, petroleum deposits, and timberland had been harnessed for power generation. All the regional capital markets had been linked together, so that profitable firms in every part of the country could obtain funds for rapid expansion. After 1920 immigration was drastically curtailed and with it New England manufacturers' traditional supply of low-cost unskilled labor.

The total impact of all these changes became readily apparent when employment in New England's textile industry started to decline in the 1920's. The big crash came after the war (WW II). New England textile employment dropped from 280,000 in 1947 to 170,000 in 1954 and to 99,000 in 1964. During 1949 the average unemployment rate reached new highs in many Massachusetts cities: 26 percent in Lawrence, 18 percent in New Bedford, and 12 percent in Fall River and Lowell. The Providence–Pawtucket, Rhode Island, areas had 13 percent unemployed during the same year.

Throughout the 1950s and 1960s the decline of traditional manufacturing industries continued as the textile and leather industries were recruited to lower cost, nonunionized locations in the southeastern United States. It is worth noting in this context that New England had never been a high wage region; the South was simply lower. In 1950 the leather and textile wage rates in Massachusetts averaged $1.36 per hour compared with $1.61 for auto workers—a differential of roughly 20 percent.

The textile and leather trades were particularly sensitive to rising production costs, and the southeastern United States offered substantial pools of nonunionized lower-wage labor that was leaving the agricultural sector. Southern educational levels were adequate, and job training was provided at the expense of state governments. Issues of wage sensitivity that pulled industry to the South were further exacerbated by a combination of state and local tax and regulatory policies that were unfriendly to business investment and pushed industry away from New England.

Yet, by and large, the early to mid-1960s were generally times of optimism, and the region, with its concentration of highly sophisticated academic institutions, played an aggressive role in the development of the technical hardware related to the U.S. space and defense programs. The concentration of academic institutions in New England is unparalleled in the United States—over 250 colleges and universities in the region with sixty-five in greater Boston alone. New England has thirty-seven institutions of higher education with engineering programs, and Massachusetts is among the top five states in the nation in producing engineering degrees. In the 1960s research and development contracts from the Defense Department poured into the universities in the greater Boston area—all contributing to the broadening and deepening of the research base from which the high technology industry as we know it today would emerge.

This optimism was abruptly terminated in 1968 by large Defense Department and NASA cutbacks that continued well into the 1970s. New England felt the impact of those cutbacks as unemployment rose to 10.4 percent. Unemployment in Massachusetts led the region with 11.2 percent. These unemployment statistics reflected not only the dislocations caused by the NASA defense cutbacks but also a continuing flight of traditional manufacturing industries to lower-wage production sites. Then in the 1974–75 national business cycle downturn, New England experienced its worst recession since the Great Depression. Buffeted by rapidly increasing oil prices, energy-sensitive industries followed labor-sensitive industries in shifting their production to other areas of the country. Unemployment reached its highest levels since the 1930s and the post-World War II transition to a civilian economy.

At this point there were few economic observers in the nation or the region who held out much hope for New England—ourselves included. We looked out on the region and saw that reflecting its status as the oldest industrialized area of the country, New England shared with Europe, more than other areas of the United States, what Gottfried Haberler[1] has characterized as the "excesses of the welfare state—high taxes and an oppressive regulatory climate." Indeed, in

Massachusetts at this time the state's political leadership was interested more in redistributing wealth than in creating a positive business investment environment. State and local elected officials in the late 1960s through the mid-1970s did not see the interrelationship between high taxation, business investment, and plant locational decisions. Capital gains, already taxed nationally at prohibitive levels, were taxed again in Massachusetts. This, combined with excessive property tax levels, had earned for the state the unwelcome title of "Taxachusetts." Further the state had among the strictest regulatory environments in the country, and various permitting and zoning procedures were widely used as a method of discouraging development in many of the prime areas, preferring instead to attempt to push business investment back into the already congested older cities. In a widely publicized case in western Massachusetts, a site permit was refused for an already funded suburban shopping center in an effort to force the investment into the city of Pittsfield. In the end the deal collapsed, leaving the city, the area, and the state as the economic losers. There seemed to be little cause for optimism.

Yet it is at precisely this point that history confirmed once again the maxim that "The only thing certain about the future is change." The new high technology firms, which in the late 1960s and early 1970s were quietly spinning out of defense-related R&D firms, had gone through the process of product development and testing and were beginning large-scale production and marketing. The region— unknown even to itself—was poised on the edge of an economic revitalization that took even its most seasoned observers by surprise.

In the next three sections of this paper, we will discuss in more detail the magnitude of the revitalization process and examine two key factors which we believe account in large measure for its job intensity.

The Revitalization: Overall Dimensions

Looking back over the past decade, it is clear that not only have we had a major economic recovery, but the structure of New England's economy has also undergone a fundamental change. Relative to the first half of the 1970s, manufacturing has swung abruptly from a laggard in overall regional growth (down 5.6 percent) to the second

Table 1

	1968 to 1975	1975 to 1980
Percent change in New England nonagricultural employment	+5.2%	+17.5%
Relative sectoral contribution		
Construction	−0.5	+0.3
Manufacturing	−5.6	+4.4
Trade	+3.0	+3.7
Services	+5.2	+7.3
Government	+3.1	+1.8

sharpest growth sector (up 4.4 percent) as shown in table 1. Indeed, approximately one-fourth of the region's employment growth in the second period can be explained by the improved performance in manufacturing.

That manufacturing activity would demonstrate such economic vitality in the oldest industrialized region of our country is most interesting. It tends to provide clear refutation to those who have argued that older regions must necessarily be condemned to a future of slow economic growth, or even stagnation, as a result of a failing manufacturing base. New England's economic strength—especially as seen in the high technology industries—demonstrates persuasively that regional growth can be led by manufacturing if the industry is technologically innovative and government policy responsive.

The results are, indeed, impressive. In the 1975 to 1980 period alone, the New England economy has generated more than 225,000 new manufacturing jobs. The Economics Department of the Bank of Boston has worked with Data Resources, Inc. to establish the contribution of the high technology industries in this process, and according to our estimates, in the period from 1975 to 1980 they accounted for 45 percent of this increase. Looking at the 1982 to 1987 period, we estimate that high technology firms will continue to be a positive growth force, albeit at a reduced rate. And as the employment benefits from these industries slow, other manufacturing firms—primarily in the defense sector—will become stronger contributors to regional job growth, thus ensuring the continuation of a strong manufacturing base.

The region's unemployment rate—at 4.5 percent—remains well below the national average of 7.0 percent, and Massachusetts continues to have the lowest unemployment rate of any industrial state in the nation—currently 3.7 percent.

As can be seen from the preceding data, a surge in service sector employment was also part of the recovery. Although a number of these jobs were, undoubtedly, in low-wage–low-skill areas, the number of jobs in sophisticated services—financial services, accounting, advertising, consulting, etc., also jumped as newly developing high technology firms demanded sophisticated supporting services. The growth in sophisticated services in Massachusetts for the period 1982 to 1984 outpaced the national U.S. performance, and within Boston alone, institutions offering financial services control over $300 billion of capital. These institutions are increasingly becoming an integral part of the state's export base. Also of importance is the role of the state's medical and educational complexes. In Massachusetts education has become a major industry, with well over 500,000 students in institutions of higher education throughout the state.

Simultaneously, employment growth in the governmental sector has moderated. As is clearly evident from table 2, the rate of job growth in Massachusetts' state and local government in the late 1970s outpaced the country. In the period 1982 to 1984 the growth in this sector turned about dramatically—an actual decline in employment occurred while the rest of the United States posted a modest increase. This improved balance between public and private sector employment was due to a number of factors, including greater management control in state and local government, tax reductions in the late 1970s and early 1980s, and, more important, the passage of Proposition 2½, a property tax limitation measure.

In conclusion, the period from the mid-1960s to the mid-1980s has seen not only a major economic revitalization in terms of employ-

Table 2

Employment growth in state and local government[a]	Actual, 1975 to 1980	Forecast, 1982 to 1984
United States	2.4	0.3
Massachusetts	2.9	−0.4

a. At annual rates of change.

ment gains but also a major structural shift in the Massachusetts economy. This occurred to a more limited extent in the economies of other New England states as well. The region is no longer overly reliant on traditional manufacturing and defense industries. There is now a more balanced picture: significant increases in employment in new nontraditional manufacturing—the high technology sector— increases in sophisticated services, decreased reliance on defense and NASA spending as the sole source of strength in the economy, and substantially moderated governmental employment.

It is also worth noting that the political climate had shifted substantially. In 1978 the new governor of Massachusetts was elected on a strongly pro-business platform, and his administration worked aggressively to enhance the opportunities for industry in the state. Capital gains taxes were lowered, property taxes limited as a result of a grass-roots campaign, and regulations simplified. This pro-business attitude has been continued in the succeeding administration, with the current governor devoting a high priority to maintaining productive relationships between government and the business community. This is evident in the aggressive use of state programs to help businesses—industrial revenue bonds, export assistance, and training centers. Most recently, the state established five "Centers of Excellence," designed as incubators for new enterprises in photovoltaics, microelectronics, marine sciences, plastics, and biotechnology. This new attitude has also spilled over into the state's legislative body— the Massachusetts General Court and, indeed, many elected officials in Massachusetts can now be characterized as "born again" capitalists.

Job Growth in New England's Technology-Based Industries

The fortuitous juxtaposition of a number of unplanned and probably unplannable factors converged in New England to create the seedbed for the new high technology industry. These factors included a unique market opportunity for sophisticated microcomputer systems—indeed, a new and virtually untapped market, a concentration of engineers/entrepreneurs/business leaders in an environment that encouraged entrepreneurial risk taking, the presence of great technical universities, a long history of federal government-sponsored technical research and development work, and aggressive financial institutions. A number of secondary factors were also important,[2] but the essence of the New England experience was an environment of risk taking. The issue before us today is not why the high technology industry was born in New England, but why it created so many jobs.

Inasmuch as these events are still very much in the region's recent economic history, additional research still needs to be undertaken to document fully the factors that played a dominant role in the industrial revitalization process. Nevertheless, the analysis to date does identify two important factors that significantly affected the unusually strong job creation capacity of the revitalization process in New England:

• A birth-to-maturity cycle in high technology firms created substantial new job growth.

• A highly competitive manufacturing wage structure encouraged greater relative reliance on labor—than capital—in the production process.

In the brief comments that follow, we will discuss each of these factors.

The life cycle process in business development theory is well established, and it is always surprising to realize how little understanding and appreciation economists have of it. A brief summary of the U.S. experience will be helpful in understanding this issue. Broadly speaking, the development of the high technology industry in the United States has fallen into a model of "early stage development" which is best exemplified by Boston-Route 128 and San Francisco-Silicon Valley or, alternatively, a model of "late stage development" which is exemplified by North Carolina and Texas. The "early stage" model takes the industry from its conceptual beginnings through its research and development (R&D) phase, test production, initial marketing, and initial production for market penetration.

The late stage model has typically involved the attraction of established, technology-driven manufacturing processes to facilities in lower production cost—especially low-wage rate—areas. This model is based on the fact that as an industry matures, production cost sensitivity begins to assume a much greater role in a firm's overall profitability. These pressures lead companies to seek out production sites in areas which, though maintaining consistency with marketing objectives, usually have the lowest wages. Increasingly, this site selection process has begun to lead New England's high tech companies to Pacific Basin countries. But the success of areas such as Lyon, France, and Peterborough, England, indicates that it is possible to attract high technology production facilities—the late stage model—desiring direct access to the EEC countries. Even in these industrial relocations the employment benefits can be significant, but the industry will be more mature, more cost sensitive, and less inclined to the dramatic growth of the early stage model.

The critical point here is that it is the growth process in the early stage model that generates the greatest impact on the job creation process. As firms mature, they typically become increasingly interested in managing costs as the initial surges of growth slow and companies adjust to changing market conditions. This nearly always results in reduced labor input. Not all firms grow large, of course, but for those that have properly identified new and emerging markets, the dynamics of job creation can be most significant. In New England, the high tech—principally computer systems—industries had identified a nearly virgin market, and the industry's early growth rates—41 percent in the period from 1969 to 1974—reflect this market opportunity and the youth of the industry. The relevant data are shown in table 3.

It is also clear from this table that the process of industry maturation and increasing cost sensitivity has already begun to affect New England's high technology firms. In the 1975 to 1980 period the job generation process among high technology firms had slowed from 41

Table 3
Average annual compounded rate of increase in employment in selected companies by stage of maturity

Firm's stage of industrial maturity	1945 to 1974	1975 to 1980
Mature	1.9%	0.0%
Innovative	10.8	4.3
Young high tech	40.7[a]	24.0

a. For the years 1969 to 1974.

percent to 24 percent per year, and 1985 has seen a modest contraction in high technology employment in Massachusetts.

A brief comment must be made about the press coverage of these recent high tech industry layoffs. Although it is clear that this industry will no longer make the significant contribution to increases in employment that it did in the past, it is equally clear that the industry will continue to employ large numbers of production workers in Massachusetts. It is also important to recognize that among the 160 companies belonging to the Massachusetts High Technology Council, only eight firms have released relatively large numbers of employees, and even here, the magnitude of these adjustments must be kept within the perspective of the aggregate employment in this industry. Total employee layoffs in 1985 have amounted to 2,780 in an industry that currently employs over 140,000—20 percent of total manufacturing employment. Moreover, though it's true that these laid off workers are a part of the current adjustment process in this industry, over 70 percent have already been reemployed in expanding high tech industries in Massachusetts. Nevertheless, it is clear that there has been a dramatic slowing of employment growth.

To conclude, one important factor in explaining why the New England recovery generated so many jobs was that the industry was new, the market unexploited, and young firms typically show the most rapid employment growth during their early "growing-up years."

The second factor contributing to the substantial increase in high tech manufacturing jobs in New England was the fact that in the 1970s New England's wage structure became relatively quite competitive—even in terms of the southeastern states where wages had risen steadily through the 1960s and 1970s. There are undoubtedly many reasons why entrepreneurs, and the venture capitalists and commercial bankers who finance them, prefer to have production sites close at hand in a start-up situation; nevertheless, it was the availability of large pools of nonunionized and relatively low-wage labor that played a key role in making the recent revitalization in New England so job intensive.

In a recent milestone study,[3] Dr. Benjamin H. Stevens demonstrated that the New England economy has become relatively more competitive for manufacturing. Specifically, this analysis shows that during the 1973 to 1980 period, there has been a relative production

Table 4
Growth of real manufacturing wages by region as percent of New England, 1980

New England	100%
Great Lakes	114
New South	104
West Coast	136

Table 5
Capital investment by worker entering the manufacturing labor force

	Capital cost per job, 1975 to 1980[a]
U.S. economy	$150,571
New England	45,868
Massachusetts	41,722

a. Costs are expressed in 1972 dollars.

cost improvement in New England vis-à-vis the New South states that ranged from 30 to 50 percent. The positive adjustment of wages dominated this change to the point that today New England now has one of the lowest real wages of all regions in the United States. The relevant wage data ratios are shown in table 4.

Moreover, recent trends in the level of nominal wages are also indicative of this regional wage disparity. At about $6.20 per hour, manufacturing wages in both New England and the South stand over $2.00 below the comparable figures for the West and Great Lakes regions.

This regionally competitive wage structure provided a tremendous cost incentive for the region's high tech industries to substitute labor for capital or simply to utilize high ratios of labor as the configuration of the production function developed. Consider the data in table 5. This information provides strong support to the view that entrepreneurs are indeed sensitive to relative wage levels and will find the most cost-effective labor-capital mix in the production process. Since relative wages were highly competitive in Massachusetts in the 1970s, labor was relied on more intensively, and the residents of the region were the economic beneficiaries. Further the fact that New England's high tech industry has been nonunionized has played

Table 6
Real hourly compensation in manufacturing (average annual percent change)

Country	1975–1980	1980–1984
France	3.5	3.1
United Kingdom	1.9	0.9
West Germany	3.3	0.6
United States	0.2	0.4

an important role in the flexibility of the work assignment on the production line as well as keeping upward wage pressure at a minimum.

For years economists have argued extensively about the issue of wage levels and unemployment rates. From our vantage in Boston, it seems abundantly clear that the extraordinary high labor costs in the U.S. auto, steel, and other heavy industries concentrated in the Great Lakes have provided a powerful incentive for business managers to steer away from expensive labor in favor of cheaper machinery. Similarly, the current unhappy situation of high unemployment in Europe was significantly influenced by a growing imbalance between rapid wage increases and narrowing profit margins in the late 1970s and early 1980s.

Table 6 compares the annual average increase in real hourly compensation of production workers in manufacturing for major European countries and the United States. In the late 1970s real wage increases in Europe were more than ten times the rate in the United States. In the 1980s wage increases in the European countries slowed substantially, except in France, but there continued to be greater downward wage rigidity in Europe than in the United States. When one also takes into account lower relative capital costs, resulting from somewhat lower real interest rates and in some cases direct capital subsidies, it is understandable to find European managers substituting capital for labor.

The solution of many economists to these unacceptably high unemployment levels is a wage cut. This is usually labeled as unfeasible. Although we acknowledge the political dimensions of the proposal, we would be quick to point out that the New England high tech experience has demonstrated conclusively the positive employment benefits of a wage cut on employment.

During the post-World War II period up to the mid- to late 1960s, the relatively high wage structure in the Massachusetts textile and leather industries vis-à-vis the South was a principal factor in driving that industry out of New England. These locational shifts alone increased regional unemployment, and as this wage differential accelerated because of union pressure, even higher unemployment resulted as those businesses that did remain in New England substituted capital for labor in the production process.

Although Massachusetts state government did not advocate wage cuts to achieve full employment, the dynamics of the labor market—that is, a prolonged period of very soft labor demand—meant that wage increases in Massachusetts would ultimately rise far less rapidly than in the highly competitive South. Tight labor markets in the South pulled wages upward and by the mid-1970s, wages in most southern states were roughly equal to those in Massachusetts. By the end of the decade relative wage rates had tilted in New England's favor. The labor market results of this gradual relative wage transformation was the equivalent of a de facto wage cut. The benefits of this adjustment are what we have been talking about in this paper, namely, the economic revitalization of New England.

Would the results have been different if wages continued to be differentially high in New England? Undoubtedly, the high tech revolution would have still grown out of the Boston technology complex, but most of the production-line work would probably have been undertaken outside the region. Double-digit unemployment would still exist today in New England.

To summarize, then, the birth-to-maturity cycle of a new industry and a highly competitive manufacturing wage structure ensured that the employment and income benefits of the high technology revolution would have significantly positive impacts on New England.

Emerging Issues for New England

If the prodigious increase in jobs created by the high technology industry has constituted an unambiguous good, the impact of the spatial location of the new manufacturing activity, at least in New

England, and the character of the newly created jobs are less clear. Let us look at each of these issues in more detail.

Seen from a distance, the recent history of the region's medium-sized cities—the so-called "old mill towns"—appears to have been one of steady progress under the impetus of New England's widely acclaimed recovery. Yet in an analysis undertaken by the Bank's Economics Department for a soon-to-be-published book on the comeback of "Snowbelt" cities, the results appear less optimistic.[4] The analysis reveals a dramatically uneven impact of the region's technological revitalization. In fact, we have found that only about one in four of the region's cities has been able to "start over" industrially by capitalizing on the growth of high tech industries. The rest have been forced into other channels or left behind.

The New England economic landscape contains 111 cities, representing 43 percent of the region's total population and 43 percent of aggregate employment. To make our analysis manageable, we selected thirty-five medium-sized cities for detailed investigation, and concentrated our attention on the disaggregated economic performance data for each individual city. We selected these cities because they were generally representative of all cities within the region, and because we had firsthand familiarity with their attempts to revitalize the economies. We excluded Boston because of its very special circumstances.

In large part, the revitalization process had its greatest impact in suburban areas and the smaller towns. Some benefits did spill over into the cities, but the effects were by no means uniform. In fact, an analysis of the data suggests that the thirty-five sample cities can be conveniently grouped into three broad categories, depending on the extent of their participation in the high technology revitalization process. Although we recognize that there are limits to any scheme of categorization, our examination of dozens of variables revealed the emergence of some general patterns across the thirty-five cities:

• Only nine of the cities analyzed appear to have been significant economic gainers as a result of the high tech revitalization process during the latter half of the 1970s.

• Twenty of the cities analyzed were found to have economic situations that were little improved, and in some cases actually worse, during the decade of the 1970s. These "old mill towns" appear to have been left behind in New England's economic revitalization process. They now must struggle with the problems of industrial maturity and declining competitiveness.

• Six of the thirty-five cities did not easily fit into either of the two preceding categories. A careful review of the statistics, however, suggests that they are emerging as regional service centers with high employment ratios in the nonmanufacturing sector. This development has been welcomed by some as an important step in breaking away from manufacturing, but it is not necessarily beneficial to the city itself. Three southern New England cities in this category are increasingly beginning to take on the unenviable characteristics of much larger old industrialized cities, with high ratios of unemployment, many families living in poverty, and large minority populations.

To summarize, to the extent that the experiences of these thirty-five cities are representative of the 111 cities in New England, the message about the comeback of Snowbelt cities as a result of high technology seems to have been exaggerated.[5] The high tech revitalization process appears to have been largely a suburban-rural phenomenon.

There is a second troubling issue emerging as well. As the high tech revitalization process works itself out, another new issue has begun to emerge. This relates to the quality level and skill level of the production worker jobs created. There is no doubt that many sophisticated engineering and scientific positions were required as the high technology firms grew, but the strong occupational bias for low-skill production workers is somewhat surprising. This issue is usually discussed under the heading of a dual labor market.

We should caution that the data that support the contention that a dual labor market is emerging are still somewhat fragmentary. The occupational estimates of the U.S. Department of Labor for the country and Massachusetts do show 20 percent higher employment in the professional and technical occupations in Massachusetts vis-à-vis the country as a whole, but the blue-collar ratios are less differential.

Nevertheless, literally hundreds of conversations with Massachusetts high tech managers confirm that their most common labor market demands are for low-skilled, entry-level workers, willing to cope with the boredom of tedious bench work. The plant managers have apparently adjusted production to accommodate high turnover ratios—for some firms in excess of 50 to 75 percent per year—in these production worker occupations.

Although many issues remain unresolved, we may conclude that a large majority of the production jobs associated with the high technology industries in Massachusetts have been low wage, low skill with virtually no career advancement ladders. From a public policy standpoint this is a troubling development.

Concluding Comments

The high technology industry undoubtedly presented New England with a unique opportunity to revitalize its economy. Because of its stage of development, however, we do not expect that the industry will continue to create jobs in the future at the same pace that it has done in the past in New England. Nevertheless, the possibility of attracting manufacturing facilities still offers other areas significant potential for capturing large numbers of manufacturing jobs. The ability of areas to achieve this will, however, depend increasingly on cost factors and negotiated trade policies—that is, restricted market access. Yet, as we look ahead, we believe that this attraction process may become more difficult. Over the past several years high tech firms have shown an increasing preference for Pacific Basin countries as production sites. Certainly strong government policies among many of these countries toward business investment as well as extraordinarily cheap labor are finding a strong positive response among many Massachusetts firms. It is too early to judge the ultimate course of these developments, but if we had to speculate as to what the future holds, it would be one of increased international production specialization among high technology firms.

Notes

1. Gottfried Haberler, *The Problem of Stagflation: Reflections on the Microfoundation of Macroeconomic Theory and Policy* (Washington, D.C.: American Enterprise Institute Studies in Economic Policy, 1985).

2. For a complete discussion, see remarks by Dr. James M. Howell on "The Factors That Played a Dominant Role in the Establishment of a High Tech Industry in New England and Some Lessons for Other Areas" given before the

Committee for Economic Development of Australia, March 28, 1985, Melbourne, Australia.

3. Benjamin H. Stevens, "Regional Cost Equalization and the Potential for Manufacturing Recovery in the Industrial North," unpublished papers presented at a conference sponsored by the State University of New York at Albany, April 1982.

4. A detailed statement of the analysis and these findings appear in Gary Gappert (ed.), *The Comeback of Snowbelt Cities,* Sage, October 1985.

5. Clearly, this analysis is neither as detailed nor comprehensive as we would like. Future researchers should examine, in particular, three additional factors: the role of commuting patterns, physical improvement of the downtown areas, and community attitudes toward change and growth.

War Stories: Defense Spending and the Growth of the Massachusetts Economy

David L. Warsh
The Boston Globe
January 1986

Massachusetts, at least in one sense, is living a double standard. It is known as a fiercely liberal state, home to many outspoken critics of the nation's defense policies. Yet it is also one of the nation's chief beneficiaries of the spending which accompanies these same policies.

Without question, the rapid development after World War II of the state's high technology community would have happened very differently without the infusion of federal defense dollars which flowed into the region both during and after the war. According to David Warsh, a columnist covering economics for The Boston Globe, *defense spending was a key factor, if not the pivotal force, behind the area's eventual high tech boom. Department of Defense estimates show that in 1985, defense spending in Massachusetts amounted to over 8 percent of gross state product.*

In the following edited article Warsh documented the web of connections that evolved as a result of World War II among the defense research establishment, universities such as MIT and Harvard, and the corporate world. These connections, Warsh claimed, fueled the development of ideas that spawned a host of new high tech companies in the region. It was Department of Defense money, for example, that funded the basic research in computing which eventually led to the formation of the region's highly successful minicomputer industry.

Massachusetts is less dependent now on defense spending than in the past, Warsh noted. Yet he also speculated that the region's continuing economic growth may stem in part from new defense programs. The Strategic Defense Initiative—commonly known as "Star Wars"—has already brought millions of dollars for basic research to area companies and institu-

tions. And the web of sophisticated research linkages to Washington, D.C., is likely to continue to influence the region's economy for some time.

Boston's arsenal has a long and significant history. Its ropewalk, shipyards, foundries, armories, and powder factories were among the first in the Western Hemisphere; they date from the city's deep involvement in the global contest between the English and the French that began in 1689 with King William's War and ended only 125 years later with the defeat of Napoleon.[1] Many nodes have developed in the American defense industry over 300 years, but Boston, like Virginia, has kept its franchise. The powder business went to Delaware; shipbuilding went to satellite ports in New England; military outfitting went south with the textile mills; the rope business went to Iowa; even naval rifles eventually went elsewhere; but New England found new products and new niches.

If Chicago and Los Alamos gave the nation nuclear weapons, if Los Angeles gave it airframes and rockets, if its submarines came mostly from Virginia, if Maryland supplied germs and spies, if the space franchise went to Texas and Florida, then it was here, in New England, that command and control of the new war machine evolved, here that significant strands of radio, radar, sonar, engines, missiles, instrumentation, telemetry, and satellite photography were developed. Even the possibility of a retail trade emerged: it was at a little plant in Salem that agents for Pakistan sought in 1983 to buy a supply of krytons, electronic switches that can serve as triggers for its nuclear bombs.[2] Yet it was from a small office above Sparr's Drug Store, in the center of Boston's medical-school ghetto, that the International Physicians for the Prevention of Nuclear War organized the crusade that won it the Nobel Peace Prize last year, and this was only the most recent of many periodic attempts by organizations whose roots are in New England to diminish the influence of the military.

Anyone who thinks dispassionately will recognize that over the years the war business consistently has enlarged its sphere of operation in the city and the region that surrounds it, even as the business has become less visible. True, the Boston Army Base is being converted into an "international design center"; the navy's old Fargo Building is now an office building; the shipyard in Charlestown is a condominium complex for yuppies; the Watertown Arsenal is now a

---

mall full of shops and restaurants. The antiwar movements that have found fertile soil here have been powerless to deflect the trend. The weapons laboratories' formal ties to universities may have been severed, but the effect of the severing has been largely cosmetic. The arms business in New England has been camouflaged by careful landscaping and a remarkable burst of growth in the region's ploughshare industries—first and foremost, the computer industry—but it is bigger than ever.

Let me say a word about the geography of the defense industry in New England, as I understand it. We think regionally because we think historically and politically: it is Congress, after all, which votes the appropriations for defense contracts. There was a time when each important city in the six New England states was a separate part of the military establishment, its special significance stemming from its proximity to a river: Hartford, Springfield, Boston, Portsmouth, New London, New Haven, Providence. Today, with the vastly altered realities of transportation and communication, to say nothing of the rise of modern corporate management, I believe it is better to think of Boston as the central locale and to regard other cities in New England as subordinate to it, at least in this connection, even though this occasionally does damage to the facts: Burlington, Vermont, for example, is an important beneficiary of military R&D spending on advanced computer techniques, but most of the revenue stream for these projects comes through New York City rather than through Boston. The really important exception is Hartford, which is a nearly independent entity. But for the sake of simplicity, in this article I treat Boston as though it were nearly synonymous with New England.

What is the role of defense in the economy of New England? How does the military economy work? How deeply is it embedded here? How did it grow? Is it good or bad for business? What are the chances that the hopes raised by peace movements of one sort or another will pan out? And what would be the consequences if they did? It is said by economists that New England does well these days because it is aloof from the problem industries: steel, autos, farming, energy; what will happen on that happy day when peace breaks out and the defense industry becomes a problem? We don't need to worry—not much—about the day the war breaks out. As my colleague M. R. Montgomery says, "One airburst over Minuteman National Park and you get rid of Lincoln Labs, Mitre, Itek, Bolt

Beranek and Newman, the Peking Gardens restaurant, and the Daniel Chester French statue. One burst would get them all."[3]

Computers: A Case in Point

It has long been a commonplace that the cold war and the space race were not especially productive of the kinds of spin-offs generated by World War II. Nose-cone ceramics for baking dishes, Teflon for frying pans, microwave ovens, and a few other trivial consumer-oriented items were all we got for the billions we spent—or so the story goes. This is, to put it simply, a completely mistaken interpretation. The main spin-off of the cold war was the computer; the main spillover of the space race was the semiconductor; and the economic ramifications of each are still reverberating throughout the world economy.

To be sure, the need for fast numerical calculation had been in the air for a century, as advances in engineering technique intensified the demand for complicated calculations. The prehistory of computers includes the analytical engine of Charles Babbage, a never-built assemblage of gears, cams, and racks the size of a small house; the widely used punch cards of Herman Hollerith; and the glorified adding machines of Howard Aiken, which could do three calculations a second. True, Alan Turing had published his intellectual blueprint for a computer in 1937, well before the war; but none of the men who actually built computers (John Atanasoff, Conrad Zuse, George Stibitz, Howard Aiken, J. Presper Eckert, or John Mauchley) read it. Statesmen and soldiers scarcely comprehended that fast calculations would prove useful in wartime; Germany drafted its leading computer architect.

Yet it was unmistakably in the caldron of the war that the calculator gave way to the computer. Between Bletchley Park in England, where the problem was code cracking, and the Moore School at the University of Pennsylvania, where the problem was ballistic trajectories, a few dozen inventors, backed by large sums from the defense establishment ("large puddles of money," in the words of one MIT engineer), created the first electronic, digital, stored-program computers. John von Neumann recognized the significance of ENIAC (Electronic Numerical Integrator and Computer—the first true computer) only after Herman Goldstine told him, while waiting for a train at the Aberdeen ballistics lab in Maryland, that he was going to visit a machine that could do three hundred calculations a minute. Within weeks, von Neumann had succeeded in diverting ENIAC from the purpose for which it had been built—the calculation of firing tables for navy guns—to a more pressing project. When ENIAC was switched on in February 1946, its first task was making calculations on the feasibility of the hydrogen bomb.

It was the cold war that put Massachusetts back in the computer business. Before the war, Vannevar Bush and a team at the Center for Analysis had been working on a very fast calculator, but with the advent of the war, the team dispersed to other projects. After the war, Warren Weaver and the Rockefeller Foundation pumped $100,000 into resuscitating the project, but by that time another candidate for funds had arisen within the university and from a fairly unexpected quarter. It simply muscled the Rockefeller Foundation and everyone else out of the way.

No single citizen of Massachusetts is responsible for more jobs in the state—or is more nearly anonymous—than Jay W. Forrester. Nebraska-born, Forrester came to MIT in 1939. His wartime assignment in the Servomechanisms Laboratory was to build a universal airplane trainer, one that would simulate the operation of any airplane; after the usual number of twists and turns, he decided that what he needed was a digital computer rather than a machine full of axles and gears. He visited von Neumann and the Moore School machines, and concluded they'd never suit his purposes: they were too unreliable, not fast enough. And so while the rest of the infant computer industry labored away, planning to sell a dozen cartoon-style electronic brains a year, Forrester pounded away for the navy on a real time machine, capable of instantaneous calculation, in order to "put men in the loop."

Saved by the Bomb

For all his considerable success, Forrester's Whirlwind computer project probably would have been canceled had it not been for the Russian atom bomb that was exploded in August 1949. The idea of nuke-laden Russian planes flying over the North Pole—plus the outbreak of the Korean War—was enough to call into being the Semi-Automatic Ground Environment project, or SAGE, an "electronic radar fence" to be coordinated by computer. Forrester got the job, and he devised little iron doughnuts to replace vacuum tubes as the on-off basis for memory. With a fat air force contract to MIT in his pocket, the company he picked to build these memories—in preference to Raytheon, Remington Rand, and Sylvania—was International Business Machines Corporation. The graduate student he sent to Poughkeepsie to supervise the process was a bright young man named Kenneth Olson.

So it was that in the early 1950s the U.S. government substantially bankrolled IBM's entry into the computer business. For the first few years after the war, the computer market had belonged mainly to Remington Rand, the firm that absorbed the company started by Moore School's Eckert and Mauchley. Raytheon and Engineering Research Associates (later to become Control Data Corporation in Minneapolis) were also active forces. Already a large and highly successful corporation, IBM was interested in electromechanical calculators (particularly those of Howard Aiken at Harvard), mainly as a way of selling more punch-card equipment to big accounts like Commonwealth Edison. A large faction within IBM, often led by Thomas Watson, Sr., was opposed to developing its electronics at all: "There were not unlimited funds within the IBM company," sniffed its director of engineering.[4] Yet the firm's younger executives saw the new wave coming. Thomas Watson, Jr., related years later that he had become "absolutely panicked" upon learning that two UNIVACs had been installed at the Census Bureau.[5]

The same Korean War that kept Jay Forrester in business at MIT brought IBM's Tom Watson, Jr., to President Harry Truman to offer the services of the firm to the nation. The offer was pointedly not limited to existing systems, Watson said, and his company decided to go ahead and build a computer for the government and as many other takers as it could find—that was the Defense Calculator. But not until an IBM engineer named John McPherson went to a committee meeting in June 1952 to organize the Second Joint Computer Conference did he learn that Jay Forrester at MIT was looking for a commercial manufacturer for his iron core memory. "One of the best payoffs that belonging to a professional society could produce," he said later. "I should have gotten a finder's fee."[6]

Suddenly, the government was precisely the huge honey pot for which Thomas Watson, Jr., had hoped two years earlier. To that point, computer building at IBM had been a tentative affair. But with SAGE, the company began by hiring thirty engineers—heavy-hitters like Gene Amdahl, Erich Bloch, Charles Bashe, Werner Bucholtz, Robert Crago, and Lawrence Kanter, among others—who were trained in the new electronic style and who promptly pushed out of the main engineering lab the old Edisonian tinkerers who had built the punch-card business. Under the SAGE contract, the company hired between seven and eight thousand engineering, programming, and maintenance workers, most of whom stayed on. During the 1950s, more than half of IBM's domestic electronic data processing revenues came from SAGE and from work on the B-52 bomber program in the Korean War.

IBM's big breakthrough—the Model T of the computer industry, Stan Augarten calls it—was its Model 650, announced in July 1953 and delivered in December 1954. Within a year, 120 machines had been installed and another 150 had been ordered, despite the product planning department's having declined to forecast a single sale. A series of improved models followed; yet as late as 1955, there were still company directors who wanted to get out of the business. But by then the company was ready to make the first of a series of dramatic gambles with its own money instead of government funding.

Nor was IBM the only one to roll the dice in those years. At about the same time, Kenneth Olson—the graduate student who had acquired a permanent disdain for IBM's strategic style while supervising the production of SAGE's memory—headed off to open his own memory company in an old abandoned mill in Maynard, Massachusetts. He called it Digital Equipment Corporation. Dozens of other young electrical engineers were going into business for themselves then, too. The rest, as they say, is history—rich, complicated, absorbing.

The $100 Billion Un-sure Thing

By this reckoning, virtually the entire modern computer business can be said to have been a fairly direct outgrowth of those few years, say, from 1940 to 1955. In 1985, that amounted to around 265,000 jobs, or about 9 percent of the three million jobs in Massachusetts. Traditional manufacturing jobs accounted for 675,000 of the total. So does it matter, thirty years later, that IBM in 1953 "ate Raytheon's lunch," as the businessmen say? Does it matter that the first computer factory went to Poughkeepsie? The fact remains that, thanks mainly to the Servomechanisms Laboratory at MIT, Massachusetts was able to make a firm entry into the fledgling electronic computer industry in the 1950s. The Commonwealth's history in semiconductors, however, hasn't been nearly as triumphant. Even though Lincoln Laboratories pioneered in investigating the electrical properties of silicon, interest in the technology flagged after World War II, and when William Shockley, who had invented the transistor at Bell Laboratories, returned to Stanford University to pursue his research, the result was that the area around San Francisco became dominant in the new technology—the Boston area fell far behind.

Nor was it simply new business in Massachusetts that benefited from the wartime spending boom. General Electric had arrived in Massachusetts in the 1890s, when Thomas Edison's firm bought one of its strong competitors, Lynn's Thompson Houston Electric Company. The smaller company's management promptly took over the larger firm, and GE acquired a strong connection with MIT. (It was Gerard Swope, for example, who in 1930 recruited Karl Compton to preside over the modern transformation of the school.) Raytheon Corporation had been a by-product of GE's struggle with Bell over who would control the market for commercial radio. Both firms grew large and diverse on military contracts during World War II. The manufacture of airplane engines, which had flourished along the Connecticut and Housatonic rivers since World War I because of the presence there of the nation's most sophisticated metal-cutting trade, boomed accordingly: when General Electric decided to enter the market in 1941, the government built a plant for it in Everett. Some firms gorged on military spending, grew fat, and eventually failed: Curtis Wright is a prime example. But around a solid industrial core, dozens of little companies took root and grew: a rocket-fuel plant learned to make bleach for newspaper pulp instead, a company that invented shock-proof mounts for shipboard radars turned to pylons for jet engines, and so on.

Looking backward, 1942 seems to be the year in which the rules of the game changed decisively. That was when the Radiation Lab was established at MIT to pursue the development of the British invention of radar. Again, the details are illuminating: Boston got the job, in preference to Bolling Field in Washington, after MIT's James Killian arranged hangar and lab space in a few hours. The Radiation Lab undertook three jobs—to build a flying radar, a gun-laying system, and a long-range navigation system that became LORAN—and to this end assembled a large collection of theoretical physicists. It was no foregone conclusion that this would work: MIT had to overcome objections of the man who put Bell Labs together, Frank Jewett, who couldn't believe that a group of young scientists working in an academic environment could do the job. By the end of the war, 20 percent of the nation's top physicists had passed through the lab and had compiled an unprecedented record of scientific and technological success.

It is worth inquiring a little further into the nature of this watershed. Frank Jewett's objection to the establishment of the Radiation Lab was not unique. Before World War II, America had relatively little experience with large-scale organization for research. But whether in the Manhattan Project, the Radiation Lab, the Office of Strategic Services, the "whiz kids" in the army air force, the group around William Norris at the Office of Naval Intelligence, or a hundred other groups of slightly lesser magnitude, the successes were so immediate and so far-reaching that they changed forever the way business is done: this was nothing less than the very invention of "high tech." The nub of the process has been identified by Gerald Holton in *Thematic Origins of Scientific Thought*:

What took place was analogous to impedance matching, the method by which an electronics engineer mediates between the different components of a larger system. That is, special coupling elements are introduced between any two separately designed components, and these allow current impulses or other message units to pass smoothly from one to the other. Similarly, in these quickly assembled groups of physicists, chemists, mathematicians, and engineers, it was found that the individual members could learn enough of some one field to provide impedance matching to one or a few other members of the group.[7]

I want to emphasize that this threshold phenomenon is at the heart of the success of all the large units with which we are concerned here: universities, cities, and nations, as well as research teams.

Situation Normal, All Fouled Up

Not that the transfer of military technology to civilian markets has ever been easy. The commercial success of the computer has been one of the big surprises of the postwar era, even to its enthusiasts, and not the least surprising part was the applicability of computers to relatively intimate situations. That the extent of this potential was not apparent, even to the smart guys who pioneered in the development of the machine, is fascinating. Aiken had pooh-poohed it; Eckert had doubted; even the great von Neumann had thought of computers mainly as calculators, and had failed to foresee their ultimate utility as storehouses of information. Even IBM failed to appreciate how flexible the machines could be made; that was "the MIT idea," as Kenneth Olson of Digital Equipment has described it, and the role played by the Massachusetts firms—DEC, Wang, Data General—in forcing IBM's hand is still underappreciated. True, the record of the computer industry is littered with sad stories of companies, Raytheon and General Electric among them, that tried to get into the industry and failed. But in 1982, there were a half million general-purpose computers in use, and the number was growing by 40 percent a year.

Nor is it that the military never makes mistakes—least of all that. The navy tried hard to pull the plug on Jay Forrester's Whirlwind computer, for example. The National Bureau of Standards, working in deepest secrecy for the navy, began Project Tinkertoy in 1950 to create components that could be put together hierarchically with ease. More than $5 million later, it turned out that Tinkertoy was based on vacuum tubes instead of newly invented transistors. Similarly, the Signal Corps spent $25 million on RCA's attempt to create the same kind of modules, this time with transistors, just as the integrated circuit was coming into use. On the other hand, the government often bets right. In the 1960s and early 1970s, the Defense Advanced Projects Research Agency funded much of the early work on time sharing and networking, two of the standard techniques for getting computers to work together. The military research is like the old saw about advertising: half of it is wasted—if only we knew which half.

Close to the truth is what Leo Steg says about the effect of military targeting. For twenty-three years Steg was head of General Electric's Science Laboratory; he says the trick is for the government to announce a standard, to set a target for which everyone can shoot.[8] Then smart guys, like the Texas Instruments crew in the case of semiconductors, can either hang along on the outside of the camp or join the governmental effort, and it doesn't really matter who hits the jackpot. Integrated circuit coinventor Jack Kilby of Texas Instruments worked on RCA's Micromodule despite his loathing of the technology involved. Something of the same sort was at work when MIT's John C. Sheehan succeeded in synthesizing penicillin where a huge wartime effort had failed. In addition to this "outsider" mechanism, there is the effect of all that money: the government can afford to back a lot of losers in order to find one winner.

It was in this way that semiconductors made their way into the commercial marketplace, via the Apollo space program and a hundred less conspicuous military uses. The first integrated circuits were offered for sale in 1961, but government sales constituted 100 percent of the market until 1964, and the federal government remained the largest buyer of chips for years after that, according to T. R. Reid. But just as had been the case with computers, as manufacturers made more and more chips, their manufacturing costs fell. By 1969, when IBM bowed to the inevitable and began using chips in all logic circuitry, chip makers finally "had a market that would dwarf the space and defense business," Reid says.[9] By the late 1970s, when the attention of the semiconductor firms had drifted away from defense, the Defense Department concocted a program that brought their representatives back to the program: the Very High Speed Integrated Circuit project.

It is in this light that the headlines about military spending should be read, with skepticism for strong stands on either side of the issue. Unexpected ties between government spending and civilian industry are everywhere.

Local Politics, National Agendas

What place is there for politics in this story? Well, certainly there is a very large one, and it deserves to be told in detail elsewhere. No one understands the political realm better than my colleague Martin Nolan, who spent fifteen years in Washington, D.C., before taking over the editorial page of *The Boston Globe*. When I asked him about the role the congressional delegation had played in shaping the composition of the defense industry in Massachusetts, he said that the politicians had won some and lost some.

For instance, the NASA mission control center should, by all rights, be in Cambridge, Massachusetts. But Albert Thomas of—guess where?— Houston, Texas, happened to be head of the Independent Agencies Subcommittee of the House Appropriations Committee at the time, and even with their guy in the White House, Massachusetts wasn't able to get it. The Texans stole it fair and square. The Massachusetts delegation was pretty good over the years, but there was nobody better than the Texans at getting on the important committees. One of their guys was on the Armed Services Committee because his district had a lot of goats and he figured you could sell goat skins to the military easier than to anyone else. The influence of the Massachusetts delegation began to fade in the 1960s; Leverett Saltonstall didn't stand for reelection in 1966; Bill Bates died and was replaced by Michael Harrington in 1970; Phil Philbin was defeated by Father Drinan on a strong antiwar program in the primary the very year before he would have taken over the Armed Services Committee. The Vietnam War slowed down; so did the moon program. Then Richard Nixon sent Elliot Richardson— Elliot Richardson, of all people—to shut the bases. There was gloom and doom all around.[10]

That was, of course, the dark before the dawn. The biggest boom since the end of the nineteenth century was about to energize the Massachusetts economy. What happened? Well, in the view presented here, the main motors of the boom were the commercial phases of the high tech and minicomputer revolutions, engines that had started turning some thirty years earlier. That interpretation is all right with Nolan—as far as it goes. He cites the thesis of Don K. Price, who in his book, *The Scientific Estate,* credits Rep. Thomas P. O'Neill with being "the hero of a turning point in [scientific] history."[11] When O'Neill, in January 1963, declined a very favorable proposition from NASA to hire engineers for Washington jobs on a strictly nonpartisan basis, Price wrote, he was acting on the basis of a deep understanding of the relationship between political and economic power: "If he turned down Washington jobs on behalf of his constituents, it was because he was interested in a far more substantial form of patronage: contracts in Boston for industrial corporations and universities."[12] The balance had decisively shifted away from standing armies to technological weapons and the experts who built them—wizards, in Churchill's phrase, or boffins, in the British slang of the war—and increasingly, the politicians realized it. The definitive version of the political history of these remarkable last forty years awaits Nolan's own accounting of the period, but until then, Price's book makes the best reading.

Boffins Regnant

The intricately connected social world in which all this activity took place is the vital counterpart to the abstraction of the cost web that we met earlier. Politics are just part of it, and in the short run, not the most important part. At least as important as the legislative leadership had been the administrative apparatus of science and technology—the boffinate, if you will. MIT's Vannevar Bush was science adviser to President Roosevelt. MIT's James Killian and Harvard's George Kistiakowsky were advisers to President Eisenhower, MIT's Jerome Wiesner adviser to President Kennedy, Princeton's Don Hornig (a Harvard College graduate and Harvard Ph.D.) to President Johnson. Lee DuBridge, who had directed MIT's Radiation Lab during the war, was adviser to President Nixon; so was Exxon's Edward David, Jr., whose doctorate came from MIT. H. Guyford Stever, who had spent twenty-five years at MIT, served Presidents Nixon and Ford; MIT's Frank Press was adviser to President Carter. Ronald Reagan's science adviser, George Keyworth II, was the first man to hold the job who never went to school or taught in Boston—and he was born in Boston.

These high-ranking bureaucrats, who commanded the pinnacle of what was an extensive administrative machinery of science, were in a position to send important business to New England, and often did. Nor did the appeal of the universities to business operate only through their influence on the federal machinery. Harvard University, too, has been highly successful in furnishing advisers to government, but there is an important flip side to MIT's efforts: since the school is far less rich than Harvard, it has had to forge intricate connections to industry as well as to government in search of funds. The modern phase of this outreach began in 1948, with its industrial liaison program. The result is that MIT has a degree of clout with the corporate community that far exceeds that of Harvard.

If the dense educational and research establishment is the single dominant feature of the business infrastructure in Boston, it is hardly the only element that matters. Important also is the city's venture capital community, its banks and investment managers: the availability of cash to bring along fledgling enterprises has been another linchpin in Boston's development since it lured Alexander Graham Bell more than one hundred years ago. Also important is the willingness of the Commonwealth to let inventors keep their wealth, if and when they earn it. Walter Muther, president of the Associated Industries of Massachusetts and dean of the State House lobbyists, contends that the legislative supervision of inheritance and capital gains is the unheralded key to the state's success in attracting and keeping start-up companies.[13]

It may be that low taxes attract businesses and high taxes drive them out. Still, the map of states, viewed through this lens of defense spending, will turn up cities—like hot spots of infrared emissions—whose postwar growth has been built in large part around their universities: Cal Tech/UCLA, Berkeley/Stanford, MIT/Harvard, Columbia/New York University, the University of Texas at Austin, the University of Chicago/Northwestern University, the cluster of universities around Washington, D.C., and so forth. Only geographic distinction confers greater advantage when it comes to competing for Pentagon dollars. Indeed, it is possible to make some comparisons of size and shape here. According to a recent study by Data Resources, Inc., Massachusetts is among the top ten states in defense spending as a share of total state product, the local contribution to GNP. At 6.6 percent, it is behind Virginia (10.4 percent), Connecticut (9.7 percent), Hawaii (8.7 percent), Washington (7.9 percent), California (7.9 percent), Maryland (7.3 percent), and Alaska (7.3 percent), and ahead of Missouri (6.5 percent), Mississippi (6.4 percent), and New Hampshire (6.4 percent). Moreover, DRI calculates that Massachusetts will share disproportionately in the growth of military spending through the rest of the decade, along with a handful of other states. Connecticut, Massachusetts, Maryland, Vermont, Virginia, and Washington are all expected to obtain 15 percent or more of their growth from military spending during the next five years.

What Next?

We are currently caught up in a remarkable new evolution, one as laden with potential economic benefits as with terror. I mean, of course, Star Wars, as the president's Strategic Defense Initiative has become known. In fact, it has less to do with nail guns and x-ray lasers than with software. The opposition to Star Wars is bucking a huge wave that is breaking over the engineering and electronic business, having to do with the conquest of new frontiers, namely, the design and manipulation of very complex systems—the issues that crop up when engineers try to design chips with a million and more gates or to write computer programs with hundreds of thousands of lines.

What about Star Wars as a weapon? Certainly I am deeply skeptical, but my skepticism is grounded in little more than a newspaperman's common sense. A low level of research and development is one thing. But is it possible to fund the research and keep the weapons at home? Perhaps. Certainly to do so will require a considerable amount of fairly stiff-backed opposition on the part of a wide segment of the research community. One needs to keep firmly in mind the idea that technologies are systems with enormous momentum, and that opposition on a local level, along only one part of their advancing salient, is doomed to fail. Yet, as Thomas Hughes says, external forces can redirect even high-momentum systems.

It can be said with confidence, I think, that once again some huge payoffs await breakthroughs made along the lines taken by government funding. Whether they come inside the research effort or outside it is, as always, open to doubt. It is this ambiguity that has rendered the Europeans relatively enthusiastic backers of the SDI—the Star Wars program is "a mini-Marshall Plan" that will get England growing again, says Sir Peter Emery, a British MP and businessman[14]—while the Japanese remain relatively skeptical; despite more than a year of formal study at the cabinet level, the Japanese government has yet to declare its support. What seems likely to emerge from the next twenty years of research is not so much new ways of manufacturing computers as new ways of controlling and linking them. These techniques may offer a unique competitive advantage to the companies that possess them. After all, America has seen its domestic television-manufacturing industry move offshore without noticeably bad results. Does it matter who makes the cathode-ray tubes if the real money is in the television networks? It may be the same with software and the design and manufacture of the most advanced computers.

Considerations like these make it devilishly hard to think about defense economics. But to ignore them is to willfully misunderstand the questions. In the past century, military spending has often been a powerful accelerant to economic growth. That is one reason—perhaps the main reason—it is so very difficult to curb.

Notes

1. The best single account of Boston's military beginnings is the abridged edition of Gary B. Nash, *The Urban Crucible* (Cambridge, Mass.: Harvard University Press, 1986).

2. See Alain Cass and Simon Henderson, "The Nuclear Threat Behind Pakistan's Grim Pursuit," *Financial Times* (13 June 1985): 3.

3. M. R. Montgomery, personal conversation with the author, 23 January 1986.

4. Franklin M. Fisher, James W. McKie, and Richard B. Mancke, *IBM and the U.S. Data Processing Industry: An Economic History* (New York: Praeger, 1983), 12.

5. David Ritchie, *The Computer Pioneers* (New York: Simon & Schuster, 1985), 243.

6. Emerson Pugh, *Memories That Shaped an Industry* (Cambridge, Mass.: MIT Press, 1984), 93.

7. Gerald Holton, *Thematic Origins of Scientific Thought* (Harvard University Press, 1973), 410.

8. David Warsh, "Star Wars: Boon or Bane for Economy?" *The Boston Globe,* 21 November 1985, 57.

9. T. R. Reid, *The Chip* (New York: Simon & Schuster, 1984), 126.

10. Martin F. Nolan, personal conversation with the author, 7 February 1986.

11. Don K. Price, *The Scientific Estate* (Cambridge, Mass.: Harvard University Press, 1965).

12. Ibid., 21.

13. Walter Muther, personal conversation with the author, 26 January 1984.

14. Flora Lewis, "Foreign Affairs," "Upside Down Values," *The New York Times*, 9 February 1986, sec. 4, 23.

Higher Skills and the New England Economy

John C. Hoy
New England Board of Higher Education
June 1986

New England is unique in its extraordinary concentration of institutions of higher learning. In all, there are sixty-five colleges and universities in the greater Boston area, and nearly 265 in the entire region, with over 800,000 undergraduate and graduate students. In the following edited article, John Hoy, president of the New England Board of Higher Education, credited this rich educational environment with providing the raw ingredients crucial to the economic revival of the 1970s.

Indeed, Hoy claimed, New England's educational complex provided the steady supply of people with the broad mix of skills in science, technology, and management necessary to start and sustain the new technologies-driven economy. Ideas, as well as people, have continually flowed from academe to industry, Hoy maintained. Such products as the minicomputer got their start in academic research labs, and the nearly 80 biotechnology companies that more recently emerged in the region have had strong links to academic laboratories.

Significantly, Hoy pointed out that although other regions are seeking to duplicate New England's success, even New England does not know much about the process by which the ideas and people generated in its educational institutions have found their way to the marketplace.

New England may be unique among American regions in its common history, its close interrelationships, and physical compactness. But the phenomena it is experiencing today—the "mature" economy, the groping for a "post-industrial" alternative, the worry about accommodating so many millions of people in a fragile life space—may be, if they are not already, the problems of the rest of the United States tomorrow. If New England "fails," its failure might presage a failure of the whole nation. Thus New England presents a fascinating laboratory and test case in the United States of the metes and bounds of what can be accomplished on a regional basis.—Neal R. Peirce, The New England States, *1976*

International conflict, military affairs, and world markets have shaped New England. The history of New England's wartime vitality (1939–1945), attenuated postwar decline (1945–1975), and ultimate resurgence (1975–1985) is inextricably linked to the skills of its people and their capacity to grow, adapt, and create. The basis of vigorous postindustrial renewal—generated over the course of four decades through basic and applied research and development—was in large measure the product of the region's academic institutions. The complex story of New England's economic revival is essentially the fact of having the professional and intellectual leadership and the skilled work force required to bring about economic renewal. New England's vitality has taken the form of a knowledge-intensive structure that provides sustained job growth, record employment, expanding capital investment, and, during the past two years, the lowest level of regional unemployment in the nation and its highest level of regional, personal, and per capita income.

New England, the smallest geographic region in the United States, with one-twentieth of the nation's total population, has more successfully shifted from a traditional manufacturing-based economy to a knowledge-intensive, high technology, high service economy than any economic unit in the industrialized world. The shift has been accomplished in large measure because of the flexibility provided by the skills of working people and the eclectic vision of the region's colleges and universities. Institutions of higher education have offered a concentrated pool of highly skilled people and have consistently made scientific and technological breakthroughs in basic research, applied research, and management processes. Their graduates have created and directed the investment of 25 percent of the venture capital available in the United States.[1]

New England has outproduced other regions of the nation in awarding degrees in those professional fields required by a sophisticated service and technology-driven economy. This has been done in the absence of state or regional manpower planning. For the most part, state policies also reveal a limited understanding of higher education's capacity and limitations. To date, higher education in New England has enjoyed a free market philosophy in the conduct of its own affairs and in establishing which academic priorities to pursue.

Ironically, across the nation, state governments are mounting major, well-funded programs which, in part, seek to emulate New England's success. The competitive thrust of these programs is aimed at successfully encouraging the commercialization of research results. Very slowly, ventures elsewhere have begun to influence public policy in New England and to draw the deliberate attention of political leadership here; and none too soon. State government in New England invests less public revenue in research and development than does any other region of the United States.

As New England becomes vulnerable to foreign and domestic competition, it can no longer afford to be smug about low unemployment, arrogant about regional academic prominence, or satisfied with its gifted corporate entrepreneurship. Our institutions of higher education will confront severe challenges in the 1985–1995 decade and will require farsighted state and regional policy if the region is to sustain and expand the skilled human resources and meet the levels of productivity demanded by global participation. The strategic interests of higher education and corporate New England will converge during this decade. The strategy will focus on (1) enhancing support for basic research; (2) creating state incentives for improving the commercialization of research and development through university-industry partnerships; (3) developing a coherent manpower policy to meet the most acute shortages of scientific, engineering, and other highly skilled personnel; (4) upgrading the quality of public school education; and (5) increasing the participation rate of adult men and women, particularly minorities, in a responsive continuing education system. All these issues require more planning, greater collaboration, and a promise of the highest level of corporate support any region in the United States has yet exhibited.

The Economic Recovery

Today New England has fully recovered from a harrowing period of high unemployment, mounting inflation, and depressed investment.

Since the height of regionwide unemployment at 11 percent in 1975, shortages in fields requiring highly trained professionals and skilled technical and sophisticated service-industry workers have continued to increase. The current employment picture also reveals shortages of unskilled sales, construction, retail, and production personnel. Unemployment in New England stands below 4.0 percent, and Massachusetts each month continues to boast the lowest unemployment rate among all industrial states in the nation.

Growth in the Service Sector

The regional economy has steadily moved into the service sector—with an emphasis on financial, insurance, health care, consulting, professional, and sales employment—providing sophisticated services to the region as well as the nation and the world. Since 1947, when 370,000 New Englanders were employed in services, the service sector has grown fourfold—to 1.5 million in 1985—the largest single sectoral gain in the nation during that period.

The growing importance of the service sector reflects to a large extent broad trends in the national economy. At the same time, New England is developing a sophisticated "high service" component that is increasingly international in dimension. Generally, as economies mature, there is a shift in the composition of employment toward services. While this is a natural outcome of industrial maturity, the process in the New England region has evolved in its own unique way. The traditionally strong service areas of education, finance, and health care have been strongly supplemented by the service-related needs of high technology, international marketing, and consulting.

Since the mid-1970s, the service sector has grown by nearly 40 percent in the region. New England now employs 24 percent of its labor force in services.

Within the service sector, more than one in three jobs are in a health-related field and more than 15 percent are in education. In 1985 alone, services employment has grown by more than 5 percent in the region, and the jobs created have not all been low paying.

Between 1975 and 1983, over 140,000 jobs were created in the health care industry in the region, as compared to 80,000 in high technology. Moreover, these jobs now create payroll expenditures exceeding $7 billion. However, the health services sector is fragile and is under extreme cost-containment pressure. Increasing dependency on services in general does not create a foundation for future growth.

Manufacturing and services are inextricably linked. If industrial competitiveness is lost, it will be that much harder to maintain the growth of the service sector, especially since it is apparent that the volume of international service-sector exports, while growing, remains small, even within the banking and insurance industries. In effect, in the long run the loss of manufacturing may result in a loss of the very services that advanced products and processes have the capacity to generate.

High Tech

High tech remains the most visible symbol of New England's economic resurgence. Among all regions of the nation, New England currently has the highest proportion of its total work force in high technology-related jobs. Massachusetts, with over half of all high tech employment in New England between 1975 and 1980, led the nation in growth of technology industries at 6.6 percent per annum, topping the national rate of 4.2 percent per annum during the same period. During 1982–1984, the rate of growth in Massachusetts slowed to 5.3 percent per annum, still above the national growth rate of 2.9 percent per annum during the period.[2]

Despite considerable worrisome attention that high tech employment has received—given the spate of layoffs in 1985–1986 amounting to ten thousand jobs—the long-term prognosis is favorable. College graduates constitute 20 percent of the employment in high tech industries generally and 33 percent in the computer industry specifically.[3] New England's concentration of professional and skilled technical workers as a percentage of the total work force is without peer in the United States.

Total New England employment passed the 6 million mark for the first time in 1984. Continued expansion throughout 1985 and 1986 despite high tech layoffs points conservatively toward 6.5 million employed New Englanders by 1990, perhaps even more.[4]

Table 1

1980 employment of technological workers in top ten states and other New England states, percentage of total employment

State	Employed persons (16 and over, nonagricultural)	Engineers	Percent	Technicians and technologists	Percent	Precision production occupations	Percent	Technical workers total percent
California	10,640,405	213,232	2.0	261,012	2.5	469,828	4.4	8.9
New York	7,440,768	93,602	1.3	144,310	1.9	304,822	4.1	7.3
Texas	6,311,845	95,967	1.5	142,950	2.3	280,090	4.4	8.2
Illinois	5,068,428	68,692	1.4	97,183	1.9	237,746	4.7	8.0
Pennsylvania	4,961,501	68,046	1.4	98,910	2.0	245,779	5.0	8.3
Ohio	4,558,442	69,584	1.5	86,133	1.9	241,656	5.3	8.7
Michigan	3,750,732	68,867	1.7	68,913	1.8	199,908	5.3	8.9
New Jersey	3,288,302	55,846	1.7	75,223	2.3	143,743	4.4	8.4
Massachusetts	2,674,275	51,510	1.9	64,850	2.4	126,207	4.7	9.1
Florida	4,002,330	43,906	1.1	78,799	2.0	129,705	3.2	6.3
Connecticut	1,482,309	31,838	2.2	34,416	2.3	81,774	5.5	10.0
New Hampshire	432,622	8,604	2.0	11,026	2.5	24,929	5.8	10.3
Maine	459,522	4,330	0.9	6,389	1.4	22,647	4.9	7.3
Rhode Island	426,812	4,795	1.1	7,070	1.7	27,373	6.4	9.2
Vermont	227,195	3,821	1.7	4,689	2.1	9,748	4.3	8.1
Totals for New England	5,702,735	104,898	1.8	128,440	2.2	292,678	5.1	9.1

Source: New England Board of Higher Education Analysis of 1980 Census, Bureau of the Census, U.S. Department of Commerce.

The comparative advantage enjoyed by the New England states in the employment of technologically skilled workers is revealed in table 1. The region in its entirety developed and continues to maintain a distinctive advantage which, in large measure, provided the mobility necessary to sustain the loss of 263,000 nondurable manufacturing jobs (down 31 percent), as 241,000 new durable manufacturing jobs were created (up 34 percent) between 1947 and 1979.

During the same period, 2,085,000 new nonmanufacturing jobs were created. Of these, 561,000 were in wholesale and retail trade (up 94 percent); 500,000 in government (up 148 percent); and 770,000 in other services (up 209 percent).[5]

A Unique New England Capacity: Producing Professionals

With 5.3 percent of the total U.S. population in 1982, New England produced the following proportions of advanced degrees:[6]

- 7.3 percent of medical residents (specialists)
- 8.0 percent of Ph.D.s in all fields
- 8.3 percent of Ph.D.s in all scientific disciplines
- 8.6 percent of law school graduates
- 9.3 percent of MBAs
- 10.0 percent of Ph.D.s in humanities
- 10.1 percent of Ph.D.s in engineering
- 11.0 percent of Ph.D.s in physical sciences

In specific disciplines within the sciences, such as computer science, electrical engineering, mathematics, physics, and astronomy, New England production of Ph.D.s is twice the national rate. The advantage such output represents to the region is reflected in the location new Ph.D. recipients choose for employment. Of all recipients of Ph.D.s awarded in the nation in 1984, the percentage of those in selected disciplines who are employed in New England include the following (see page 338):[7]

	Percent
Political science/international affairs	5.0
Business and management	6.2
Engineering	6.3
Economics	7.8
Mathematics	8.6
Physics/astronomy	8.3
History	9.4
Computer science	10.7
Biochemistry	11.9
Foreign language	13.7

In the absence of quality comparative data on corporate demand, the degree of "overproduction" by New England institutions during the past two decades has provided the most significant human resource "insurance policy" available in the technologically advanced regions of the nation and perhaps the world.[8]

Massachusetts ranked third among the nation's top ten states enrolling seven thousand or more graduate students in science and engineering. The rates of growth in matriculated graduate students during the period 1976–1983 are presented in table 2.

The pursuit of undergraduate degrees in business and management is remarkably high in New England, exceeding national output by an estimated 50 percent (see table 3). New England institutions of higher education and their students are far less liberal-arts oriented than their image projects. The highly visible concentration of nationally selective independent colleges and universities undoubtedly explains the image, but not the reality, of liberal learning in New England.

A Distinguished Level of Production

The baccalaureate sources of male and female doctorate recipients in the United States reveal that the most productive New England campuses continue to be the region's independent colleges and universities, including those listed here (see page 339):[9]

Universities	Colleges
1. Boston University	1. Amherst
2. Brandeis	2. Bennington
3. Brown	3. Bowdoin
4. Dartmouth	4. Hampshire
5. Harvard	5. New England Conservatory
6. MIT	6. Smith
7. Wesleyan	7. Wellesley
8. Yale	8. Williams

Table 2
Rates of growth in number of matriculated graduate students, science and engineering, in top ten states, 1976–1983

Number of graduate students		State	Average annual percent change, 1976–1983	Rank in growth
1976	1983			
35,807	40,058	California	1.6	10
31,159	40,203	New York	3.7	5
17,380	23,170	Texas	4.2	3 ⎱ tied
15,031	20,067	Massachusetts	4.2	3 ⎰ for 3rd
14,633	16,802	Ohio	2.0	8
13,923	17,598	Pennsylvania	3.4	6
13,744	16,786	Illinois	2.9	7
7,397	11,319	Florida	6.3	1
7,284	8,207	Indiana	1.7	9
7,186	9,619	New Jersey	4.3	2

Source: New England Board of Higher Education Analysis of *Surveys of Science Resources Series,* National Science Foundation (Washington, D.C., 1985).

Table 3

Percentage of students enrolled in business and management programs (1976, 1978, 1980) in New England and the United States, and degrees awarded (1982)

State	1976	1978	1980	1982[a]
Connecticut	11.1	17.4	20.3	22.1
Maine	13.7	14.6	15.7	13.6
Massachusetts	16.2	16.5	15.7	19.0
New Hampshire	21.4	24.7	26.5	23.8
Rhode Island	17.6	19.8	19.8	24.0
Vermont	9.0	10.5	11.6	11.2
United States	11.7	13.2	13.7	N.A.

Sources: New England Board of Higher Education Analysis of National Center for Educational Statistics (NCES) data, 1976, 1978, 1980; and 1982 unpublished NCES regional data.
N.A. signifies that information is not available.
a. Percentage of bachelor's degrees awarded.

The leading public university in the region is the University of Massachusetts at Amherst, which ranked twenty-third among all U.S. colleges and universities in output of baccalaureates who received Ph.D.s in 1984. MIT ranked fourth, Harvard ninth, and Yale twentieth among the top thirty nationally.[10]

Another way to compare the relative concentration of scientific and engineering talent (see table 4) in a given state is to use the ratio of academically employed scientists and engineers to state population. Massachusetts ranks an undisputed first in the nation by this measure. With a ratio of 3.5 scientists and engineers per 1,000 population, the colleges and universities of the Commonwealth possess by national standards an exceptional pool of talent for teaching and research.

Research: The Critical Factor

Quality higher education is the crucial factor in the knowledge-intensive New England economy. We need greater understanding of how competencies are taught and learned and how well colleges and universities are assessing what students know. Schools are the central capital investment and infrastructure of a knowledge society, as Peter Drucker has pointed out: human capital, "defined as the skill, dexter-

Table 4
Engineering degrees in New England and the United States, 1971, 1978, 1979, 1980, 1982

Degree	1971	1978	1979	1980	1982
Bachelor's					
New England	3,419	3,719	4,309	4,619	5,296
United States	43,167	46,091	52,598	58,117	66,990
Percent (New England)	7.9%	8.1%	8.2%	7.9%	7.9%
Master's					
New England	1,414	1,421	1,316	1,541	1,627
United States	15,899	15,736	15,624	16,927	18,289
Percent (New England)	8.9%	9.0%	8.4%	9.1%	8.9%
Professional engineering					
New England	113	110	62	77	69
United States	494	446	412	302	254
Percent (New England)	22.9%	24.7%	15.0%	25.5%	27.2%
Doctor's					
New England	335	264	232	244	293
United States	3,640	2,573	2,815	2,753	2,887
Percent (New England)	9.2%	10.3%	8.2%	8.9%	10.1%
All degrees					
New England	5,281	5,514	5,925	6,481	7,285
United States	63,190	64,846	71,449	78,099	88,420
Percent (New England)	8.4%	8.5%	8.3%	8.3%	8.2%

Source: New England Board of Higher Education Analysis of *Surveys of Science Resources Series,* National Science Foundation (Washington, D.C., 1985).

ity, and knowledge of the population, has become the critical input that determines the rate of growth of the economy and well-being of the population."[11]

A national yardstick of the importance of New England academic institutions and nonprofit research institutes is the region's capacity to compete for research and development grants and contracts awarded by the federal government. Analysis of 1982 National Science Foundation data published in 1984 profiles considerable evidence of the region's competitive position.[12]

New England institutions (academic, nonprofit, and corporate) are highly competitive with all other regions of the United States in award of federal obligations. Support to the region is the most concentrated in the nation. With only 5.3 percent of the total U.S.

population, New England receives 11 percent of the total federal obligations for research and development to industrial firms and 12 percent of the total federal obligations for research and development to colleges and universities. In selected categories, New England receives 12 percent of NASA and 13 percent of Department of Transportation research and development expenditures, together with 15 percent of the total obligations of the National Science Foundation.

In biomedical areas, 15.5 percent of National Institutes of Health (NIH) research grants are awarded to the region's colleges and universities, institutes, and nonprofit hospitals, as are 19 percent of NIH fellowships and training grants. The National Institutes of Health awards 38 percent of research and development obligations to non-university-owned, but university-affiliated, voluntary hospitals in New England.

Of all the contracts and grants the Department of Defense (DOD) awards to university and nonprofit research institutes in the United States, 40 percent go to New England institutions. DOD contracts and grants for 1985 are presented in table 5. The nation significantly depends upon New England's nonprofit defense-related research network. The $1 billion of New England DOD academically related research budget should be compared with the $1.5 billion in total expenditures of the six New England states provided in 1987 for the support of the public and independent colleges and universities, including all state student financial aid.

The Example of Biotechnology

Biotechnology is one example of a direct link between our successes in securing federal research grants and developing new products commercially. The strong links between the biomedical and biotechnical industries and universities have encouraged the emergence of more than 130 biotechnology corporations in the region, almost all of which are continuously linked to academic laboratories.

Biotechnology is entering a fragile stage in its development. Much of the past development of the industry has focused on research efforts to develop recombinant DNA, cell fusion, and bioprocessing techniques. After twelve years of research following the first successful insertion of foreign DNA in a host organism in 1973, the biotech-

Table 5

Department of Defense (DOD) research and development contracts to colleges/universities and nonprofit organizations in New England, FY 1985

	Amount awarded	Type of institution
New England colleges and universities		
1. Massachusetts Institute of Technology	$360,104,000	Private
2. University of Massachusetts	6,141,000	Public
3. Yale University	5,507,000	Private
4. Harvard University	4,637,000	Private
5. Trustees of Boston University	3,691,000	Private
6. Brown University	3,530,000	Private
7. University of Rhode Island	3,413,000	Public
8. Wentworth Institute of Technology	3,199,000	Private
9. Northeastern University	2,476,000	Private
10. Emmanuel College	2,436,000	Private
11. University of Connecticut Foundation	1,346,000	Public
12. Dartmouth College	1,152,000	Private
13. Trustees of Boston College	1,048,000	Private
14. University of Lowell	650,000	Public
Subtotal, New England private	$387,780,000	97.1%
Subtotal, New England public	$ 11,550,000	2.9%
Total, New England public and private	$399,330,000	
New England nonprofit research institutes		
1. Charles S. Draper Laboratory	$305,238,000	
2. Mitre Corporation	260,995,000	
3. Woods Hole Oceanographic Institution	11,548,000	
Total, nonprofit research institutes	$577,781,000	
Total, colleges/universities, nonprofit research institutes	$977,111,000	

	U.S. population	Proportion of DOD nonprofit grants
New England	5.3%	40.06%
Balance of United States	94.7	59.94

Source: New England Board of Higher Education Analysis of U.S. Department of Defense data as published in the *Chronicle of Higher Education*, 26 June 1986 (institutions receiving $500,000 or more).

nology industry is bringing products to market. Potential industrial applications include production of pharmaceuticals, animal and plant agriculture, specialty chemicals and food additions, environmental applications, commodity chemicals, and bioelectronic instruments, including biosensors and new conducting devices called biochips. The drive now is to move scientific ideas into the marketplace safely.

Universities in New England play a major international role in the development of biotechnology products worldwide by carrying out research independently or in cooperation with industry. The success of biotechnology commercial development in the region will critically depend on translating scientific processes from the universities into safe, competitively priced, well-marketed products. Undoubtedly, the acceleration of this process requires an increasing emphasis on (1) promoting commercial-academic research, (2) encouraging the development of entrepreneurs in the universities, (3) developing university-business liaison functions to protect intellectual property rights and secure adequate funding for product development, (4) arranging viable university-industry partnerships, (5) investing more of a university's endowment fund in the commercialization of potentially successful research ideas, (6) securing equity involvement for academic participants in any products developed, and (7) utilizing the region's capability of securing federal funding for research ideas to upgrade and maintain laboratories in state-of-the-art fashion. Extensive partnerships in research development among universities will prove to have a vital role in generating commercial potential and ultimately employment from research ideas.[13]

The dramatic increase in the development of partnerships between universities and emerging biomedical industries reveals the accelerating pace of technological changes as well as the new mode of collaboration. Biomedical collaboration is a generation ahead of the more collegial high tech university patterns of a decade ago.

Both universities and industries are testing the mutual benefits emerging from new patterns in research-licensing agreements that permit industry access to new science and encourage privileged development of products in advance of competitors. Corporate access to personnel with outstanding credentials at relatively low cost will allow leading universities to develop additional intellectual resources through collaborative arrangements as corporations continue the investment cycle. The pattern is intimate and risks limiting the dissemination of significant discoveries.

Conclusion

Skilled human capital is the rockbed of New England's economic strength, the vital resource in establishing the future capability of the region to compete nationally and internationally. Education is critical to increasing productivity and improving the quality of New England products and their acceptance worldwide. The region cannot rest on current success. Now is the time to use education to build the foundation for future regional prosperity.

Science and engineering, the availability of skilled labor, a decided edge in professional leadership, and a unique concentration of venture capital have provided the basis for New England prosperity since 1975. We must recognize the growing importance of basic research to our economic competitiveness. Before it is too late, New England must increase the quality of education and training at all levels throughout the region. Business must respond with imagination and long-term commitment to education to assure the quality training of young scientists, engineers, and educated manpower generally. We must act together to develop a comprehensive growth policy for New England aimed at developing a particularly flexible regional labor force skilled to meet the pace of economic change.

As international competition intensifies, the emerging threshold of New England's economy will require that knowledge be qualitatively applied more rapidly to the solution of technical, economic, and social problems than at any point in our history. In learning how to do so, we must strengthen the entire educational system.

There is no time for bickering—political, academic, bureaucratic, or corporate. Strong, farsighted leadership is required and bold collaborative steps must be extended to correct the tragic pattern of human waste the region has permitted to prevail in the conduct of its public schools. While partnerships in behalf of genuine reform are emerging throughout the region, the patterns of action have been studiously slow.

A major premise of this discussion returns to the question of whether or not New England is prepared to invest in the creative priorities that have generated economic growth in the first place. A corollary question is whether or not the policy lesson is fully understood. The connection between quality basic education, research and development, and skilled job creation is axiomatic. The possession of an unequaled concentration of skilled people, rich and flexible modes of venture capital, and an expanding role in national and world affairs will quicken the pace of innovation throughout New England. The centrality of knowledge to continued regional prosperity is indisputable. Do we have the vision to address the unresolved issues hindering the provision of educational equity and quality for all our people? Will greater numbers be left behind without skills? As the answers to these questions become clear in the next decade, we will be in an all too prominent position to judge how well New England has invested her renewed prosperity.

Notes

John C. Hoy has been president of the New England Board of Higher Education since 1978 and was vice-chancellor of the University of California, Irvine, from 1969 to 1978.

1. This information was presented by Frank Morris, president of the Federal Reserve Bank of Boston, in a speech before the Council of Northeast Governors (CONEG), Rye Brook, New York, 29 July 1986.

2. "The Economic Outlook for Massachusetts," Bank of Boston, Economics Department Report, September 1985.

3. Melvin H. Bernstein, "Fine-tuning New England's Labor Force," in New England Board of Higher Education publication, *New England's Vital Resource: The Labor Force* (Washington, D.C.: American Council on Education, 1982), 3.

4. New England Board of Higher Education Analysis based on data from the 1980 U.S. Census and the Departments of Employment Security of the six New England states.

5. Peter Doeringer, Patricia Flynn Pannell, and Pankaj Tandon, "Market Influences on Higher Education: A Perspective for the 1980s," in New England Board of Higher Education publication, *Business and Academia: Partners in New England's Economic Renewal* (Hanover, N.H.: University Press of New England, 1981).

6. *Summary Report, 1984: Doctorate Recipients from United States Universities,* National Research Council (Washington, D.C.: National Academy Press, 1986); and information provided by the American Bar Association (ABA); the Law School Admissions Council (LSAC); the Association of Academic Health Centers (AAHC); and the National Center for Education Statistics (NCES).

7. *Summary Report, 1984.*

8. For a more complete discussion of manpower issues, see John C. Hoy, "The Professional Manpower New England Has Been Provided May Be the Answer to What the Region Needs," *The Alden Seminars, A White Paper, Massachusetts Higher Education in the Eighties: Higher Education and Engineering Workplace Needs* (Boston: Association of Independent Colleges and Universities of Massachusetts and the University of Massachusetts, 1986).

9. *Summary Report, 1984.*

10. Ibid.

11. Peter Drucker, *Wall Street Journal,* 3 March 1981.

12. New England Board of Higher Education Analysis of *Surveys of Science Resources Series,* National Science Foundation (Washington, D.C., 1985).

13. Neville S. Lee, "Biotechnology: A New Phase of Development in New England," a report prepared for the Bank of Boston, October 1985.

The Massachusetts Experience

Linda D. Frankel, Diane Fulman,
and James M. Howell
Bank of Boston
May 1987

A success story as dramatic as that of Massachusetts creates the temptation for many to bask in its glory, and perhaps to claim some credit. But as these authors pointed out in a paper which Howell delivered at a May 1987 international OECD conference on venture capital and new entrepreneurship held in Istanbul, Turkey, no specific organizations and no public policies played much of a role in orchestrating the region's revival.

The authors contended that the real catalysts behind the region's revival were individual entrepreneurs working in an environment that encouraged innovation. And the special expertise in new technologies which these individuals brought to the marketplace came not only from the state's extensive network of research and educational institutions but also from the ever-growing infrastructure of existing high tech firms in the New England region.

In making recommendations for newly industrialized nations seeking to tap the potential of high technology in their plans for economic development, the authors caution that the basic dynamics of the cultures and economies in such emerging nations are likely to be fundamentally different from those of Massachusetts and the more industrialized nations. Thus it may be necessary for regional governments to play a larger role in hurrying along economic development than they did in Massachusetts. The key to success, they concluded, would be to devise a strategy that encourages technology transfer into a region and that fosters entrepreneurialism while building on a region's inherent strengths. Furthermore they should let go of the more traditional views of nationalism in order to open economies to new investment from the highly developed countries.

By 1975 Massachusetts had experienced nearly twenty-five years of industrial stagnation resulting from the out-migration of older industries to the more rapidly growing U.S. South. During the seven-year period ending in 1975, 112,000 manufacturing jobs had been lost—roughly one job out of five.

State and local taxes were pushed to levels that made them the highest of all the states. The unemployment rate jumped to nearly 12 percent. Welfare rolls reflected the pervasive nature of our dilemma; namely, that of the 5.7 million persons living in Massachusetts in 1975, 1.25 million were receiving some form of state welfare assistance. Yet, during the second half of the 1970s there was a dramatic turnabout in Massachusetts as nearly 100,000 new manufacturing jobs were created. The microcomputer and computer peripheral industries engineered drastic reductions in the size and cost of their products which, together with advances in technical and software design, generated an explosion in private sector applications.

By the early 1980s the Massachusetts unemployment rate had fallen below 4 percent—the lowest of all industrial states—sharp state revenue growth led to lower taxes, and the vigorous demand for labor virtually eliminated the welfare problem. To many of us this dramatic revitalization was the second most significant step in market capitalism—the first was the Industrial Revolution that took place in the north of England—and the confirmation that an industrially mature and stagnant area can be revitalized through a rebirth of manufacturing activity utilizing technology and the vigorous growth of sophisticated services.

Although most of us agree that the "Massachusetts experience" will not be easily replicated, it is nevertheless relevant to newly industrialized countries struggling to define and manage economic development strategies predicated on higher levels of technology. And although there are always disadvantages in starting second, we believe that an understanding of the Massachusetts revitalization can provide valuable insight into ways in which the process of technological development can be "hurried along."

As we review the Massachusetts revitalization, three key factors appear to have played a dominant role: high levels of entrepreneurship, a rapid process of technology transfer, and aggressive capital financing. We will explore each of these factors in greater detail.

High Levels of Entrepreneurship

The revitalization process in Massachusetts was shaped and driven by individuals—not by organizations. The business development environment in Massachusetts is one in which innovation and new enterprises are actively encouraged and expected.

Indeed, Dr. Frank Newman, president of the Education Commission of the States, has remarked that what distinguishes Massachusetts from other parts of the United States is the presence of an "opportunistic" environment that favors innovation and that, in turn, attracts "risk lovers"—the very kind of individual who is likely to pursue a new technical idea with tenacity and determination to become a successful entrepreneur.[1]

For many years individual entrepreneurial behavior was poorly understood. Although the early works of Joseph Schumpeter, five decades ago, underscored the importance of individual effort in the process of innovation, it was not until the mid-1960s that we were able to develop a more complete picture of the entrepreneur. Based on research undertaken by Professor Edward Roberts of MIT, we now know that entrepreneurs usually share similar family backgrounds, motivations, and educational attainment. Not surprisingly, entrepreneurs have a high level of goal orientation and motivation. A large part of this has been demonstrated to have grown out of the day-to-day activities of their families during their "growing up" years. Goal orientation and family relationships in turn affect the level of education, especially of the technical entrepreneur who generally has at least an undergraduate degree, and more likely advanced degrees in both management and engineering. Further, 50 to 60 percent of entrepreneurs come from families where the father was self-employed. Finally, the new enterprise founder is usually in his thirties at the start of the new business development venture, and new venture starts fall off rather dramatically as one's age increases.

These personal characteristics are in themselves interesting, but perhaps the more interesting question is why entrepreneurs tend to be clustered in selected areas, rather than randomly distributed throughout society. A large part of the answer appears to be related to the presence of outstanding colleges and universities—particularly engineering and medical schools.[2]

Massachusetts institutions of higher education—sixty-five in the greater Boston area alone—with their internationally recognized scientists, engineers, and research labs have played a critical role in attracting the "best and brightest" from all over the United States and the world. Further, having attended these academic institutions, graduates tend to stay in the area. For example, over 90 percent of the electrical engineers who received their final schooling in New England remained in the region for their employment.

Universities can also influence an entrepreneur's decision to start a new technology firm. This has particularly been the case in certain technical universities, such as MIT, where senior university administrators have encouraged entrepreneurial behavior among faculty. This "outer directedness" stands in sharp contrast to the more traditional academic emphasis on research and publication as the means to advancement and tenure. In this connection senior faculty can become significant agents of change as well as "role models" for junior faculty and students.

High Levels of Technology Transfer

Once the process of technology-driven revitalization has started, it becomes strongly reinforcing. Successful high tech companies in Massachusetts produced spin-offs as ambitious employees and researchers assumed an entrepreneurial role and ventured out on their own. Each new company in turn provided a role model for another. The magnitude of this process is truly significant. Between 1965 to 1975 roughly one-half of the new computer company products were the result of direct technology transfer from previous employers. Roberts' analysis here is particularly insightful. He identified thirty-nine new business enterprises started by forty-four former employees of one large Boston-based electronics company. And, only a short time later, the thirty-two surviving firms had aggregate sales double that of the "parent company" from which the entrepreneurs had spun off.[3] Thus one of the most conspicuous advantages of having many small technology-driven firms has been the acceleration of other new firms in related technologies. A small number of these firms have grown to become major manufacturing companies, thus contributing significantly to new job growth.

Further Massachusetts has benefited from the tendency of some entrepreneurs to start multiple enterprises—leaving one established successful venture to found another. Among the better-known examples are Philippe Villers who cofounded Computervision, Inc. of Bedford, founded Billerica-based Automatix, Inc., and recently started Cognition, Inc. in Billerica; J. William Poduska, a cofounder of Prime Computer, Inc. of Natick, founder of Apollo Computer, Inc. of Chelmsford, who is now launching Stellar Computer, Inc. of Newton; and Henry E. Kloss, who successively founded Acoustic Research, KLH, Advent, and Kloss Video. This again underscores the self-reinforcing nature of the technology transfer process.

In addition, though this corporate spin-off process was an integral part of the Massachusetts economic revitalization process, academic, government, and not-for-profit research labs also played a critical role. In one MIT study, over 200 new technical ventures were founded by former employees of MIT labs and academic departments, and government labs during the late 1950s to the mid-1960s. Moreover follow-up studies have shown that four out of five of these firms have survived.[4] If documentation from the experiences of other Boston–Cambridge-based academic institutions were added, the full economic impact could be more accurately judged, but the current level of prosperity in Massachusetts tells us that it has been significant.

Before turning to the role of aggressive capital financing, it is important to note that the process of technology transfer in Massachusetts was facilitated by the presence of a substantial regional manufacturing and business infrastructure which provided support to the area's newly created, technologically based industries. Massachusetts—especially the greater Boston area—contains a strong technological infrastructure or network of support firms in manufacturing and services as well as a large pool of skilled labor. Historically, this technological base grew out of the late nineteenth and first half of the twentieth centuries. As the electronics industry grew, this infrastructure has adjusted and expanded to meet new needs. Today this network also includes sophisticated business services—accounting, new business development services, patent protection, and complex technical product licensing sensitive to the specialized needs of technology start-ups.

Aggressive Capital Financing

Quite often, the financing needs of high tech companies are discussed in terms of their access to venture capital. Equity, in the form of venture capital, is the major source of financing for new enterprises. Venture capital provides the bulk of the early or development stage funding for high tech firms, and we are well aware that other speakers at this conference plan to address this subject in great detail. Therefore we would like to concentrate on how banks, at the proper stage of development, have helped put together the overall financing packages that have allowed "coming companies" to become "going and growing" concerns.

Without doubt, the creation and growth of new high technology firms have required new bank-financing strategies. Traditionally, banks have waited until emerging firms achieve the following: a sustained level of commercial activity; a history of profitable operations; an accumulation of business assets such as accounts receivable, inventory, and plant and equipment; and a large capitalization in order to support fully the bank's commitment to lend at the time the commitment is extended to the company. This financing strategy, though appropriate in many cases, does give rise to the often quoted customer complaint that banks "are only willing to lend me money when I don't need it."

High tech financing has required a shift in the timing of these fundamentals. The Bank of Boston's lending experience in the 1960s and 1970s with these industries traces out what we like to regard as a new and innovative banking pattern.

First, target the bank loan commitment to the best entrepreneurial talent—not necessarily to the established company or the developed product. It is the entrepreneur who drives growth and who will capitalize on new product ideas in the face of difficulties. It is the entrepreneur who has identified the market opportunity and new technology; who has attracted a sufficient level of venture capital to underwrite the development stage, which may last two to three years or more; and who has assembled a team of managers and directors who are capable of developing and implementing the firm's business plan. These elements are, first and foremost, essential for any successful venture.

Second, as this development stage process unfolds, the entrepreneur and the venture capitalists will look to the banks to make an initial commitment to fund the future levels of business activity once the firm becomes self-sustaining. Banks in New England have learned to make commitments at the earliest stage of business creation—to complement, but not compete with, the role of the venture capitalist's equity investment—not after the business has become established in the market.

Banks in other countries will undoubtedly find that, as in the case of Massachusetts, entrepreneurs given the proper flow of venture capital, do not need to draw heavily upon these bank commitments. Yet these bank loan commitments to high tech firms serve as a signal of endorsement to investors, thereby enabling the entrepreneur to raise private capital on favorable terms. Often a bank's own venture capital arm may invest in the early stage rounds of equity financing, and even a modest level of asset-based financing for plant and equipment is now commonplace during the development stage.

Third, just as the venture capital support must be continued, if not increased during the high growth periods of the firm's development, it is particularly important that the entrepreneur be able to rely on the bank's loan commitment at that very time of above-average leverage. High tech companies typically operate within short-term windows of opportunity and, at times, startling growth rates, even in an environment of a national economic downturn. It is during such times that the confidence and fortitude of the banker is often put to the greatest test.

In short, the prerequisites must come full circle; that is, the entrepreneurial spirit of a region's manufacturing base must eventually extend into what are usually regarded as the most conservative business institutions, mainly banks.

The Massachusetts Experience in Perspective: Relevant Lessons for Newly Industrialized Countries

As already stated, the central force in the Massachusetts revitalization process has been the individual entrepreneur; the organizational and policy role of the state has been quite minimal. This is not likely to be the case in newly industrialized countries, where entrepreneurial values are generally not as widely held or long-standing as they are in more industrialized countries. Moreover, because there is a less-developed private sector, the government in newly industrialized countries offers the best initial departure point for implementing a strategy of technological growth. In this situation governmental policies that enhance technology transfer become the most logical route to innovation and economic development. This process will enable newly industrialized countries to overcome some of the disadvantages of starting second.

Relevant literature on technology transfer in newly industrialized nations is growing, and in this concluding section we want to make several brief observations. These comments are based, in part, on a study of technology transfer to small manufacturing firms in three countries—Spain, Ireland, and Mexico.[5]

The following key observations are relevant to our discussion:

• The most valuable source of technology transfer across countries is the foreign firm or foreign supplier to the domestic firm. In the cross-country technical and innovative messages analyzed by Allen, Hyman, and Pinckney, more than one-half were from this source.

• Of much less significance were the efforts of governmental-sponsored research institutes, universities, and trade fairs. Collectively these methods of facilitating technology transfer accounted for only slightly more than 5 percent of the innovative messages.

• The "international gatekeeper"[6] is a critical player in the technology transfer process. The gatekeeper serves as the conduit for technical knowledge and information and exchange.

These observations provide the basis for a series of recommendations. The first is based on the evidence that the parent firm in a highly industrialized country serves as a rich source of technology to its foreign subsidiaries, and that the process of transferring that technology can have a positive effect on the economic development of the recipient country. As positive as this may be, attitudes toward industrial nationalism may foreclose this avenue of technology transfer. However, as the process of internationalization of technology takes place, a development differential will become increasingly evident between those nations that welcome foreign investment—even when it means foregoing ownership control of local companies—and those that do not. In a very rough way this differentiation has already become clear between Pacific Basin vis-à-vis Latin American countries.

The second recommendation—though acknowledging the limited effectiveness of government-sponsored research institutes as agents for technology transfer—recognizes that no country can develop without an intellectual and research infrastructure. Thus there is a clear need to allocate additional financial resources to academic research laboratories in newly industrialized countries. Unfortunately, academic research laboratories often operate independently from industry. In addition to increased funding the task is to improve the laboratory-industry linkages.

One of the most innovative approaches in this area is in Brazil where established industries are given research grants, or vouchers, that can only be spent to support industry-relevant research in a Brazilian university or scientific laboratory. It is still too early to determine the long-run success of this approach and, given the contemporary political and economic instability in Brazil, it may well never take root. It is, however, an innovative technique to encourage technology transfer, and other newly industrialized countries can certainly adapt the idea to their own economic realities. Another approach has been tested and is working: the MIT Industrial Liaison Program provides incentives in the form of additional research funding to academic departments that engage in projects that link their research with industry. The key point here is that measures to enhance technology transfer can be successful, and are certainly worth trying.

Our third recommendation builds on the role of the international gatekeeper. When one analyzes the professional backgrounds of gatekeepers, they typically have either been employed by a foreign technology-based firm or have visited another country to work on a sabbatical or research fellowship. The gatekeepers increase the flow of technical information by serving as a link between research laboratories and industries in one country and scientific and technology-oriented individuals in another. When successful, this linkage results in increased technology-driven economic development. The key question is: How can individuals be encouraged to pursue this role on a sufficiently large scale to make a difference?

One interesting example of this process involves the Technical University at Aachen in West Germany and the Council for Economic Action, Inc., a nonprofit organization based in Boston. These two organizations are attempting systematically to organize graduates of the university's science, engineering, and medical programs now in the United States into a network to transfer technology to Aachen. In effect, the international gatekeeper—in this case, Aachen graduates working outside the country—are the cornerstone of this economic development effort. Thus we may conclude that a government wishing to actively promote technology transfer would be well advised to consider supporting this type of program.

Finally, one important cumulative outcome of the technology transfer process is likely to be attitudinal change. The utilization of new approaches to innovation and development will, in turn, promote other factors critical in the Massachusetts experience; namely, entrepreneurship and aggressive capital financing. Thus, a strategy based on "outward directedness" to enhance technology transfer will pay important dividends by encouraging a more opportunistic society. A technological strategy that builds on your inherent strengths and increases the linkages with the sources of technological know-how in other countries will enable your country to "hurry along" the process of economic development.

Notes

1. Everett Rogers and Floyd Shoemaker, *Communication of Innovations: A Cross-Cultural Approach* (The Free Press, 1974). See also Thomas Allen, *Managing the Flow of Technology* (The MIT Press, 1985).

2. See Seymour Lipset, "Values, Education, and Entrepreneurship," in *Elites in Latin America,* Seymour Lipset and Aldo Solari, editors (Oxford University Press, 1967).

3. See Edward Roberts, "A Basic Study of Innovators; How to Keep and Capitalize on Their Talents," *Research Management* 11 (4), 1968.

4. Ibid. The role of defense spending for long-term research and development should not be minimized as an additional causative factor in technology transfer from defense to non-defense products.

5. For more details, see Thomas Allen, Diane Hyman, and David Pinckney, "Transferring Technology to the Small Manufacturing Firm; A Study of Technology Transfer in Three Countries," *Research Policy* 12, 1983. In this study, significant steps to diffuse technology across national boundaries were categorized as innovative messages.

6. For elaboration of the role of the international gatekeeper, see "The International Technological Gatekeeper," *Technology Review,* March 1971.

List of Documents Used
in This Study

"The Dilemma of a Mature Economy and Excessive Government Spending," *New England Letter*. Economics Department, The First National Bank of Boston. December 1971.

"The Massachusetts Economy," Gov. Francis W. Sargent, Address to the Boston Citizens Seminar, March 13, 1972. *The Sargent Years, Selected Public Papers of Francis W. Sargent, Governor, 1969–1975*. Assembled with an Introduction by Jack Flannery. Commonwealth of Massachusetts. Boston, 1976.

"The Governor's Message on the Economy of Massachusetts," *New England Letter*. Economics Department, The First National Bank of Boston. April 1972.

"The State's Fiscal Crisis," Gov. Francis W. Sargent. Address to the Massachusetts Taxpayers Foundation, April 8, 1972. *The Sargent Years, Selected Public Papers of Francis W. Sargent, Governor, 1969–1975*. Assembled with an Introduction by Jack Flannery. Commonwealth of Massachusetts. Boston, 1976.

"The Impending Fiscal Crisis," *New England Letter*. Economics Department, The First National Bank of Boston. August 1972.

Look Out, Massachusetts!!!, Economics Department, The First National Bank of Boston. November 1972.

"The Economic Development of Massachusetts," Bennett Harrison. Report to the Joint Committee on Commerce and Labor, Massachusetts State Legislature. Commonwealth of Massachusetts, November 1974.

"Alternatives for the Northeast: Choices and Costs," James M. Howell. *Balanced Growth for the Northeast, Proceedings of a Conference of Legislative Leaders on the Future of the Northeast*. New York State Senate. Albany, New York. December 1975.

"An Economic Development Plan for Massachusetts," Governor Michael S. Dukakis. Commonwealth of Massachusetts. Boston. August 1976.

"A Four-Point Program for the Northeast," Diane Fulman and James M. Howell, Speech before the Boston College Citizens Seminar. March 1977.

"A New Social Contract for Massachusetts," Massachusetts High Technology Council. February 1979.

"New England's Economy in the 1980s," Lynn E. Browne and John Hekman. *New England Economic Review,* Federal Reserve Bank of Boston. January/February 1981.

"The Massachusetts Economy in the 1980s," Economics Department, The First National Bank of Boston. November 2, 1981.

"The Role of Small Business in New England," David L. Birch, MIT Program on Neighborhood and Regional Change. November 1983.

"Route 128: The Development of a Regional High Technology Economy," Nancy S. Dorfman, MIT Center for Policy Alternatives. *Research Policy,* vol. 12, no. 6. December 1983.

"High Technology and Business Services," Lynn E. Browne, *New England Economic Review,* Federal Reserve Bank of Boston. July/August 1983.

"Lowell: A High Technology Success Story," Patricia M. Flynn, Bentley College. *The New England Economic Review,* Federal Reserve Bank of Boston. September/October 1984.

"Economic Revitalization and Job Creation in America's Oldest Industrialized Region," Linda D. Frankel and James M. Howell. Remarks before the American Enterprise Institute/Institute La Boetie Conference. October 24–25, 1985.

"War Stories: Defense Spending and the Growth of the Massachusetts Economy," David Warsh. *New England Journal of Public Policy,* vol. 2, no. 1. Winter/Spring. 1986.

"The Next Threshold: Higher Skills and the New England Economy," John C. Hoy. *New England Journal of Public Policy,* vol. 2, no. 2. Summer/Fall 1986.

"The Massachusetts Experience," Linda D. Frankel, Diane Fulman, and James M. Howell. Remarks before the International Experts Conference on Venture Capital and New Entrepreneurship. May 1987.

Index